Ask Like a Therapist, Sell Like a Pro
A Therapy-Inspired Sales Approach

Jared Kelner, M.Ed.

Ask Like a Therapist, Sell Like a Pro: A Therapy-Inspired Sales Approach

Copyright © 2025 Jared Kelner, M.Ed.

All rights reserved.

ISBN: 979-8-9929177-1-0

Title: Ask Like a Therapist, Sell Like a Pro

Subtitle: A Therapy-Inspired Sales Approach

Publisher: The Infinite Mind Training Group

Author: Jared Kelner, M.Ed.

Website: www.asklikeatherapist.com

Editor: The Infinite Mind Training Group

Cover Art: Shoib Brohi

ISBN: 979-8-9929177-1-0

All rights reserved. No part of this book may be reproduced, stored in a retrieval system, or transmitted in any form or by any means, electronic, mechanical, photocopying, recording, or otherwise, without the prior written permission of the author.

Copyright © 2025 by Jared Kelner, M.Ed.

First Edition, 2025

Published in the United States of America

Ask Like a Therapist, Sell Like a Pro: A Therapy-Inspired Sales Approach

DEDICATION

This book is dedicated to the people in my life who challenge me to grow and encourage me to share what is in my head, heart, and guts.

To my family, for always being there as honest and supportive sounding boards for my non-stop waterfall of ideas. I know I can be exhausting at times, so thank you for your patience and for loving me anyway.

To Lindsey Wilson College, the School of Professional Counseling, and the Master of Education in Counseling Department, with special a Thank You to Dr. Bradley Grot my academic advisor, and Dr. Susan Patterson and Dr. Gregory Bohner, two of my favorite professors, for the education and encouragement for me to carve my own path in the field of Mental Health Counseling. www.lindsey.edu. A special Thank You to Kenneth Freedman, MSW, LICSW, Sergeant First Class Daniel Shalikar, Diane L. Parker, and Gary Gruber for writing Letters of Recommendation to help me complete my application to graduate school, which altered the course of my life. Without your generous, kind, and supportive words, I would not have been accepted to Lindsey Wilson College.

To The Center For Therapy and Counseling Services in New Jersey, with a heartfelt Thank You to Melissa Higgins, MSW, LCSW, for the opportunity to learn and grow as a Therapist under your masterful supervision. www.centerfortherapy.net

To my sales managers, mentors, and colleagues that have shaped me into the professional salesman I am today. Thank You to the late Margaret Schoening, and to Ellen Berlan, Dan Whalen, Gordon Galzerano, Kent Wisenor, Dwight Alabanza, Joel Weidert, Jose Pontoriero, Jen Vasin, Guido Russo, Gary Gruber, Ed Romero, Anna Ganzman, Cris Cronin, Z Tonoco, and Mariano Dy-Liacco X.

And finally, Thank You to my Therapy and Sales clients that have trusted me enough over the years to have generously shared their thoughts, emotions, perspectives, challenges, and truths with me. I am forever in your debt.

TABLE OF CONTENTS

FOREWORD	1
OPEN–MINDEDNESS	2
WHY THIS APPROACH MATTERS	3
FOSTERING TRUST WITH THERAPY-INSPIRED QUESTIONS	7
BUILDING TRUST THROUGH MIRRORING	18
APPLYING THERAPY TECHNIQUES TO SALES CONVERSATIONS	45
LEVERAGING MOTIVATIONAL INTERVIEWING	83
UNDERSTANDING AND ADDRESSING BIASES	88
PRESENTING YOUR SOLUTION	135
MOVING THROUGH OBJECTIONS	152
CLOSING THE SALE	159
MID-PROJECT CHECK-IN	173
POST-SOLUTION DEBRIEF	181
ROLE PLAY EXERCISES	194
CLOSING THOUGHTS	212
BONUS TECHNIQUE: THE MIRACLE QUESTION	215
ADDITIONAL BONUS TECHNIQUE: SILENCE	216
STAY CONNECTED	217
ABOUT THE AUTHOR	218
REFERENCES	219

FOREWORD

Therapists and sales professionals share a fundamental goal: guiding someone through an internal process of discovery and commitment to action. In therapy, a client may struggle with uncertainty, fear, or limiting beliefs[1] before making a life-altering decision. Similarly, in sales, a client may hesitate due to risk aversion,[2] status quo bias,[3] or unclear value perception.[4] The role of the therapist—and the sales professional—is to create an environment where the client can work through these hesitations and confidently choose their next step.

With nearly three decades of experience selling technology services to some of the world's largest companies, I've come to realize that one key factor has driven my success: the ability to build trust and rapport with clients. This insight deepened after earning a Master of Education in Mental Health Counseling later in my career. I discovered that many of the principles central to therapy—such as holding space, trust-building, active listening, empathy, motivational questioning, and thoughtful observation—were already embedded in my sales approach. This revelation revealed a powerful intersection between sales and therapy, inspiring me to write this book. My goal is to help sales professionals develop the skills to build meaningful, long-term client relationships, ultimately driving greater success in their careers. I offer *Ask Like a Therapist, Sell Like a Pro: A Therapy-Inspired Sales Approach* with deep respect for both sales and counseling, hoping it transforms not only your professional life but your personal growth as well.

OPEN–MINDEDNESS

This book is not about debating psychological theory or classifying techniques by modality—it's about applying therapy-inspired strategies to sales in a way that builds trust, deepens understanding, and drives real results.[1] Whether or not you agree with how these methods are categorized, their effectiveness speaks for itself. The order of the therapeutic modalities, biases, and all other content throughout the book is intentionally designed to reflect the dynamic, unpredictable nature of real-world interactions.[2] Therapy and sales are both fluid processes, often requiring us to adapt in the moment, sometimes in ways that defy traditional structures.[3] By stepping away from conventional categorizations, we open ourselves up to a more flexible and authentic approach that meets clients where they are.[4] Instead of focusing on labels, I invite you to explore how these techniques work, why they matter, and how they can transform your sales approach. The order may be unexpected, but I urge you to trust in the process and embrace the power of adaptability. It's about what works in the moment, not what's predictable, popular, or fashionable, and that's where true connection and success happen.

WHY THIS APPROACH MATTERS
ଔଔଔଔଔଔ

In the sales profession, success is often measured by numbers—quotas hit, deals closed, revenue generated. But behind every sale is a human being, complete with emotions, motivations, and internal struggles. Traditional sales methodologies focus on persuasion and objection handling, yet they often neglect the deeper psychological drivers that influence decision-making.[1] This book offers a revolutionary approach—one that integrates proven mental health counseling techniques into consultative sales conversations, transforming the way professionals build relationships, uncover needs, and guide clients toward meaningful solutions.

By leveraging therapeutic modalities such as Cognitive Behavioral Therapy, Motivational Interviewing, and many others, sales professionals can move beyond surface-level conversations and tap into the deeper motivations that drive client decisions. Instead of simply selling a product or service, this approach helps clients clarify their own needs, challenge their biases,[2] and align their decisions with their core values. The result? More authentic connections, stronger trust, and higher-value deals that serve both the client and the salesperson.

Therapists are extensively trained to create safe environments and to hold space for their clients.[3] This nurturing, non-judgmental, and non-confrontational setting is the foundation for individuals to feel seen, heard, and understood—an environment in which people loosen their grip on their firmly held beliefs and open up, share, reflect, contemplate, challenge their thoughts, emotions, and actions, and make meaningful decisions which lead to a healthier life.[4] What if consultative sales professionals could develop the same level of trust with their clients? How might that transform the seller-client relationship, and what might this foundation of irrefutable trust mean for both? The foundation of a therapeutic relationship is built on active listening,[5] thoughtful inquiry, and the ability to guide someone toward their own insights rather than forcing an agenda.[6] When applied to sales, this approach shifts the conversation from persuasion to collaboration, from selling a solution to uncovering what truly matters to the client.

In this book, we will explore how techniques such as Motivational Interviewing, mirroring, and strategic questioning can be adapted to enhance consultative sales conversations. We will examine how cognitive biases shape decision-making and how recognizing these biases can lead to better client interactions. Through this approach, sales professionals will learn to facilitate meaningful discussions that help clients gain clarity, recognize needs they may not have considered, and take ownership of their decisions.

The chapters ahead will delve into the specific skills and strategies that bridge the gap between therapy and consultative sales, including:

- **Fostering Trust with Therapy-Inspired Questions** – How to ask insightful questions that create trust and discovery.
- **Building Trust Through Mirroring** – The power of reflecting a client's language, tone, gestures, and emotions to deepen connection.
- **Applying Therapy Techniques to Sales Conversations** – Adapting and integrating counseling strategies to enhance consultative selling.
- **Leveraging Motivational Interviewing** – Encouraging clients to explore their own motivations and commit to change.
- **Understanding and Addressing Biases** – Understanding how cognitive biases impact decision-making and how to navigate them effectively.
- **Presenting Your Solution** – Learn how to position your offering in a way that resonates with your client's needs, values, and motivations, ensuring alignment and engagement.
- **Moving Through Objections** – Discover how to navigate objections using therapeutic questioning techniques, reframing concerns as opportunities for deeper exploration rather than points of conflict.
- **Closing the Sale** – Explore strategies rooted in trust and collaboration to guide clients toward confident, commitment-driven decisions without pressure or manipulation.
- **Mid-Project Check-In** – Understand the importance of maintaining strong client relationships post-sale by proactively addressing concerns, reinforcing value, and ensuring continued alignment.
- **Post-Solution Debrief** – Learn how to conduct thoughtful debrief conversations that solidify trust, extract key insights, and lay the groundwork for long-term partnerships.
- **Role-Play Exercises** – Engage in practical, real-world scenarios that reinforce key techniques, helping sales professionals internalize and master the consultative approach through guided practice.

This book is not about psychological or sales tricks. It is about mastering the art of human connection. By adopting these techniques, sales professionals will transform their conversations, their relationships, and ultimately their success. Welcome to a new way of thinking about consultative sales—one rooted in empathy, authenticity, and meaningful engagement.

I carefully considered the title of this book, exploring numerous options before selecting *Ask Like a Therapist, Sell Like a Pro*. For your enjoyment, here are the finalists that made the shortlist but were ultimately set aside.

- **Therapeutic Selling:** Transforming Sales through Counseling Techniques
- **From Couch to Close:** Therapy-Inspired Sales Techniques
- **The Counselor's Close:** Applying Therapy Techniques to Transform Sales

I want to take a moment to acknowledge what has been intentionally omitted from this book. The field of mental health counseling (therapy) includes many valuable therapeutic modalities, each offering meaningful benefits to clients. Some modalities, techniques, and approaches have been omitted intentionally and their exclusion here is not a reflection of their significance to the mental health counseling profession or its community of clients but rather a necessity to maintain focus and practicality. Covering every therapeutic approach and its application to consultative sales would result in an overwhelming, thousand-page volume. Instead, I have carefully selected the modalities that, through years of exploration, have proven most impactful for sales professionals and business clients. This streamlined approach ensures that the insights provided are both actionable and directly relevant to real-world sales conversations. I look forward to guiding you through these powerful techniques.

○ PERSONAL EXPLORATION ○

Before you begin, I encourage you to take a moment to reflect on and respond to the questions below. Writing your answers in the space provided will allow you to document your initial thoughts and perspectives before embarking on this journey. At the conclusion, you will have the opportunity to revisit your responses, assess your growth, and evaluate how your approach to sales has evolved in a meaningful way.

How do you currently approach sales conversations, and what do you believe is your greatest strength in building client relationships?

_____
_____
_____

When was the last time you felt truly connected to a client during a sales conversation? What made that interaction different from others?

What do you expect to learn from this book, and how open are you to shifting your mindset from persuasion to collaboration?

On a scale of 1-10, how confident are you that integrating therapeutic techniques into sales will enhance your success? How did you arrive at that number?

If you could transform one aspect of how you engage with clients, what would it be, and what impact do you think it would have on your sales results and professional fulfillment?

ೊ YOUR FINAL THOUGHTS ೋ

Use The Space Below To Capture Your Thoughts And Reflections On What You've Learned In This Section

FOSTERING TRUST
WITH THERAPY-INSPIRED QUESTIONS
☙❧☙❧

In consultative sales, true connection is built through empathy, mutual understanding, and genuine dialogue.[1] Building rapport and establishing an authentic relationship with clients, which leads to earned trust, is an essential part of the sales process.[2] Often, relationships are forged during casual conversations before or after meetings, as well as at client meals and outings.[3] The questions in this section are designed to cultivate authentic conversations that allow clients to explore their experiences, values, and aspirations in a safe, non-judgmental space.

By going beyond surface-level inquiries that are present in many impersonal sales relationships, these relationship-building questions invite clients to slow down and take the time necessary to reflect on key moments in their personal and professional lives, providing insight into what motivates them, what drives their decisions, and what they and the company value most. When clients feel seen, heard, and understood, especially in relaxed settings outside of the boardroom, they're more likely to trust you and engage in meaningful, long-lasting business relationships.[4] These questions foster a safe space for vulnerability and introspection, empowering clients to share deeply personal reflections, while giving you the opportunity to think about how you might align your solutions with their unique business needs and goals. The result is not just a transaction, but a partnership grounded in empathy, trust, and understanding.

As you read the questions below, answer them out loud as if someone asked you. By responding to these questions, you will gain a deeper, more embodied, and connected understanding of their impact and value to the relationship-building process.

Can you think of a time when you had every reason to play it safe, but something inside you told you to take a leap? What pushed you over the edge to go for it, and what did you discover about yourself in the process?

> **Therapeutic Commentary:** Risk-taking isn't just about boldness; it's about self-trust and personal evolution.[5] This question encourages reflection on the inner conflict between fear and intuition, revealing how individuals navigate uncertainty. By examining the motivations and outcomes of taking a leap, clients can gain deeper insight into

their decision-making process and build confidence in their ability to adapt and grow.[6]

Think of a belief or strong opinion you once held that you no longer stand by. What led you to reconsider, and how did that shift impact the way you see yourself or others today?

> **Therapeutic Commentary:** Changing one's mind is often framed as weakness, but in reality, it's a sign of intellectual humility and personal growth.[7] This question invites exploration into the evolution of thought and highlights the ability to critically assess and revise one's perspectives. It fosters self-awareness, adaptability, and a greater appreciation for diverse viewpoints, which are essential in leadership and decision-making.[8]

Think about a time when someone earned your trust completely. What did they do—specifically—that made you feel safe, valued, and understood?

> **Therapeutic Commentary:** Trust is rarely built in a single moment but through consistent actions that signal reliability, empathy, and genuine care.[9] By identifying the behaviors that created a sense of security, this question helps individuals recognize what they need in relationships. It also provides insight into how they, in turn, can foster trust in their own interactions, both personally and professionally.

What's a time in your life you'd like to revisit and relive exactly as it happened the first time?

> **Therapeutic Commentary:** Nostalgia is a powerful emotional tool that strengthens our sense of identity and connection to meaningful experiences.[10] Reflecting on cherished memories can highlight what brings joy and fulfillment, providing valuable insight into one's core values. Additionally, this exercise can serve as a reminder of past successes and happiness, reinforcing confidence and gratitude.

What's a time in your life you'd like to revisit and reimagine the event to create a new experience?

> **Therapeutic Commentary:** Reflection on past experiences can uncover unresolved emotions and patterns in decision-making.[11]

By reimagining a different outcome, individuals gain insight into their growth, resilience, and how they can approach future situations with greater awareness and intention.[12] This exercise promotes self-compassion and helps clients break free from cycles of regret or self-doubt.

What's the best advice someone gave to you that you pass on to others often?

Therapeutic Commentary: The wisdom we carry forward often reflects our deepest values and guiding principles.[13] By revisiting meaningful advice, individuals gain insight into what has shaped their perspective and decision-making.[14] This question also promotes storytelling and personal connection, reinforcing the importance of mentorship and shared learning in both professional and personal relationships.[15]

What personal values guide your decisions and actions?

Therapeutic Commentary: Core values act as an internal compass, influencing choices and relationships.[16] Clarifying these principles helps individuals align their actions with their authentic selves, fostering integrity and consistency.[17] Recognizing personal values also strengthens confidence in decision-making and enhances emotional intelligence in interactions with others.[18]

Can you share a moment when you felt truly understood by someone?

Therapeutic Commentary: Feeling deeply understood is one of the most validating human experiences.[19] This question encourages reflection on what made that connection so impactful—whether it was active listening, shared experience, or empathy.[20] Identifying these elements can help individuals cultivate more meaningful relationships and develop stronger communication skills.[21]

What are some challenges you've overcome that you are particularly proud of?

Therapeutic Commentary: Overcoming adversity fosters resilience and self-efficacy.[22] By reflecting on past challenges, individuals can recognize their own strength and problem-solving skills.[23]

This question also helps shift the focus from struggles to accomplishments, reinforcing a growth mindset and an ability to navigate future obstacles with greater confidence.

What's a goal you're currently working towards, and what motivates you to achieve it?

Therapeutic Commentary: Goal-setting provides purpose and direction, and understanding motivation reveals deeper aspirations and values.[24] Exploring what drives someone toward achievement helps reinforce commitment and can uncover obstacles that may be hindering progress.[25] This question also promotes accountability and self-reflection, key components of sustained personal and professional growth.

How do you recharge and take care of yourself during stressful times?

Therapeutic Commentary: Self-care is crucial for mental and emotional well-being, yet many people neglect it under pressure. This question encourages individuals to reflect on the strategies that help them restore balance. By identifying and prioritizing these methods, they can improve resilience, prevent burnout, and enhance overall productivity and well-being.[26]

What's a book or movie that has had a significant impact on you, and why?

Therapeutic Commentary: Stories shape our perspectives and values, often revealing what resonates deeply with us.[27] This question allows individuals to express their influences and personal philosophy through media. By discussing these works, they can explore themes of identity, transformation, and inspiration, which can lead to greater self-awareness and connection with others.

How do you handle conflicts or disagreements in your relationships?

Therapeutic Commentary: Conflict resolution is a vital skill in both personal and professional settings.[28] This question encourages reflection on communication styles, emotional regulation, and problem-solving approaches. Understanding how one navigates disagreements can lead to more constructive interactions, stronger relationships, and greater emotional intelligence.

What are some traditions or rituals that are meaningful to you?

Therapeutic Commentary: Rituals and traditions provide a sense of continuity and identity.[29] This question explores what holds deep personal or cultural significance, revealing how these practices influence beliefs and behaviors. By discussing these traditions, individuals can reflect on their roots and the values they wish to preserve or pass on.

What do you consider to be your greatest strengths, and how do they manifest in your daily life?

Therapeutic Commentary: Recognizing strengths fosters self-confidence and motivation.[30] This question helps individuals identify qualities they may take for granted, reinforcing a positive self-image. By understanding how these strengths show up in daily life, they can better leverage them in both personal and professional contexts.

Can you recall a time when you felt particularly inspired or motivated? What sparked that feeling?

Therapeutic Commentary: Identifying sources of inspiration can reignite passion and purpose, supporting ongoing personal and professional development.[31] This can also help uncover intrinsic motivators that drive fulfillment and success.

What's a lesson you've learned from a difficult experience that you carry with you?

Therapeutic Commentary: Reflecting on lessons learned from adversity promotes resilience and the ability to find meaning in challenging situations.[32] This process encourages post-traumatic growth, shifting focus from struggle to strength.

What does success mean to you, and how do your daily choices bring you closer to it?

Therapeutic Commentary: Clarifying definitions of success helps clients align their actions with their values and aspirations, fostering goal-directed behavior.[33] It also highlights any misalignment between perceived success and personal fulfillment.

What's an activity or hobby that brings you joy, and how did you discover it?

> **Therapeutic Commentary:** Discussing joyful activities highlights the importance of leisure and creativity in well-being, and can inspire new interests.[34] It also fosters self-care awareness, which is crucial in managing stress and preventing burnout.

What's a dream or aspiration you have that you've yet to pursue, and what's holding you back?

> **Therapeutic Commentary:** Exploring unfulfilled dreams can uncover barriers and promote problem-solving, encouraging clients to take proactive steps toward their goals.[35] This discussion can reveal underlying fears or limiting beliefs that hinder progress.

What's a piece of feedback you've received that has significantly impacted you?

> **Therapeutic Commentary:** Reflecting on feedback fosters self-awareness and growth, highlighting areas for improvement or validation of strengths.[36] It also provides insight into how individuals process constructive criticism and praise.

How do you balance your personal and professional life, and what strategies have you found effective?

> **Therapeutic Commentary:** Discussing work-life balance promotes the importance of boundaries and self-care,[37] which are essential for overall well-being. It also allows individuals to assess whether they are prioritizing their needs effectively or experiencing burnout.

What's a quality you admire in others, and how do you cultivate it in yourself?

> **Therapeutic Commentary:** Identifying admired qualities encourages individuals to strive for personal growth,[38] fostering positive change. This question also helps uncover values that shape character and decision-making.

How do you stay motivated during difficult times or setbacks?

Therapeutic Commentary: Exploring motivation strategies provides individuals with tools for resilience and perseverance,[39] supporting long-term success. It also sheds light on their coping mechanisms and whether they are adaptive or maladaptive.

What role does gratitude play in your life, and how do you practice it?

Therapeutic Commentary: Discussing gratitude practices promotes a positive mindset and well-being,[40] encouraging individuals to focus on the positive aspects of their lives. Research in positive psychology supports gratitude as a key factor in resilience and happiness.

What's a habit or routine that has made a significant difference in your life?

Therapeutic Commentary: Exploring beneficial habits or routines emphasizes the importance of consistency and self-discipline[41] in achieving goals and maintaining well-being. This also helps identify structures that support success.

Who has had the most profound influence on your life, and what did they teach you?

Therapeutic Commentary: This question fosters emotional depth by uncovering key relationships and the lessons they imparted.[42] Understanding who has shaped someone's values, work ethic, or worldview provides insight into their motivations and personal aspirations. It also strengthens self-awareness by highlighting the qualities they admire in others.

If you could go back in time, what advice would you give your younger self?

Therapeutic Commentary: This question encourages self-reflection on personal growth, resilience, and hard-earned wisdom. This exercise can help individuals process past regrets with self-compassion[43] and recognize how challenges have shaped their journey. It also offers a roadmap for future decision-making based on lessons already learned.

What's one thing that brings you joy no matter the circumstances?

> **Therapeutic Commentary:** Identifying sources of consistent joy helps clients recognize emotional anchors that provide stability in times of stress.[44] This question also highlights what truly matters to them, reinforcing the importance of prioritizing moments of happiness and well-being in daily life.

If someone were to write a book about your life, what would the title be?

> **Therapeutic Commentary:** This question combines creativity with self-reflection, allowing individuals to frame their life narrative in a meaningful way.[45] This question can reveal how they see themselves, the themes that define their journey, and any underlying aspirations or challenges they've overcome.

What's one thing you've always wanted to learn but haven't yet pursued?

> **Therapeutic Commentary:** This question explores personal aspirations and untapped passions, shedding light on areas of curiosity or growth.[46] Identifying these learning goals can reignite enthusiasm, highlight potential roadblocks, and create a path for self-improvement and fulfillment.

Who or what inspires you the most right now?

> **Therapeutic Commentary:** This question focuses on current motivations and sources of inspiration, offering insight into where their energy and attention are directed.[47] It also encourages deeper connections by creating opportunities to explore shared values and aspirations.

If you could change one thing about the world, what would it be?

> **Therapeutic Commentary:** This question uncovers deeply held values, beliefs, and a sense of social responsibility.[48] This question encourages individuals to think beyond themselves, reflecting on their role in creating positive change and how they align their actions with their convictions.

When was the last time something completely surprised or delighted you?

> **Therapeutic Commentary:** This question encourages reflection on moments of joy and spontaneity, which are key to emotional resilience and openness to new experiences.[49] Recognizing these moments can help individuals cultivate gratitude and a more positive mindset.

What do you consider to be your greatest accomplishment?

> **Therapeutic Commentary:** This question reinforces self-worth and confidence by highlighting moments of pride and achievement.[50] Reflecting on accomplishments can also help individuals combat imposter syndrome, recognize their own growth, and set the stage for future success.

If you could instantly master one skill, what would it be and why?

> **Therapeutic Commentary:** This question sheds light on personal aspirations, self-perceived gaps, and ambitions for growth.[51] This question can also reveal underlying insecurities or areas where they feel they need improvement, helping guide professional or personal development strategies.

What's an experience that significantly changed your perspective on leadership or teamwork?

> **Therapeutic Commentary:** This question provides insight into their leadership philosophy and how they navigate collaboration.[52] Understanding these experiences allows for deeper discussions on adaptability, problem-solving, and how past challenges have influenced their current approach to leadership.

What's a common misconception people have about your industry, and how do you see it differently?

> **Therapeutic Commentary:** This question encourages individuals to share their expertise and unique perspectives while challenging industry stereotypes.[53] This question fosters thought leadership and can reveal frustrations or insights that shape how they approach their profession.

What's something about you that people often misunderstand?

> **Therapeutic Commentary:** This question creates space for self-clarification and fosters empathy by allowing individuals to express aspects of their personality or leadership style that may not be immediately obvious.[54] This question can help bridge communication gaps in both personal and professional settings.

When you reflect on the most important relationships in your life, what do they all have in common?

> **Therapeutic Commentary:** This question identifies recurring values and dynamics in meaningful relationships, providing insight into what they prioritize in human connection.[55] Recognizing these patterns can guide future interactions, helping them cultivate stronger personal and professional relationships.

If you could share one lesson with someone new to your industry, what would it be and why?

> **Therapeutic Commentary:** Reflecting on key industry insights fosters a sense of expertise and confidence.[56] This question invites individuals to distill their knowledge into practical advice, reinforcing their own growth while positioning them as a mentor or leader. It also sheds light on what they perceive as the most critical takeaways from their professional journey.

How has your view of success evolved over time, and what experiences shaped that change?

> **Therapeutic Commentary:** Personal definitions of success are rarely static—they shift as individuals gain experience, face challenges, and reassess their priorities.[57] Exploring this evolution can reveal personal growth, changes in values, and a deeper understanding of fulfillment. It also provides a framework for setting future goals that feel authentic and achievable.

◌ PERSONAL EXPLORATION ◌

Now it's time for you to practice what you've learned.

Which two or three questions from this chapter will you commit to asking in your next client meeting? What do you expect their response to be, and how will you adapt based on what they share?

Think about a recent conversation where you could have gone deeper. Which question from this chapter would have helped you uncover more valuable insights, and how would it have changed the outcome?

Put your creative cap on now and write your own reflective question that would stimulate a thoughtful and introspective response from your client. What is that question and what do you believe you would learn about their values, motivations, or beliefs?

Over the next week, challenge yourself to ask one thought-provoking question each day, whether in a business setting or a personal conversation. Keep a journal of the responses and note any patterns or surprising insights. What did you learn about others—and yourself?

◌ YOUR FINAL THOUGHTS ◌

Use The Space Below To Capture Your Thoughts And Reflections On What You've Learned In This Section

_____
_____
_____
_____
_____
_____

BUILDING TRUST THROUGH MIRRORING

Mirroring is a powerful technique used in both therapy and consultative sales to establish rapport, foster trust, and deepen client relationships. By reflecting back the client's words, vocal variations, body language, breathing patterns, and emotions, the professional seller creates a sense of validation and understanding, making the client feel heard and seen.[1] In therapy, mirroring can help clients process their thoughts and emotions,[2] while in consultative sales, it strengthens the connection between the salesperson and the client, facilitating a deeper conversation.[3] When used skillfully, mirroring is not merely mimicry of the client's behavior, but an empathetic and intentional reflection that promotes openness, clarity, and connection.

Mirroring is both an art and a science. The practitioner must become hyper-observant and tuned into the natural behaviors of the client and in so doing, can intentionally employ a subtle application of the mirroring technique.[4] This sends quiet signals to the client's subconscious, resulting in the client feeling, without them knowing why, that a foundational connection exists and that they have been understood and validated.[5] In the following sections, we'll explore various aspects of mirroring, providing examples that consultative sales professionals can use to enhance their client interactions.

Words (Repeating Critical Words)

Mirroring through words is a deceptively simple yet powerful technique that involves repeating back a few key words or phrases the other person has just used. This serves both to confirm understanding and to signal curiosity, which encourages further sharing. The basic idea is to repeat or reflect back a few key words or phrases from what the other person has just said, often spoken in an inquisitive tone, as if asking, "Could you tell me more about that?"[6] By mirroring, you encourage the other person to elaborate, clarify, or share more, which signals that you're engaged, genuinely listening, and interested in understanding their point of view.[7] This helps build rapport and fosters a deeper connection. It also has the added benefit of giving the person a sense of being heard, which is essential for trust-building.

The reason this technique is so impactful is that it taps into a core human need for validation and empathy. When a salesperson mirrors a client's words, it not only reinforces the message that they're listening, but also invites the other person to explore their thoughts more deeply. It provides space for reflection and further dialogue without interruption. The simplicity of repeating just a word or two creates an open invitation for the other person to clarify, expand, or reconsider their perspective.[8] This encourages further engagement and creates an opportunity for deeper conversation.

Therapist Example:

- Client: "I was so mad at him."
    - Therapist: "Mad at him?"
- Client: "He doesn't care about me at all."
    - Therapist: "Doesn't care?"
- Client: "It's like I'm always the one putting in effort and nothing ever changes."
    - Therapist: "Nothing ever changes?"
- Client: "I feel like I'm running out of time to make a decision."
    - Therapist: "Running out of time?"
- Client: "I just don't trust people anymore."
    - Therapist: "Don't trust?"
- Client: "I've been feeling overwhelmed lately with everything piling up."
    - Therapist: "Piling up?"
- Client: "I don't think I can ever forgive him for what he did."
    - Therapist: "What he did?"
- Client: "I'm afraid I'll mess things up again."
    - Therapist: "Mess things up?"
- Client: "It's been hard to move on from that experience."
    - Therapist: "Hard to move on?"
- Client: "I'm not sure I can do this on my own."
    - Therapist: "On your own?"

Consultative Sales Example:

- Client: "We don't have the budget for this project."
    - Salesperson: "This project?"
- Client: "We're concerned about the long-term impact of this solution."
    - Salesperson: "Long-term impact?"
- Client: "It's too complex to roll out across the entire organization."
    - Salesperson: "Too complex?"
- Client: "The current system isn't working as we expected."
    - Salesperson: "Not working?"
- Client: "Our team isn't on the same page with this project."
    - Salesperson: "Same page?"
- Client: "This solution doesn't align with our strategic goals."
    - Salesperson: "Doesn't align?"

- Client: "We need something that's more adaptable to changes."
    - Salesperson: "More adaptable?"
- Client: "The lack of integration is a major problem."
    - Salesperson: "Lack of integration?"
- Client: "We're worried about the implementation timeline."
    - Salesperson: "Implementation timeline?"
- Client: "This issue has been dragging on for too long."
    - Salesperson: "Dragging on?"

Why Mirroring Words Works

This technique works because it shows active listening, helps clarify meaning, and invites further exploration. Repeating key words reinforces that you're paying attention and helps focus the conversation on what matters most to the other person. This is particularly powerful in situations where emotions or concerns are running high. It calms the other person, as they know their thoughts and feelings are being acknowledged. Mirroring also encourages the speaker to reflect on their own words, which may lead them to uncover new insights or emotions they hadn't considered before. This process deepens the conversation and builds trust, because it signals that you value their input and are invested in understanding them.[9]

In the context of sales, this technique can guide the conversation toward areas of pain points or needs that the client may not have fully expressed yet. It helps uncover hidden obstacles or motivations, creating the foundation for a solution that genuinely addresses the client's needs.[10] The simplicity of repeating just one or two words keeps the dialogue open, leaving room for more expansive and productive conversations.

Practice

Your challenge is to practice mirroring in a low-stakes, low-risk social setting where sales pressure does not exist. When you find yourself in a conversation with family or friends, listen with intentionality and pick up on the key words or short phrases the other person says. When they pause, repeat the word or words in an inquisitive tone and then stop talking. Allow the silence to be the invitation that encourages the other person to share more.[11] Listen intently again and mirror a second time. This may go on for a while, so enjoy the experience of mirroring words with your family or friends.

Once you're comfortable with mirroring words in social settings, it's time to bring word mirroring into work. First, explore it with peers and colleagues, and when you feel comfortable, leverage it within your client conversations. Even though this technique is simple, you will be amazed at the results.

ଔ୶୶ଔଔ

Use of Sensory Words (NLP Predicates)

Neuro-Linguistic Programming (NLP) predicates refer to the sensory-based language patterns people use to process and express their thoughts.[12] These predicates align with the way individuals experience the world—whether through sight (Visual), sound (Auditory), touch (Kinesthetic), smell (Olfactory), taste (Gustatory), logical reasoning (Auditory Digital), or time perception (Temporal).[13] Understanding and mirroring a client's preferred predicate helps sales professionals establish deeper rapport, build trust, and enhance communication effectiveness.

Clients naturally use predicate-based language when they think, describe experiences, or make decisions.[14] By actively listening for these linguistic cues, a sales professional can adjust their communication to match the client's internal processing style, making interactions feel more intuitive and personalized.[15] This approach fosters stronger connections, ensures clarity, and increases the likelihood of a successful sale.

Below is an in-depth explanation of each NLP predicate, why it matters in sales conversations, and key verbal cues to listen for when determining a client's preferred mode of communication.

1. Visual (Seeing, Imagining, Perceiving)

People with a visual preference process information through images, spatial awareness, and visualization.[16] They think in pictures and describe concepts using words that evoke clarity, brightness, and structure. Visual individuals appreciate diagrams, charts, and demonstrations because they help them "see" the solution.[17] If sales conversations feel vague, they may struggle to engage.

What a Client Might Say:

- "I don't see how this will fit into our existing setup. Can you illustrate the process?"
- "I want to get a clearer picture of what this means for our long-term goals."
- "I can't quite visualize how this will integrate with our current system."
- "Show me what this would look like in action."

Effective Sales Phrases:

- "I see what you're looking for. Let me paint a clearer picture for you."
- "Can you visualize how this solution will streamline your workflow?"
- "Let's take a look at the bigger picture."
- "From your perspective, what does success look like?"
- "I'd like to highlight a few key benefits that stand out."
- "We can sharpen the focus on what matters most to your team."
- "This gives you a clearer vision of how everything connects."
- "What's your view on this approach?"
- "Let me illuminate the advantages for you."
- "You'll gain a crystal-clear perspective once you see it in action."

Why It Works

Visual clients think in images and process information by forming mental pictures.[18] By aligning your communication with their natural thinking process, you create a sense of clarity and confidence, making them more likely to connect with and trust your proposal.[19]

2. Auditory (Hearing, Listening, Discussing)

Auditory clients process information through sound, tone, and verbal communication.[20] They prefer discussions, presentations, and explanations that emphasize auditory clarity. They are sensitive to voice modulation and often repeat key phrases to ensure understanding.[21] Background noise can be distracting to them, and they may be drawn to rhythmic or structured speech patterns.

What a Client Might Say:

- "That sounds like something to consider."
- "Let's talk through the details so we can make a decision."
- "I need to hear a lot more about how this could work for us."
- "Can you talk me through this step by step?"

Effective Sales Phrases:

- "That sounds like the right solution for your team."
- "I hear what you're saying, and I'd like to explore that further."
- "Let's talk through the specifics and tune in to your key priorities."
- "Does this ring a bell with what you've been considering?"
- "If we listen carefully to your challenges, the solution becomes clear."

- "I'd love to echo some of your thoughts to ensure we're aligned."
- "From your point of view, what resonates the most about this option?"
- "Let's amplify the impact by fine-tuning the details."
- "This should be music to your ears when it comes to efficiency gains."
- "You'll love the sound of what's possible with this approach."

Why It Works

Auditory clients rely on verbal communication, rhythm, and tone to process information.[22] If a sales pitch lacks engaging discussion or structured explanation, they may feel disconnected. Using auditory-focused phrases ensures they "hear" the value in your solution, reinforcing clarity and understanding. This also helps them retain information better, as they tend to recall conversations based on sound and structured dialogue.[23]

3. Kinesthetic (Feeling, Sensing, Experiencing)

Kinesthetic clients process information through touch, movement, and emotions.[24] They often need to physically experience or emotionally connect with a concept before making a decision. They use language related to feelings, grip, texture, and motion. If a presentation lacks a tangible or emotional aspect, they may struggle to engage with the message.[25]

What a Client Might Say:

- "This has to feel right before we move forward."
- "I need to get a better grasp on how this solution works."
- "I want to make sure this sits well with our team."
- "Let me get a sense of how this will affect our workflow."

Effective Sales Phrases:

- "I can tell this decision has to feel right for you."
- "Let's get a solid grasp of what success means for your business."
- "This will give you a firm foundation for long-term growth."
- "I sense that this is something you're passionate about."
- "How does this option sit with you?"
- "You want a solution that's smooth and easy to implement."
- "This approach will give you a strong hold on your challenges."
- "You'll feel the impact of these results right away."
- "Does this direction feel aligned with your goals?"
- "Once you try this, you'll notice the difference immediately."

Why It Works

Kinesthetic clients make decisions based on how something feels, both emotionally and physically.[26] If they don't develop a tangible connection to a solution, they may hesitate to commit. Using sensory language related to movement, touch, and emotions allows them to experience the solution in a way that feels real and compelling. This approach helps build a deep, intuitive connection that makes your pitch resonate on a personal level.[27]

4. Olfactory (Smelling, Sensing Intuition)

Olfactory clients associate experiences with scents, intuition, and environmental triggers.[28] While less common, these individuals often rely on instinct and gut feelings when making decisions. Their language references smells, freshness, and instinctual cues. Addressing their need for an intuitive, natural flow in decision-making can strengthen rapport.[29]

What a Client Might Say:

- "Something about this doesn't smell right—I need to look into it more."
- "This proposal has a fresh take that I really like."
- "We need to clear the air on some concerns before we proceed."
- "This deal has the scent of success—it feels like the right move."

Effective Sales Phrases:

- "I sense there's something in the air about this decision—what are your thoughts?"
- "Does this solution pass the sniff test for your team?"
- "I get the feeling that something doesn't smell right—let's address it."
- "There's a fresh approach we can take to this challenge."
- "Let's clear the air on any concerns you might have."
- "This opportunity has the scent of success."
- "Something about this option feels fresh and invigorating."
- "We'll filter through the details to find the best path forward."
- "You want to work with a partner that smells success before it happens."
- "There's an unmistakable aroma of innovation in this approach."

Why It Works

Olfactory clients rely on intuition, scent-based memories, and instinct to guide their decisions.[30] While less common, their decision-making process is deeply tied to how something "feels in the air" rather than just facts and figures.[31]

Using phrases that reference freshness, instinct, and environmental cues makes the conversation feel more aligned with their natural way of evaluating opportunities.[32] This helps them trust their gut feeling, making them more comfortable moving forward with a decision.[33]

5. Gustatory (Tasting, Digesting Information)

Gustatory clients relate to the world through taste, preference, and absorption of information.[34] They use language that references flavors, digestion, and nourishment. While rare, this predicate often aligns with people who talk about experiences in terms of enjoyment, satisfaction, or personal preference. Ensuring your offer is "easy to digest" can make a significant impact.[35]

What a Client Might Say:

- "I need time to chew this over before making a decision."
- "This option leaves a bad taste in my mouth—what else do you have?"
- "I want a proposal that's easier to digest."
- "That sounds like a sweet deal, but I need more details."

Effective Sales Phrases:

- "Does this solution leave a good taste in your mouth?"
- "Let's chew over the details before making a final call."
- "I want this proposal to be easy for you to digest."
- "This approach is designed to be palatable and effective."
- "You don't want a deal that's hard to swallow."
- "Success should taste sweet, and this strategy delivers just that."
- "Savor the benefits this solution brings to your business."
- "This will leave a lasting impression, much like a fine meal."
- "Let's avoid any bitter outcomes by refining our approach now."
- "We want to create a recipe for long-term success."

Why It Works

Gustatory clients associate decisions with taste, preference, and satisfaction.[36] If a solution seems unpalatable or hard to digest, they'll likely hesitate. By framing the offer as something enjoyable, easy to absorb, and fulfilling, you make it more appealing and relatable. This language helps them process the information in a way that feels comfortable, ensuring they "digest" the value of your solution with ease.[37]

6. Auditory Digital (Thinking, Logic, Internal Dialogue)

Auditory Digital clients process information internally through analysis, reasoning, and structured thought.[38] They tend to use logical, precise language and prefer conversations that are clear, structured, and data-driven. They need evidence, frameworks, and well-reasoned arguments to support a decision. If a discussion is too emotional or abstract, they may disengage.[39]

What a Client Might Say:

- "Let's break this down logically before moving forward."
- "I need to analyze all the variables before making a choice."
- "Does this approach align with our strategic objectives?"
- "I want to see the numbers behind this before committing."

Effective Sales Phrases:

- "Let's analyze the key data points together."
- "That logically aligns with your objectives."
- "I think this approach makes the most sense."
- "We'll break this down into logical steps."
- "From a rational standpoint, this is the optimal path."
- "The numbers strongly support this direction."
- "It's all about weighing the facts and making a sound decision."
- "Does this conclusion align with your analysis?"
- "From a strategic perspective, this holds strong value."
- "The logic behind this approach is undeniable."

Why It Works

Auditory Digital clients process information through logic, reasoning, and internal dialogue.[40] They need structure, data, and clear rationale to feel confident in their decisions.[41] If a conversation is too emotional or unstructured, they may disengage. By using precise, analytical language, you align with their thought process, making them feel intellectually secure and more likely to commit.[42]

7. Temporal (Time, Future Orientation)

Temporal clients are focused on time—past, present, and future.[43] They prefer discussions that highlight sequencing, deadlines, and long-term impact.[44] They often reference schedules, timing, and projections in decision-making. If a sales pitch lacks clear timelines or future-oriented framing, they may struggle to engage.[45]

What a Client Might Say:

- "What's the long-term impact of this decision?"
- "How does this fit into our timeline for the next year?"
- "Can you walk me through the implementation schedule?"
- "Looking ahead, what kind of results should we expect?"

Effective Sales Phrases:

- "In the future, how do you see this playing out?"
- "Let's set a timeline for implementation."
- "Over time, this will become even more valuable."
- "Looking ahead, how does this fit into your roadmap?"
- "This solution is built for long-term success."
- "Let's map out the next steps to ensure a smooth transition over time."
- "This decision will shape the future of your business—how do you see it unfolding?"
- "Imagine looking back a year from now—what impact would you want this solution to have had?"
- "Timing is everything—when would be the ideal moment to implement this for maximum impact?"
- "This investment isn't just for today—it's about creating momentum for what's ahead."

Why It Works

Temporal clients think in terms of timelines, sequences, and long-term outcomes.[46] If a proposal lacks clear timeframes or future-oriented planning, they may struggle to see its relevance. Using temporal language helps them map out how a solution fits into their schedule and long-term strategy.[47] This makes the decision-making process feel structured and future-proof, increasing their confidence in moving forward.

Mastering NLP predicates is a game-changer in consultative sales. By aligning your language with how clients naturally process information—whether they see possibilities, hear concerns, feel decisions, or think logically—you build trust, enhance clarity, and create a seamless flow of conversation. This isn't about persuasion; it's about connection.[48] When done with authenticity, mirroring sensory language not only strengthens relationships but also helps clients envision the future impact of their choices, making decisions feel more natural and inevitable.[49] By reducing fear of change and structuring the decision-making process, you empower clients to move forward with confidence.[50] The result? A consultative sales experience that feels intuitive, strategic, and mutually beneficial.

Practice

It's time for you to practice using NLP predicates in your daily conversations. As mentioned before, practice this approach first in a non-business setting to avoid anxiety or discomfort when cultivating this new skill. Actively listen for cue words from the other person and align your response to match their preferred predicate. Take note of how they respond and watch as the conversation flows naturally as you "speak their language".

Once you're comfortable with using NLP predicates in social settings, try using them at work. Explore this approach with peers and colleagues, and when you feel comfortable, bring this covert tool into your client conversations. This technique takes a bit more effort than the simple mirroring of words that was explored in the previous section, but the value derived from this technique far outweighs any learning curve that may exist.

Mirroring in Body Language, Movement, and Facial Expressions

Mirroring body language is a powerful technique in consultative sales that fosters trust, rapport, and a sense of connection with clients. When done correctly, it creates an unconscious alignment between the salesperson and the client, making interactions feel effortless and natural.[51] The key to effective mirroring lies in subtlety—being too obvious or mechanical can make the client feel manipulated, while being too passive can fail to create meaningful engagement. The goal is not to mimic or act as a perfect mirror, but rather to provide a natural, slightly delayed reflection of the client's body language, energy, and movement—something skilled therapists do with intentionality.

Timing is everything when it comes to body mirroring. Rather than instantly replicating a client's gestures or posture, a skilled salesperson allows a brief, natural pause before subtly adjusting their own movements to reflect the client's.[52] This slight delay prevents mirroring from feeling forced or contrived, allowing it to register subconsciously rather than as an overt technique. Additionally, mirroring should not be an exact replication; instead, the salesperson should adjust their response to be similar but not identical.[53] For example, if a client leans forward with their elbows on the table, the salesperson might lean in slightly, resting their forearms on the surface rather than copying the exact positioning. This ensures that the client perceives a sense of connection without consciously recognizing the technique at play.

Done well, mirroring body language creates a powerful psychological effect. Clients see themselves reflected in the salesperson, but they don't know why—it's an unconscious cue that fosters comfort, trust, and openness.[54] This sense of familiarity triggers a feeling of security, making the client more receptive to the conversation. When used strategically throughout the sales interaction, mirroring body language can lower resistance, encourage collaboration, and set the foundation for a strong, consultative relationship.

A successful mirroring strategy involves two key phases:

Following

Initially, the salesperson subtly mirrors the client's body language, energy level, and posture to establish a sense of connection and comfort.[55] This phase is about observation and responsiveness—watching how the client moves, holds themselves, and expresses emotion, and then gradually incorporating elements of their behavior into the salesperson's own. However, mirroring should remain subtle and adaptive; if the client shifts frequently or exhibits high-energy gestures, the salesperson should respond in a way that reflects but slightly softens their movements to maintain control of the interaction. The goal of following is to create a nonverbal bridge that allows the client to unconsciously feel seen, heard, understood, and experience a sense of ease.

Leading

Once rapport has been established through effective following, the salesperson can gradually shift their own posture, expressions, and gestures to guide the client toward a more open, engaged, and positive state.[56] Leading works best when done with careful pacing—too abrupt a shift may break the subconscious connection, while a gradual transition encourages the client to follow suit.[57] For example, if the client initially sits with crossed arms but later relaxes, the salesperson might also open their posture slightly sooner, subtly encouraging further openness.[58] Similarly, if the client is subdued or hesitant, the salesperson can begin to project slightly more confidence and enthusiasm, subtly lifting the energy of the conversation. Leading allows the salesperson to influence the emotional and psychological tone of the interaction, ultimately steering the client toward a state of greater receptivity and engagement.[59] If the salesperson leads a body movement change and then moments later sees the client move in a similar manner, the salesperson can assume one of two things:

1. The foundation of rapport and connectedness has been established, and the salesperson can settle into the conversation feeling confident in the formation of a trusted relationship, or
2. The client, if also trained in body language mirroring, may also be intentionally employing the same technique.
    - This rarely happens, but when it does, smiles usually come across the faces of both client and salesperson as they acknowledge their shared application of a mutually known rapport-building approach.[60]

By skillfully navigating the balance between following and leading, sales professionals can use mirroring as a natural and strategic tool to strengthen trust and build authentic connections with clients. When executed with subtlety and proper timing, mirroring fosters a sense of familiarity and ease, making conversations feel more engaging and collaborative.[61] By ensuring that body language adjustments remain organic rather than forced, salespeople can create an environment where clients feel understood and valued. This nonverbal alignment not only enhances rapport but also encourages open, productive discussions, ultimately leading to stronger, more persuasive client relationships. Be sure to Follow first, to establish a connection and makes the client feel comfortable. Then Lead subtly after rapport is built. Shift your body language to a more open, engaged posture to gently encourage the client to follow suit. Finally, be sure to stay authentic in your physical mirroring. Overdoing mirroring your body movements is easily perceived by the other person and can feel manipulative. The goal is to use this approach naturally and with the sole intention of nurturing and building a trust and rapport.

Below are practical mirroring techniques across different body areas to enhance consultative sales interactions and forge client rapport.

1. Head Movements

- **Subtle Nodding:** Mirroring a client's nods reinforces agreement and engagement, encouraging them to continue speaking.[62]
- **Head Tilt for Curiosity:** Slightly tilting the head when a client expresses uncertainty signals curiosity and empathy, inviting them to elaborate.[63]
- **Maintaining Stillness:** If a client pauses in thought, holding a calm, neutral head position respects their processing time and avoids disruption.
- **Forward Head Lean:** Leaning in slightly when the client shares important details demonstrates attentiveness and deeper interest.[64]

- **Gradual Leading Toward an Upright Posture:** If the client appears disengaged or slouched, mirroring their posture first and then gradually straightening up can encourage them to do the same.[65]

2. Arms and Hands

- **Matching Hand Gestures:** If the client is expressive with their hands, responding with subtle matching movements aligns energy and communication rhythm.[66]
- **Resting Hands in Sync:** Placing hands on the table a few moments after the client does fosters a sense of mutual transparency.[67]
- **Crossing Arms Briefly Before Opening Up:** If the client starts with a closed posture, mirroring it initially and then shifting to an open stance can encourage them to do the same.[68]
- **Synchronizing Hand Movements:** Matching the pacing and style of gestures when explaining a concept enhances conversational flow.[69]
- **Mimicking Thoughtful Gestures:** If the client places a hand on their chin while thinking, a subtle similar movement a few moments later can reinforce alignment.[70]

3. Body Direction

- **Turning Toward the Client When They Shift Toward You:** This subtle movement signals engagement and attentiveness.[71]
- **Leaning In to Match Their Posture:** If the client leans forward while discussing a point, mirroring this posture reinforces active listening.[72]
- **Adopting a Similar Sitting Posture:** Whether upright, relaxed, or leaning back, aligning with the client's sitting style maintains comfort and connection.[73]
- **Adjusting Torso Orientation to Match the Client's:** If they angle slightly away, mirroring this can reduce perceived pressure before leading back into full alignment.[74]
- **Subtly Mirroring Weight Shifts:** If the client shifts their weight from side to side, subtly doing the same can create subconscious attunement.[75]

4. Legs and Feet (Crossing, Placement, Direction)

Some commentary for you to ponder. It has been said that the eyes are the windows to the soul, but I would offer for your consideration that in fact it is the feet and not the eyes. Specifically, the direction in which the feet are pointed are the true windows to the other person's thoughts and desires.[76] If a client has their feet pointed toward you, this is likely an indicator that they desire to stay engaged in a conversation with you.[77] However, if their torso is facing you but their feet are pointed elsewhere, perhaps toward the bar or at another person, their body is telling them and you that in that moment, they wish to move on.[78] If this situation arises, the most beneficial thing you can do for the relationship is to allow the other person to leave. Perhaps say something like, "Thank you so much for chatting with me. I've thoroughly enjoyed our conversation. I'm sure there are many people here that you'd like to connect with. Why don't we both mingle a bit and let's reconnect later." This kind gesture to respectfully release them from the engagement with you so they can move on to other conversations will plant a seed in the other person that you are respectful of their time and have a level of self-awareness that is not common amongst pushy salespeople.[79]

- **Crossing Legs When the Client Does:** Establishes subconscious synchronization without being overt.[80]
- **Placing Feet Flat When the Client Does:** Creates a grounded, stable presence.[81]
- **Pointing Feet Toward the Client:** Indicates attentiveness and engagement in a nonverbal way.[82]
- **Matching Casual or Formal Posture:** Sitting in alignment with their comfort level helps maintain ease in the conversation.[83]
- **Gradually Leading Toward an Open Stance:** If the client starts with tightly crossed legs, mirroring first and then shifting toward a more open posture encourages receptiveness.[84]

5. Facial Expressions (Emotional Alignment and Microexpressions)

- **Mirroring a Smile:** If the client smiles, responding with a natural smile reinforces warmth and connection.[85]
- **Reflecting Concern:** Subtly mirroring a client's concerned expression when discussing challenges shows empathy and validation.[86]
- **Raising Eyebrows Slightly for Emphasis:** This signals attentiveness when the client emphasizes a key point.[87]
- **Softening Expressions During Solution Discussions:** Encourages a sense of calm and trust when guiding the client toward a resolution.[88]
- **Matching the Client's Expressiveness:** Whether animated or reserved, aligning expressiveness keeps the conversation natural and comfortable.[89]
- **Synchronizing Blink Rate and Eye Contact Style:** Creates an unconscious rhythm of engagement, reinforcing connection.[90]
- **Adjusting Facial Tension Based on Emotional State:** Tension when they are serious, relaxation when they are at ease.[91]

Mastering the art of mirroring in body language, movement, and facial expressions allows consultative sales professionals to build deeper, more meaningful client relationships. When used with intention and subtlety, mirroring fosters trust, enhances communication, and creates a natural sense of alignment between the salesperson and the client. By first following the client's cues and gradually leading toward a more engaged and open posture, sales professionals can gently guide the conversation in a positive direction without appearing disingenuous. The key to effective mirroring lies in authenticity—when done naturally and with genuine attentiveness, it strengthens rapport and helps clients feel truly heard and understood. By integrating these techniques into everyday sales interactions, professionals can not only improve their ability to connect but also influence outcomes in a way that feels seamless and organic. Ultimately, mirroring is not just about body language; it is a powerful psychological tool that, when mastered, transforms transactional sales into consultative, relationship-driven partnerships.

Practice

When people are in rapport, they unknowingly mirror each other's body language. Start "people watching" when you are in public. Observe how people physically relate and respond to each other and notice how physically in sync people are when they do and do not have a meaningful connection. Then, begin subtly adding body mirroring into your personal and professional conversations. Pay attention to how the other person's body responds and enjoy the newfound rapport created through subtle body movements.

C380806380C380

Mirroring Vocal Variety

Vocal variety is a powerful yet often underestimated tool in consultative sales. How something is said matters just as much—if not more—than the words themselves. By mirroring a client's pitch, rate, volume, tone, rhythm, and tempo, a salesperson can build deeper rapport, establish trust, and guide conversations more effectively.[92] This technique helps align emotionally and cognitively with the client, making the interaction feel natural and connected.[93]

Vocal mirroring should never feel forced or exaggerated; rather, it should be a subtle alignment that fosters engagement and psychological comfort.[94] Below are ten highly strategic examples of how a salesperson can leverage vocal mirroring to influence outcomes in a consultative sales setting.

1. Matching a Thoughtful, Deliberate Speaking Style

- **Example:** A client speaks slowly and deliberately, taking their time to articulate their thoughts. Instead of rushing ahead, the salesperson mirrors this pace, pausing slightly before responding.
- **Why It Works:** This demonstrates patience and respect for the client's decision-making process, preventing the salesperson from appearing pushy or impatient.[95]

2. Adjusting to an Energetic, Fast-Paced Client

- **Example:** A client is excited about a new project, speaking quickly and with enthusiasm. The salesperson slightly increases their own speech rate and matches the upbeat energy.
- **Why It Works:** Engaging at a similar tempo makes the conversation feel more dynamic and aligned with the client's momentum, preventing the salesperson from seeming disengaged or uninterested.[96]

3. Calibrating Volume to Establish Authority or Reassurance

- **Example:** A client speaks in a low, reserved voice, unsure about making a decision. The salesperson slightly lowers their own volume but maintains steady confidence.
- **Why It Works:** This subtle mirroring creates a sense of intimacy and trust, making the client feel safe and understood while ensuring that the salesperson remains in control of the conversation.[97]

4. Mirroring a Decisive and Assertive Tone

- **Example:** A client is direct, confident, and uses a firm tone when discussing their needs. The salesperson responds in a similarly clear, assertive tone, reinforcing certainty.
- **Why It Works:** Confidence is contagious. By mirroring a decisive tone, the salesperson signals competence and reliability, which reassures the client that they are dealing with an expert.[98]

5. Aligning with Hesitancy to Guide the Client Toward Clarity

- **Example:** A client speaks with uncertainty, using a questioning tone and pausing frequently. The salesperson mirrors the questioning tone initially but gradually transitions into a steadier, more reassuring tone.

- **Why It Works:** This technique first validates the client's uncertainty but then leads them toward confidence in their decision-making process, making them feel supported rather than pressured.[99]

6. Matching an Urgent, Time-Sensitive Tempo

- **Example:** A client is under pressure and speaks quickly, emphasizing deadlines and constraints. The salesperson mirrors the fast pace but speaks with calm clarity, offering structured solutions.
- **Why It Works:** This prevents friction by demonstrating understanding of the urgency while maintaining composure, which reassures the client that the salesperson can handle time-sensitive challenges effectively.[100]

7. Mirroring an Analytical, Data-Driven Rhythm

- **Example:** A client speaks in a measured, fact-based manner, emphasizing logical points and avoiding emotional language. The salesperson mirrors this structured approach, presenting data succinctly and minimizes the emotionality in their tone.
- **Why It Works:** Analytical clients trust those who communicate in a way that aligns with their thought process. Matching their logical delivery style increases credibility and alignment.[101]

8. Shifting Tone to Encourage Openness in a Reserved Client

- **Example:** A client is guarded and reserved, keeping their tone neutral and their responses brief. The salesperson starts with a neutral tone as well but gradually warms their voice, introducing more openness.
- **Why It Works:** This approach eases the client into greater engagement without overwhelming them. It allows trust to develop naturally while keeping the conversation comfortable.[102]

9. Adapting to an Energetic, Lighthearted Client to Foster Connection

- **Example:** A client jokes frequently and keeps conversations informal. The salesperson responds with light humor and a relaxed tone while maintaining professionalism.
- **Why It Works:** Mirroring a client's playful energy fosters connection, making interactions more natural and engaging. This builds rapport and eases the sales process.[103]

10. Pacing a Storytelling Rhythm for Engaging Narratives

- **Example:** A client shares anecdotes and speaks with a natural storytelling cadence, emphasizing certain words and pausing for effect. The salesperson mirrors this rhythm when sharing their own insights.
- **Why It Works:** Storytelling is an emotional engagement tool. By mirroring the storytelling rhythm, the salesperson fosters a more personal and compelling conversation, keeping the client engaged.[104]

The Power of Vocal Variation and Adaptation in Consultative Sales

Effective vocal variation and adaptation in sales is about connection, not mimicry. By naturally adjusting elements like tone, pace, volume, and rhythm to align with a client's speaking style, a salesperson fosters a sense of ease and familiarity. This subtle alignment helps clients feel heard and understood, strengthening trust. It is essential to note that any use of vocal adjustments must be organic, subtle, natural, and responsive. Overdoing it or applying it rigidly can seem forced, undermining authenticity, and make the client feel manipulated. Skilled sales professionals remain attuned to the client's emotional state, adjusting their vocal variety in real time to maintain a natural flow. When used thoughtfully, vocal variation and adaptation enhances engagement, deepens rapport, and creates a more comfortable, productive dialogue—leading to stronger relationships and better outcomes.

Practice

If you've ever been in a meaningful relationship, you may have heard your partner say, "It's not **WHAT** you said, it's **HOW** you said it." Or perhaps you were the one who said this to your partner. The point is that vocal pitch, rate, volume, tone, rhythm, and tempo all impact how a message is received and experienced by the other person. Your task is to listen intently to your personal and professional conversations and begin to classify the other person according to their vocal quality. One way to think about this might be to compare people's vocal variety to different musical instruments. Do they speak in a tempo like maracas shaking, resonant and smooth like a cello, or pitchy and squeaky like bagpipes?[105] By classifying their vocal style, you will be able to intentionally adjust your vocal approach to align in a subtle but meaningful way to foster a deeper, more trusted connection.[106]

Mirroring Breathing Patterns

Breathing is one of the most fundamental, yet often overlooked, aspects of human connection and communication.[107] When two people synchronize their breath, it creates an unspoken connection—a physiological alignment that fosters trust and rapport on a subconscious level.[108] Therapists will often purposefully synchronize their breathing pattern to align with their client's to help accelerate and enhance rapport.[109] In sessions when the client is breathing rapidly as a result of a deep emotional experience, instead of matching the rapid breathing pattern, the therapist may intentionally breathe in a slow, methodical manner to subtly lead the client to a more relaxed and calm state.[110] In many clinical couples therapy sessions, clients are asked to face each other, look into each other's eyes, and synchronize their breathing. In some cases, couples are asked to embrace and breathe in unison. In both cases, the act of aligning the couple's breath creates a profound connection that penetrates deep.[111] Obviously, in consultative sales, breath-mirroring is approached in a professional manner, avoiding any unwelcome, unwarranted, or undesired physical touch. Regardless, mirroring a sales client's breathing pattern can help the seller establish a sense of calm, reduce resistance, develop a connection, and create a more comfortable atmosphere for discussion.

Unlike more overt mirroring techniques, breathing synchronization is subtle and should feel natural and never forced. The goal is not to mimic every inhale and exhale mechanically but to gradually adjust your own breathing to align with the client's rhythm in a way that unconsciously enhances connection.

Practical Applications of Mirroring Breathing in Sales

1. Slowing Down to Match a Relaxed Client

- **Example:** If your client is speaking in a slow, measured tone and taking deep breaths, subtly slow your own breathing to match their pace.
- **Why It Works:** This signals to their subconscious that you are on the same wavelength, creating a shared sense of calm.[112] It also ensures that you don't come across as overly aggressive or rushed in the conversation.

2. Regulating Fast-Paced Breathing in High-Energy Situations

- **Example:** If the client is speaking quickly and breathing in shorter, more frequent bursts—perhaps due to excitement or stress—match their tempo briefly before gradually slowing your breath.
- **Why It Works:** By first mirroring their heightened state, you establish rapport, and by slowing down afterward, you help bring the conversation to a more controlled and balanced pace.[113] This is particularly useful when a client is feeling pressured by deadlines or overwhelmed with decisions.

3. Using Breathing to Diffuse Resistance

- **Example:** If a client is tense, crossing their arms, and holding their breath intermittently, take slow, deep breaths yourself. Eventually, they will subconsciously begin to follow your lead and relax.
- **Why It Works:** People tend to unconsciously synchronize with those they trust. By demonstrating a relaxed, open breathing pattern, you encourage them to lower their defenses, making them more receptive to discussion.[114]

4. Matching Subtle Shifts in Breath During Decision-Making Moments

- **Example:** When a client is deeply contemplating a decision, you might notice a shift in their breathing—perhaps a long pause followed by a sigh. Mirror this by pausing before you speak, then exhaling gently before continuing.
- **Why It Works:** This technique reinforces that you are tuned into their thought process, creating a feeling of mutual understanding. It also prevents you from rushing in to fill the silence, allowing the client the space they need to process their thoughts.[115]

5. Aligning Breath for a Smoother Sales Closing

- **Example:** As you move toward closing the sale, subtly synchronize your breathing with the client's and then slightly slow it down. Maintain steady, confident breathing as you present the final decision or next steps.
- **Why It Works:** This stabilizes any last-minute nerves and encourages the client to feel grounded in their choice.[116] It also prevents you from appearing anxious or overly eager, which could create doubt in their mind.

6. Controlling Breath to Maintain Authority in Difficult Conversations

- **Example:** If a client becomes defensive or argumentative, they may start breathing rapidly or erratically. Instead of mirroring this, maintain steady, controlled breathing while speaking in a measured tone.
- **Why It Works:** This demonstrates composure and reassures the client that you are confident and in control of the conversation. It helps de-escalate tension and keeps the discussion productive.[117]

7. Creating an Engaged, Present Atmosphere During Meetings

- **Example:** During a long meeting, if a client starts sighing or showing signs of disengagement, subtly adjust your breathing to a more intentional, energized rhythm.
- **Why It Works:** Energy levels are contagious. By maintaining an engaged, attentive breathing pattern, you help refocus their attention and subtly shift the meeting's energy in a positive direction.[118]
  - However, if the client continues to yawn, that is a clear signal that it is time to take a break.

The Power of Breathing in Sales Conversations

Mirroring breath is one of the most natural yet powerful ways to create connection in consultative sales. Unlike verbal mirroring, which is conscious, breath synchronization operates on a subconscious level, helping clients feel at ease without them realizing why. When used with skill and subtlety, this technique enhances trust, lowers resistance, and fosters an environment where productive, open conversations can thrive. The key is to remain adaptable—adjusting your breathing based on the client's state while leading the interaction toward a more balanced and confident rhythm.

Practice

Adjusting and aligning your breathing pattern to the people you interact with in your personal life is a wonderful way to practice this technique without putting your business transactions at risk. Once you feel comfortable subtly employing this technique with your family and friends, the logical next step is to practice it with coworkers and then with clients. Always remember to be natural and subtle when applying these principles. Ease into breath alignment with your client's breathing rhythm and pattern and notice just how more connected the relationship becomes.

Mirroring Emotionality

Mirroring emotionality is one of the most powerful techniques in consultative sales. While logic and data play a role in decision-making, emotions often drive purchasing decisions.[119] By accurately reflecting and mirroring a client's emotions, a salesperson can foster trust, deepen rapport, and create a psychological sense of alignment that makes the client feel truly heard and understood.

This approach goes beyond merely repeating words—it requires emotional intelligence to recognize, reflect, and appropriately respond to the client's underlying feelings.[120] The goal is not to mimic but to attune oneself to the client's emotional state and respond in a way that validates their experience. Below are ten strategic examples of how sales professionals can mirror emotional tone to create meaningful client relationships, just like a therapist.

1. Mirroring Frustration to Show Understanding

- **Example:** A client is frustrated with their current provider, speaking in a clipped tone and expressing dissatisfaction. Instead of immediately offering a solution, the salesperson mirrors their concern by saying, *"I completely understand why that would be frustrating. That's not the experience you should have."*
- **Why It Works:** By matching the frustration in a concerned yet composed tone, the salesperson signals empathy and validation, rather than dismissing the client's emotions or rushing to problem-solve too soon.[121]

2. Matching Excitement to Reinforce Positive Energy

- **Example:** A client is enthusiastic about a new initiative and speaks with energy and optimism. The salesperson mirrors this excitement with a slightly elevated tone and enthusiasm: *"That's incredible! It sounds like a huge opportunity for your team—tell me more!"*
- **Why It Works:** Matching the client's excitement amplifies their positive feelings, making the salesperson feel like a trusted collaborator rather than just a vendor.[122]

3. Reflecting Hesitation to Build Comfort

- **Example:** A client is hesitant, speaking slowly and with uncertainty, saying things like, *"I'm not sure this is the right time for us to make a change."*

The salesperson mirrors this tentative tone and responds with, *"I hear you—it's a big decision, and timing is everything. Let's explore what makes sense for you right now."*
- **Why It Works:** Instead of countering the hesitation with high energy or pressure, the salesperson aligns with the client's cautious mindset, creating a non-threatening non-judgmental space for exploration.[123]

4. Mirroring Disappointment to Build Trust

- **Example:** A client expresses disappointment in a previous solution, speaking with a deflated tone. The salesperson mirrors their disappointment: *"That must have been really frustrating, especially since you were expecting a better outcome."*
- **Why It Works:** Reflecting their disappointment acknowledges the emotional weight of their experience and prevents the salesperson from appearing indifferent or dismissive.[124]

5. Syncing with an Urgent or Stressed Tone to Show Responsiveness

- **Example:** A client speaks rapidly and urgently, emphasizing tight deadlines and stress over an issue that needs resolution. The salesperson mirrors their urgency but remains composed: *"I hear that this is time-sensitive, and we need to act fast. Let's focus on the fastest path to a solution."*
- **Why It Works:** Mirroring urgency shows alignment with the client's priorities while maintaining composure, demonstrating that the salesperson is both responsive and in control.[125]

6. Mirroring Skepticism to Foster Openness

- **Example:** A client sounds doubtful, using a skeptical tone and saying things like, *"I've heard this kind of promise before, and it didn't work out."* The salesperson mirrors the skepticism in a thoughtful tone: *"That makes total sense—skepticism is healthy, and I'd feel the same way. What specifically didn't work last time?"*
- **Why It Works:** By validating skepticism rather than dismissing it, the salesperson invites the client into a more open conversation rather than triggering defensiveness.[126]

7. Matching a Calm, Analytical Tone for Logical Buyers

- **Example:** A client speaks in a measured, methodical way, focusing on data and facts rather than emotion. The salesperson matches this tone,

responding with structured, logical explanations: *"That's a great point. If we look at the numbers, here's how this compares…"*
- **Why It Works** Analytical buyers trust those who communicate in a similar logical, composed manner, as it aligns with their cognitive style of decision-making.[127]

8. Reflecting Hopefulness to Reinforce Confidence

- **Example:** A client expresses cautious optimism, saying things like, *"This could be a great solution for us, but I want to be sure we're making the right move."* The salesperson mirrors this hopeful yet thoughtful tone: *"I completely understand. This has the potential to be a great fit, and it's smart to evaluate all angles."*
- **Why It Works:** By balancing enthusiasm with a measured response, the salesperson reassures the client that due diligence is encouraged, not rushed.[128]

9. Syncing with an Annoyed Tone to Defuse Tension

- **Example:** A client is irritated with service delays, speaking with a sharp, exasperated tone. The salesperson mirrors their frustration but stays constructive: *"I get it—waiting on something like this is really frustrating. Let me look into this right now so we can get it resolved."*
- **Why It Works** This validates the client's frustration without escalating the emotion. It also shifts the focus to action, helping the client feel heard and taken care of.[129]

10. Mirroring Gratitude to Strengthen Relationships

- **Example:** A client expresses appreciation for the salesperson's help, saying, *"You've been really helpful throughout this process."* The salesperson mirrors this gratitude with a warm tone: *"That means a lot to me—thank you. I truly appreciate working with you as well."*
- **Why It Works:** Expressing appreciation back creates reciprocity, deepening the relationship and reinforcing positive emotions in the interaction.[130]

Why Emotional Mirroring Works in Consultative Sales

At its core, mirroring emotionality is about *emotional validation and alignment*. People want to feel understood before they're willing to trust, and by subtly matching their emotional energy, a salesperson can build rapport and connection more quickly.[131]

Key Psychological Benefits of Emotional Mirroring in Sales:

- **Builds Trust** – Clients feel that the salesperson *gets* them on a deeper level.
- **Reduces Resistance** – Emotional alignment lowers defensiveness, making conversations smoother.
- **Increases Engagement** – Clients naturally lean in when they feel emotionally understood.
- **Strengthens Relationships** – Mirroring creates a sense of camaraderie and connection.
- **Improves Persuasion** – When clients feel heard, they are more open to solutions.

By mastering emotional mirroring, sales professionals can create *meaningful and lasting* client relationships—ones built not just on solutions but on genuine human connection.

Practice

By now, you have practiced many of the mirroring techniques above, so adding emotional mirroring to your regimen should come naturally. Emotional Intelligence is needed for a successful application of emotional mirroring, so your task is to be present and engaged in conversations when the other person is "in feeling". Begin to hone your skills of accurately articulating the emotion the other person is experiencing so that you can ease into an approach to mirror and validate what they are feeling. The more you practice the emotional labeling of what you perceive the other person is experiencing, the more skilled you will be at reflecting that back in an empathetic and connected manner. The skill of emotional mirroring is transformative and validates the client's emotional experience, resulting in true emotional connection.

⊰ PERSONAL EXPLORATION ⊱

It's time to reflect on what you've experienced throughout this chapter on mirroring. Give yourself time to reflect on the following questions:

- **Authenticity vs. Manipulation:** Mirroring can create a sense of connection and trust, but if overdone, it can feel manipulative. How do you personally draw the line between using mirroring as an authentic rapport-building tool versus a sales tactic that might come across as calculated?
- **Observation and Application:** Now that you understand the power of mirroring, think about a recent conversation you had—whether personal or professional. Looking back, can you identify moments where mirroring naturally occurred? If not, how might you have subtly incorporated it to enhance the interaction?
- **Challenging Your Comfort Zone:** Many people are unaware of their own body language and vocal patterns. What specific challenges do you anticipate when trying to apply mirroring techniques in real conversations, and how will you push yourself to practice despite potential discomfort?
- **The Ethics of Influence:** Mirroring allows you to lead a conversation by first following. Do you believe it's ethical to use mirroring to subtly guide a client's emotional state? Why or why not? How does your answer shape the way you intend to apply these techniques in your sales conversations?

⊰ YOUR FINAL THOUGHTS ⊱

Use The Space Below To Capture Your Thoughts And Reflections On What You've Learned In This Section

_____
_____
_____
_____
_____
_____

APPLYING THERAPY TECHNIQUES TO SALES CONVERSATIONS

ⳛⳛⳛⳛ

In consultative sales, the ability to foster genuine, trust-based relationships is key to success. One powerful way to deepen these connections is by applying therapeutic questioning techniques drawn from various mental health counseling modalities.[1] Each modality brings its own unique approach to understanding human behavior, motivation, and decision-making.[2] By integrating these techniques, sales professionals can engage in more meaningful conversations, helping clients feel seen, heard, and supported. The questions listed in this section are designed to guide you in exploring your clients' perspectives more thoroughly, uncovering insights that will help you align your solutions with their specific needs. As you incorporate these approaches, you'll be equipped to build stronger relationships, challenge assumptions, and facilitate positive change—all while maintaining a client-centered focus grounded in empathy and understanding, which are foundational to trusted relationships.[3]

Sales professionals can leverage therapeutic modalities by carefully observing their clients' language, emotional tone, and recurring patterns during conversations. By identifying key aspects of the client's communication style, challenges, and mindset, salespeople can strategically select the appropriate set of questions from each therapeutic approach.[4] This method allows for deeper engagement, fostering more personalized, insightful, and impactful conversations. It not only strengthens the relationship but also guides the client toward solutions, resulting in improved outcomes and a more genuine connection.[5]

ⳛⳛⳛⳛ

Identifying Client Indicators & Matching Therapeutic Approaches

You may be wondering how to determine which therapeutic modality to leverage for your consultative questioning? Furthermore, you may wonder if there are "Client Indicators" that you should look for and recognize in order to select the most applicable and effective set of modality-specific questions. Within each of the 23 therapeutic modality sections below, you will find a simple guide of "Client Indicators" to assist you in recognize what you might see and hear in prospective clients to determine which therapeutic modality's sales questions would be an effective match.

At a high level, here are nine categories and their associated therapeutic modalities to help you formulate your approach:

Clients stuck in negative thought loops?

- **Cognitive Behavioral Therapy (CBT):** Challenge unhelpful thought patterns and introduce alternative perspectives.[6]
- **Rational Emotive Behavior Therapy (REBT):** Identify and reframe irrational beliefs driving negative emotions.[7]
- **Dialectical Behavior Therapy (DBT):** Provide tools to regulate emotions and tolerate distress.[8]
- **Mindfulness-Based Cognitive Therapy (MBCT):** Guide clients to detach from negative thoughts through mindfulness.[9]

Clients struggling with past failures or unresolved experiences?

- **Adlerian Therapy:** Help clients reframe setbacks as opportunities for growth and develop a sense of belonging and purpose.[10]
- **Eye Movement Desensitization and Reprocessing (EMDR):** Help clients reprocess limiting beliefs tied to past experiences.[11]
- **Narrative Therapy:** Assist clients in reframing their professional story from failure to growth.[12]
- **Psychodynamic Therapy:** Explore underlying unconscious patterns driving their perception of past failures.[13]

Clients focused on immediate action and practical results?

- **Solution-Focused Brief Therapy (SFBT):** Guide clients toward rapid solutions and future-focused thinking.[14]
- **Reality Therapy:** Emphasize personal responsibility and actionable steps.[15]
- **Constructivist Therapy:** Help clients develop a new framework for approaching challenges based on their strengths.[16]

Clients feeling lost or seeking meaning in their career or business?

- **Adlerian Therapy:** Guide clients in identifying their core values, personal goals, and how their work aligns with a greater purpose.[17]

- **Existential Therapy:** Explore deeper themes of purpose, freedom, and responsibility.[18]
- **Humanistic Therapy:** Encourage self-actualization and authentic decision-making.[19]
- **Logotherapy:** Help clients find meaning in their current struggles and goals.[20]
- **Positive Psychology Therapy:** Shift focus to strengths, growth, and opportunities.[21]

Clients dealing with workplace conflict or relationship issues?

- **Interpersonal Therapy (IPT):** Improve communication and conflict resolution skills.[22]
- **Family Systems Therapy:** Explore how workplace relationships mirror family dynamics.[23]
- **Transactional Analysis (TA):** Identify patterns in interactions and help clients shift unproductive communication styles.[24]

Clients experiencing internal conflict, self-doubt, or personal resistance?

- **Internal Family Systems (IFS):** Identify competing "parts" of themselves that create conflict.[25]
- **Acceptance and Commitment Therapy (ACT):** Guide clients to accept internal struggles and take value-driven action.[26]
- **Gestalt Therapy:** Use present-moment awareness to resolve internal struggles.[27]

Clients experiencing stress that manifests physically?

- **Somatic Therapy:** Recognize how stress and emotions manifest in the body and release tension.[28]
- **Mindfulness-Based Cognitive Therapy (MBCT):** Use mindfulness to regulate physiological stress responses.[29]

Clients lacking motivation or struggling with change?

- **Adlerian Therapy:** Encourage clients to develop self-efficacy and take ownership of their progress.[30]
- **Motivational Interviewing (MI):** Help clients uncover their intrinsic motivation for change.[31]

- **Positive Psychology Therapy:** Reinforce optimism and small wins to sustain momentum.[32]

Clients needing validation and emotional support to build confidence?

- **Person-Centered Therapy:** Use deep listening and unconditional positive regard to empower the client.[33]
- **Humanistic Therapy:** Reinforce the client's self-worth and unique strengths.[34]

The 23 Therapeutic Modalities and Their Sales Questions

1. Acceptance and Commitment Therapy (ACT)

Overview: ACT helps individuals accept their thoughts and emotions rather than avoiding them. By using mindfulness techniques, it encourages people to detach from negative thought patterns. The goal is to focus on living in line with personal values and taking actions that promote well-being, even in the presence of distressing emotions.[35]

Acceptance and Commitment Therapy (ACT) Client Indicators:

- Feels stuck in avoidance behaviors or emotional distress
- Struggles with accepting uncertainties and discomfort in decision-making
- Mentions difficulty aligning actions with core values
- Uses language of pushing through rather than mindful engagement[36]

Sales Questions Using ACT Principles:

1. What challenges in your business do you feel you've been avoiding, and what would change if you faced them directly?
   - This question encourages acceptance of discomfort rather than avoidance.
2. If you weren't held back by fear, what bold move would you take in your business today?
   - This question separates thoughts from actions and focuses on values-driven behavior.
3. How do you differentiate between what you can control and what you need to accept in your business challenges?
   - This question highlights the ACT principle of psychological flexibility.

4. **What are the core values that guide your business decisions, and how aligned are you with them right now?**
    - This question emphasizes value-driven actions as a foundation for decision-making.
5. **When dealing with setbacks, do you focus more on eliminating negative emotions or on taking action despite them?**
    - This question challenges avoidance and promotes committed action.
6. **How do you currently handle difficult conversations, and how might acceptance of discomfort improve your outcomes?**
    - This question reinforces the idea that discomfort is part of meaningful engagement.
7. **What strategies do you use to stay focused on long-term goals despite short-term pressures?**
    - This question encourages commitment to values-driven action even in the face of challenges.
8. **How do you manage the internal dialogue when making difficult decisions in your business?**
    - This question promotes mindfulness and the ability to detach from unhelpful thought patterns.
9. **When your team faces obstacles, how do you encourage them to stay committed to their core values?**
    - This question reinforces values-driven perseverance rather than avoidance.
10. **How do you ensure that fear of failure doesn't prevent your organization from taking calculated risks?**
    - This question highlights the importance of accepting discomfort while making progress.

2. Adlerian Therapy

Overview: Adlerian therapy is rooted in the idea that individuals are driven by a desire for purpose, belonging, and personal growth. It emphasizes how early experiences and social relationships shape an individual's beliefs, behaviors, and decision-making patterns. This approach encourages self-awareness, goal-setting, and an understanding of how one's contributions impact the larger group or organization.[37]

Adlerian Therapy Client Indicators:

- Talks about deep-seated feelings of inadequacy or needing to prove oneself
- Values status, achievement, and societal belonging

- Seeks personal growth and clarity on purpose or legacy
- Expresses concerns about their place within a team or social hierarchy[38]

Sales Questions Using Adlerian Therapy Principles:

1. **How do you believe your leadership style influences your team's engagement and morale?**
   - This question reflects Adlerian principles by encouraging the client to examine how their actions affect the group dynamic. It reinforces the idea that leadership is not just about personal success but also about fostering a collaborative and motivated environment.
2. **Looking back, what key experiences shaped the way you solve problems today?**
   - Adlerian therapy explores how past experiences form an individual's worldview. This question prompts the client to recognize patterns in their decision-making and adapt their approach if needed.
3. **What role do you see yourself playing in your organization's overall vision and success?**
   - Adler emphasized social interest and the importance of understanding one's place within a larger system. This question helps the client reflect on their contribution and how they align with their company's mission.
4. **Who has had the biggest influence on your professional development, and what lessons have you taken from them?**
   - Adlerian therapy acknowledges the impact of mentors and role models on shaping beliefs and behaviors. This question encourages the client to assess how influential figures have shaped their leadership and approach to challenges.
5. **If you could change one perception that others have of you in the workplace, what would it be and why?**
   - This question addresses the Adlerian concept of self-image and perceived inferiority or superiority. It encourages clients to identify aspects of their professional identity they may want to refine.
6. **What personal strengths give you confidence in tackling this issue?**
   - Adlerian therapy focuses on recognizing strengths to foster self-efficacy. This question shifts the client's focus from obstacles to capabilities, promoting a solution-focused mindset.

7. **How do you think your team experiences your leadership, especially in times of uncertainty?**
   - Self-awareness is a crucial part of Adlerian therapy. This question encourages the client to reflect on how they are perceived by their team and consider ways to strengthen their leadership approach.
8. **What values guide you when making difficult business decisions?**
   - Adlerian therapy emphasizes the role of personal beliefs in shaping actions. This question helps the client clarify whether their choices align with their core values and long-term objectives.
9. **Can you recall a past success that reassures you of your ability to navigate this challenge?**
   - This question aligns with Adlerian principles by reinforcing confidence through past achievements. It helps the client draw from prior successes to build momentum in overcoming current obstacles.
10. **When you reflect on your career, what impact do you hope to leave on your colleagues and industry?**
    - Adlerian therapy encourages individuals to think about their legacy and the lasting impact of their contributions. This question helps the client connect their present efforts with their long-term professional aspirations.

3. Cognitive Behavioral Therapy (CBT)

Overview: CBT is a goal-oriented, structured, therapeutic approach that helps individuals identify and alter negative, maladaptive, and unproductive thought patterns. CBT stresses and focuses on the inherent connection between thoughts, emotions, and behaviors, and teaches individuals in their therapeutic journey practical and effective strategies and interventions to challenge unhelpful thinking and behavior.[39] By identifying, addressing and adjusting these patterns, individuals can improve their emotional responses and engage in more productive behaviors, fostering long-term well-being.

Cognitive Behavioral Therapy (CBT) Client Indicators:

- Expresses rigid thinking or all-or-nothing beliefs (e.g., This always happens to me.)
- Struggles with negative self-talk or limiting beliefs
- Feels overwhelmed by decision-making due to perceived risks
- Uses language that suggests distorted thinking patterns (e.g., catastrophizing, overgeneralization)[40]

Sales Questions Using CBT Principles:

1. **What obstacles are currently standing in the way of your business goals?**
   - This question aligns with CBT by helping the client pinpoint specific thought patterns or assumptions that may be limiting their decision-making and effectiveness.
2. **When things don't go as planned, how do you and your team typically respond, and what impact does that have?**
   - This question encourages reflection on automatic reactions, helping the client recognize patterns that may be reinforcing unproductive behaviors.
3. **Are there any assumptions you're making about this challenge that might not be entirely accurate?**
   - CBT encourages individuals to challenge cognitive distortions. This question helps uncover any limiting beliefs that might be clouding objective analysis.
4. **If you could change one aspect of your current approach to improve results, what would it be?**
   - This question supports incremental change, similar to how CBT breaks large problems into manageable steps for sustainable improvement.
5. **How do you define success, and in what ways do your current beliefs support or hinder your ability to reach it?**
   - This question helps the client explore how their mindset influences their outcomes, a key concept in CBT.
6. **What other approaches have you considered for solving this issue, and what led you to stick with your current strategy?**
   - CBT encourages re-evaluating thought processes. This question helps the client assess whether their current approach is the most effective or if biases are influencing their decision.
7. **What beliefs about your team's capabilities might be shaping how you tackle this challenge?**
   - CBT focuses on identifying underlying thought patterns. This question encourages the client to recognize and assess how their beliefs impact leadership and problem-solving.
8. **Looking back at past obstacles, do you see any recurring themes in how your organization responds?**
   - This question promotes self-awareness by helping the client recognize behavioral and cognitive patterns that might be influencing long-term outcomes.

9. **How do you determine whether a potential solution is truly effective, and what role do biases play in that evaluation?**
    - CBT promotes cognitive flexibility by challenging ingrained assumptions. This question encourages a critical examination of the decision-making process.
10. **If a colleague were facing the same challenge, what advice would you offer them?**
    - This question supports cognitive reframing, a key CBT technique that helps clients gain a new perspective by stepping outside of their immediate thought process.

4. Constructivist Therapy

Overview: Constructivist therapy operates on the principle that individuals actively create their own realities based on their experiences and personal interpretations. This therapy helps clients examine and reshape their views, beliefs, and perceptions to create healthier ways of thinking. By reconstructing their mental models, clients are empowered to approach life with greater flexibility, resilience, and adaptive coping strategies.[41]

Constructivist Therapy Client Indicators:

- Talks about how things should be based on past experiences
- Struggles to see beyond their current perspectives
- Expresses difficulty in adapting to industry changes
- Wants to reshape their personal or professional identity[42]

Sales Questions Using Constructivist Therapy Principles:

1. **How have past business experiences shaped the way you approach challenges today?**
    - This question highlights the role of personal narrative in shaping decisions.
2. **If you were to rewrite your business journey as a story, what would the next chapter be?**
    - This question encourages perspective-shifting.
3. **What beliefs about your industry or business have you held for a long time, and do they still serve you?**
    - This question challenges rigid thought constructs.
4. **How might looking at this problem from a completely different angle lead to a breakthrough?**
    - This question promotes flexible thinking.

5. **What assumptions are guiding your current business strategy, and how could you test their validity?**
   - This question encourages examining cognitive biases.
6. **If you were mentoring someone in your industry, how would you help them view obstacles differently?**
   - This question helps the client envision a new reality and role they can play in which can lead to new collaborative experiences.
7. **What do you think the current challenge is trying to teach you about your business or leadership style?**
   - This question reframes challenges as learning opportunities, encouraging growth.
8. **How has your understanding of success evolved as your business has progressed?**
   - This question encourages reflection on how past experiences shape current beliefs.
9. **What are the most important beliefs you hold about your industry, and how do they inform your strategic decisions?**
   - This question probes how constructed beliefs influence actions and strategies.
10. **How would you explain your approach to moving through obstacles to someone new to your industry?**
    - This question aligns challenges the individual to articulate and potentially reframe their business narrative.

5. Dialectical Behavior Therapy (DBT)

Overview: DBT is a cognitive-behavioral-based therapy that focuses on emotional regulation, distress tolerance, interpersonal effectiveness, and mindfulness. Originally developed for individuals struggling with emotional dysregulation, DBT teaches skills to balance acceptance and change. The core principle of DBT is dialectics—helping individuals integrate opposing perspectives and move towards a more balanced and effective approach to problem-solving.[43]

Dialectical Behavior Therapy (DBT) Client Indicators:

- Struggles with emotional decision-making or impulsivity
- Experiences high levels of stress and burnout
- Has difficulty balancing work pressures with personal well-being
- Finds it challenging to integrate conflicting viewpoints[44]

Sales Questions Using DBT Principles:

1. **When facing business challenges, do you tend to react emotionally or take a step back to assess the situation?**
   - DBT emphasizes emotional regulation and this question helps the client recognize whether their emotions drive their decisions or if they use a structured approach to problem-solving.
2. **How do you typically handle high-pressure situations, and what strategies do you use to manage stress?**
   - DBT teaches distress tolerance and understanding how a client manages business stress can reveal whether they have effective coping mechanisms or need a more structured approach.
3. **When making a tough decision, do you find yourself stuck between two conflicting perspectives?**
   - The dialectical nature of DBT encourages balancing opposing views and this question helps clients recognize if they struggle with integrating multiple perspectives.
4. **What's your process for handling interpersonal conflicts within your team?**
   - DBT focuses on interpersonal effectiveness and this question assesses how well a leader navigates workplace conflicts.
5. **Do you ever feel overwhelmed by responsibilities, and how do you bring yourself back to focus?**
   - This question relates to mindfulness, a core DBT principle, encouraging awareness and presence in high-pressure situations.
6. **How do you validate the concerns of your team while still pushing towards your business goals?**
   - DBT teaches balancing acceptance with change and this question helps clients evaluate their leadership approach.
7. **What emotional triggers impact your decision-making, and how do you manage them?**
   - Emotional awareness is critical in DBT and identifying triggers can help clients improve their business decision-making.
8. **How do you maintain balance between personal well-being and professional success?**
   - DBT encourages balancing work and self-care, making this a relevant question for leaders.
9. **How do you approach situations where you feel stuck or unable to move forward?**
   - DBT's distress tolerance skills can help business leaders manage stagnation and frustration.

10. **What's one skill you wish you had to improve how you handle business challenges?**
    - DBT emphasizes skill-building and this question encourages self-reflection on growth areas.

6. Existential Therapy

Overview: Existential Therapy explores the challenges of human existence, including meaning, purpose, freedom, responsibility, isolation, and meaninglessness. It encourages individuals to confront uncertainty, take ownership of their choices, and align their lives with their values, fostering a deeper sense of fulfillment and authenticity.[45]

Existential Therapy Client Indicators:

- Feels lost or uncertain about purpose in their career or business
- Questions the meaning of their work or leadership role
- Expresses fears about mortality, legacy, or making an impact
- Struggles with existential concerns such as freedom and responsibility[46]

Sales Questions Using Existential Principles:

1. **What is the deeper purpose behind your company's mission, and how does this decision align with it?**
    - This question emphasizes meaning and purpose.
2. **What legacy do you want your organization to leave behind?**
    - This question explores long-term impact and existential fulfillment.
3. **How do you balance the freedom to innovate with the responsibility to maintain stability?**
    - This question confronts the tension between freedom and responsibility.
4. **What fears come up for you when thinking about major change?**
    - This question helps explore existential anxiety and uncertainty.
5. **If you had unlimited resources, what would you change first?**
    - This question removes practical constraints to reveal core desires.
6. **What motivates you personally to succeed in this business?**
    - This question encourages deep reflection on personal meaning and motivation.

7. **When making tough decisions, how do you ensure they align with the core identity of your organization?**
    - This question encourages alignment between actions and deeper existential meaning.
8. **How do you help your team find purpose in their work beyond just meeting business goals?**
    - This question focuses on meaning and fulfillment in daily business activities.
9. **What role does uncertainty play in your industry, and how do you navigate it with confidence?**
    - This question addresses the existential reality of uncertainty and helps explore strategies for resilience.
10. **How do you define success in a way that extends beyond financial performance?**
    - This question challenges superficial definitions of success and fosters deeper meaning.

7. Eye Movement Desensitization and Reprocessing (EMDR)

Overview: EMDR is primarily used to help individuals process and reframe traumatic experiences through bilateral stimulation, such as eye movements. It focuses on rewiring how past experiences affect present thoughts and behaviors. Through structured phases, EMDR enables individuals to desensitize distressing memories and replace them with adaptive beliefs.[47]

Eye Movement Desensitization and Reprocessing (EMDR) Client Indicators:

- References past traumatic business experiences affecting current confidence
- Mentions strong emotional reactions to specific triggers
- Struggles with persistent fears despite logical reassurances
- Describes feelings of being stuck due to past failures or betrayals[48]

Sales Questions Using EMDR Principles:

1. **Are there past experiences in your business that continue to impact decision-making today?**
    - This question explores how unresolved past events influence current thinking and behavior.

2. **When you think about making a major change, what memories or past outcomes come to mind?**
   - This question examines how past experiences create emotional triggers.
3. **How do previous failures or successes shape your confidence in making decisions now?**
   - This question focuses on how past experiences become stored mental frameworks that affect current responses.
4. **When faced with risk, do you tend to react based on past experiences, or do you evaluate each situation independently?**
   - This question challenges automatic responses rooted in past experiences.
5. **If you could remove the emotional weight of a past business decision, how would that change your approach today?**
   - This question emphasizes reprocessing past events to reduce their emotional influence.
6. **What mental images come to mind when you think about the risks and rewards of this decision?**
   - This question connects visual and emotional processing, similar to how EMDR therapy engages traumatic memories.
7. **What past business decisions still trigger a strong emotional response for you or your team?**
   - This question identifies unresolved experiences that continue to influence present decision-making.
8. **When making a choice under pressure, do you feel more influenced by logic or by past emotional experiences?**
   - This question explores the balance between cognitive reasoning and emotional memory in decision-making.
9. **Have there been situations where a past failure prevented you from taking a necessary risk?**
   - This question examines how past negative experiences can create avoidance behaviors.
10. **If you could mentally reset your perception of risk, what opportunities might you be more open to exploring?**
    - This question encourages reprocessing and reframing past events to create new decision-making pathways.

8. Family Systems Therapy

Overview: Family Systems Therapy approaches the therapeutic process with the perspective that individuals are connected to a system of relationships – not necessarily biologically a family – and where those interconnected relationships each influence the behaviors of those in the system. There is an emphasis on roles, patters, and communication within and throughout the system as opposed to with only individual issues. Professional sellers should consider the "Family" as their work colleagues that are part of the sales and support teams.[49]

Family Systems Therapy Client Indicators:

- Talks about professional struggles in the context of team/family dynamics
- Expresses feeling trapped by dysfunctional workplace relationships
- Uses language that suggests role-based identity (e.g., I'm the fixer in my team.)
- Describes repeating conflict patterns within their organization[50]

Sales Questions Using Family Systems Therapy Principles:

1. **How do different departments within your organization influence the way decisions are made?**
   - This question acknowledges the interdependent nature of systems and how different roles shape behaviors.
2. **Who are the key influencers in your company, and how do their perspectives shape business decisions?**
   - This question explores how individuals within the system impact overall functioning.
3. **What patterns have you noticed in how your team responds to organizational changes?**
   - This question focuses on recurring behavioral dynamics within the system.
4. **How do conflicts typically get resolved in your team, and what role do you tend to play in those situations?**
   - This question examines relational roles and interaction patterns.
5. **If we implemented this solution, how do you think it would impact the relationships within your team?**
   - This question considers how changes affect the system as a whole.
6. **What strengths exist within your team that could help implement this change more effectively?**
   - This question highlights the collective strengths of the system rather than just individual efforts.
7. **What unwritten rules or expectations exist within your team that influence decision-making?**
   - This question uncovers systemic norms and hidden dynamics affecting behavior.

8. **How does leadership style within your organization impact how changes are accepted or resisted?**
   - This question aligns examines power dynamics and relational influence within the system.
9. **When a major decision is made, how does it typically ripple through different levels of your organization?**
   - This question considers the systemic impact of decisions beyond just one individual or department.
10. **Who within your organization is most likely to resist this change, and how can we support them in adapting?**
    - This question acknowledges resistance as part of the system and seeks to address relational challenges proactively.

9. Gestalt Therapy

Overview: Gestalt therapy emphasizes self-awareness, present-moment focus, and personal accountability. Instead of dissecting past events, it encourages individuals to fully experience their thoughts, emotions, and actions in the here and now. The goal is to foster deeper insight, integration, and responsiveness to current realities.[51]

Gestalt Therapy Client Indicators:

- Appears disconnected from present experiences or emotions
- Uses language that distances them from responsibility (e.g., This just happens to me.)
- Struggles with self-awareness or personal agency in decision-making
- Demonstrates unresolved emotional reactions to past events[52]

Sales Questions Using Gestalt Therapy Principles:

1. **As you reflect on your biggest business challenge at this moment, what emotions are surfacing for you?**
   - This question aligns with Gestalt principles by directing attention to the present emotional experience rather than analyzing past setbacks or future anxieties.
2. **What do you notice about your own reactions when discussing this issue?**
   - Gestalt therapy emphasizes self-awareness. This question helps clients recognize their immediate thoughts, feelings, and body language when confronted with business difficulties.

3. **What is it like for you to be in your role, making these high-stakes decisions daily?**
   - This question fosters deeper self-exploration by encouraging clients to articulate their lived experience in real-time, aligning with Gestalt's focus on the present moment.
4. **What's happening in your business right now that you feel isn't being fully acknowledged or addressed?**
   - Gestalt therapy highlights avoidance patterns. This question helps clients confront neglected areas of concern rather than sidestepping them.
5. **How do you typically navigate team conflicts, and what role do you find yourself playing in those situations?**
   - This question fosters self-responsibility, a core Gestalt principle, by prompting reflection on one's influence in team dynamics.
6. **If you were to trust your instincts in this moment, what decision would you make?**
   - Gestalt therapy values spontaneity and immediate awareness. This question shifts the focus from overanalyzing to acting on present insights.
7. **When you picture yourself implementing this change, what stands out to you most about that experience?**
   - Gestalt therapy encourages visualization to gain clarity, which may reveal overlooked considerations, excitement, or discomfort the client may not have consciously addressed.
8. **How do you currently experience the relationships and dynamics between different departments in your company?**
   - This question encourages present-moment awareness of interpersonal and organizational patterns, fostering holistic understanding.
9. **What emotions arise when you consider the possibility of encountering setbacks?**
   - Gestalt therapy values emotional processing in real time. This question helps clients identify and engage with their immediate reactions rather than suppressing concerns.
10. **What thoughts or concerns do you find yourself holding back in this decision-making process?**
    - Gestalt therapy helps individuals acknowledge suppressed thoughts and emotions. This question creates space for the client to express any unspoken reservations.

10. Humanistic Therapy

Overview: Humanistic therapy centers on personal growth and self-actualization, believing that individuals have the inherent ability to reach their full potential. It emphasizes self-awareness and encourages autonomy, with a strong focus on the therapeutic relationship as a space for support and understanding.[53]

Humanistic Therapy Client Indicators:

- Expresses a desire for self-actualization and personal growth
- Feels disconnected from their deeper values and purpose
- Struggles with self-acceptance or self-compassion
- Uses language focused on authenticity, meaning, and fulfillment[54]

Sales Questions Using Humanistic Therapy Principles:

1. **What personal or professional growth do you hope to achieve through this business decision?**
   - This question focuses on self-actualization.
2. **What strengths do you or your team have that you feel are underutilized?**
   - This question emphasizes unlocking potential.
3. **How does this decision align with your deeper aspirations and sense of purpose?**
   - This question encourages intrinsic motivation.
4. **What does success truly mean to you beyond just financial metrics?**
   - This question shifts focus from external success to personal fulfillment.
5. **If you had no constraints, what would your ideal version of your company look like?**
   - This question aligns to Humanistic Therapy because it encourages vision-driven thinking.
6. **How can I support you in creating the most fulfilling version of your business or career?**
   - This question aligns to Humanistic Therapy because it reinforces a person-centered approach.
7. **What personal qualities do you want to develop further in your leadership role?**
   - This question focuses on self-actualization and ongoing personal growth.
8. **How do you foster an environment where your team feels empowered to reach their full potential?**
   - This question encourages creating an environment that supports self-awareness and autonomy.

9. **If you could eliminate any obstacles to personal growth within your organization, what would that look like?**
    - This question promotes self-discovery and emphasizes the importance of removing barriers to self-actualization.
10. **How do you align your business practices with your personal values and beliefs?**
    - This question encourages a harmony between personal beliefs and professional actions to enhance fulfillment.

11. Internal Family Systems (IFS)

Overview: IFS is based on the idea that the mind consists of multiple "parts," such as the inner critic, protector, or vulnerable child, each with distinct roles and needs. The therapy aims to integrate these internal parts, fostering harmony and balance within the self. By understanding and healing these conflicting parts, individuals can develop a more cohesive, compassionate sense of identity and reduce internal struggles.[55]

Internal Family Systems (IFS) Client Indicators:

- Talks about internal conflict as if multiple parts of them are at odds
- Struggles with self-judgment or critical inner dialogue
- Expresses frustration with behaviors they feel they can't control
- Feels torn between different roles or responsibilities[56]

Sales Questions Using IFS Principles:

1. **When faced with a tough decision, do you ever feel like different parts of you are in conflict?**
    - This question encourages awareness of internal parts influencing decisions.
2. **Is there a part of you that resists making a particular change, and if so, what does it want to protect?**
    - This question explores protective internal mechanisms.
3. **What part of you is most excited about this opportunity, and what part is most hesitant?**
    - This question acknowledges multiple perspectives within the self.
4. **Have you ever noticed a recurring voice or inner dialogue that influences your business choices?**
    - This question helps identify dominant internal parts.

Ask Like a Therapist, Sell Like a Pro: A Therapy-Inspired Sales Approach

5. **If you could give the hesitant part of you a voice, what would it say?**
   - This question fosters dialogue between different parts of the psyche.
6. **How do you balance the different internal needs of being ambitious, cautious, and innovative in your business?**
   - This question supports harmonizing competing internal drives.
7. **What part of you feels the most resistance when it comes to changing your approach to business growth?**
   - This question identifies internal resistance and examines the protective mechanisms at play.
8. **How do you manage the tension between your long-term vision and the short-term pressures you face in your business?**
   - This question highlights the balance between different internal drives, such as ambition and practicality.
9. **When you think about expanding your business, which internal voice feels the most fearful or reluctant?**
   - This question surfaces the vulnerable or hesitant parts of the self that may resist growth or change.
10. **How do you ensure that your values are represented in your business, especially when there are competing interests?**
    - This question promotes integration of internal values and priorities into decision-making processes.

12. Interpersonal Therapy (IPT)

Overview: IPT focuses on improving interpersonal relationships and communication skills to alleviate psychological distress. It is particularly effective for people facing social or professional challenges, such as grief, role transitions, or conflicts. By enhancing relationships, IPT helps individuals develop healthier connections and reduce symptoms of anxiety, depression, and interpersonal difficulties.[57]

Interpersonal Therapy (IPT) Client Indicators:

- Mentions difficulty in professional relationships and communication
- Expresses frustration with how others perceive them
- Feels misunderstood or struggles with social confidence
- Wants to improve relationship dynamics in leadership or teamwork[58]

Sales Questions Using IPT Principles:

1. **What are the biggest interpersonal challenges you face in your workplace or business relationships?**
   - This question centers on social dynamics as a key driver of outcomes.
2. **How do you navigate difficult conversations with employees, partners, or clients?**
   - This question promotes healthy communication strategies.
3. **How have past professional relationships influenced your leadership or negotiation style?**
   - This question explores relational patterns.
4. **What do you think is the biggest misunderstanding people have about your leadership style?**
   - This question encourages self-awareness in social interactions.
5. **How do you handle feedback—both giving and receiving—in a way that strengthens relationships?**
   - This question emphasizes constructive dialogue.
6. **How do you nurture relationships that positively impact your work environment?**
   - This question emphasizes the importance of fostering strong interpersonal connections in a professional setting, a key element of IPT's focus on social support.
7. **What methods do you use to communicate your intentions clearly to colleagues and clients?**
   - This question highlights communication skills and the transparency needed to maintain effective relationships, a core concept of IPT.
8. **How do you manage disagreements when your personal values differ from those of others in your organization?**
   - This question explores conflict resolution strategies while preserving professional relationships, reflecting IPT's focus on maintaining healthy interactions.
9. **In what ways do you build trust during negotiations or sales interactions?**
   - This question encourages relationship-building tactics, which are central to successful business interactions, aligning with IPT's emphasis on interpersonal connections.
10. **What practices do you use to ensure that everyone's opinions are respected and valued during team discussions?**
    - This question addresses fostering a supportive environment where every team member feels heard, resonating with IPT's focus on communication and emotional bonds.

13. Logotherapy

Overview: Logotherapy focuses on finding meaning and purpose in life, even amid suffering. It teaches that purpose can be found in any situation by living according to personal values, offering a path toward resilience and personal growth. By shifting focus from what is out of one's control to what can be shaped through attitude and action, individuals gain a greater sense of direction and fulfillment.[59]

Logotherapy Client Indicators:

- Seeks deeper meaning in work beyond financial success
- Feels unfulfilled despite achievements, craving significance
- Reframes hardships as part of a meaningful journey
- Values legacy and impact, aligning work with core beliefs[60]

Sales Questions Using Logotherapy Principles:

1. **What deeper purpose does this business serve beyond just financial gain?**
   - This question highlights meaning-driven decisions.
2. **How do you stay motivated during difficult times in your business?**
   - This question emphasizes resilience through meaning.
3. **What is the most fulfilling aspect of your work, and how can you focus more on it?**
   - This question identifies sources of purpose.
4. **How do you want your business legacy to be remembered?**
   - This question explores long-term meaning.
5. **What values do you refuse to compromise on, no matter the circumstances?**
   - This question reinforces core values.
6. **If your business had a mission statement for its deeper purpose, what would it be?**
   - This question frames actions around a higher purpose.
7. **In what ways do you help your team find a sense of meaning and purpose in their daily tasks?**
   - This question encourages the pursuit of meaning even in routine work.
8. **When you face adversity, how do you stay focused on the deeper purpose behind your business?**
   - This question helps reconnect challenges to meaningful purpose, fostering resilience.

9. How do you ensure that your business decisions align with your personal and professional sense of meaning?
    - This question emphasizes aligning actions with a sense of purpose, creating a meaningful business journey.
10. If you had to summarize your business mission in a single phrase that captures its higher purpose, what would it be?
    - This question helps clarify the deeper existential purpose that drives business decisions and motivations.

14. Mindfulness-Based Cognitive Therapy (MBCT)

Overview: MBCT is a hybrid of Cognitive Behavioral Therapy and mindfulness practices. It helps individuals develop awareness of thought patterns and emotions while reducing automatic negative responses. By integrating mindfulness, MBCT encourages a balanced and intentional approach to challenges, making it an effective tool for consultative sales professionals who need to remain present, adaptable, and client-focused.[61]

Mindfulness-Based Cognitive Therapy (MBCT) Client Indicators:

- Tends to react impulsively rather than thoughtfully
- Struggles with being present and focused during decision-making
- Feels overwhelmed by stress and external pressures
- Expresses a desire for greater clarity and balance in their leadership approach[62]

Sales Questions Using MBCT Principles:

1. What factors do you notice influencing your decision-making in this moment?
    - This question encourages present-moment awareness, a key component of MBCT.
2. When evaluating options, do you ever find yourself reacting automatically rather than making an intentional choice?
    - MBCT helps break automatic negative thought patterns, making this a useful self-awareness question.
3. How do you stay focused and present when making important decisions?
    - This question aligns with MBCT's emphasis on mindfulness in high-stakes scenarios.

4. **What distractions or pressures tend to cloud your judgment?**
   - MBCT helps individuals recognize external influences on thought processes.
5. **How do you typically handle uncertainty, and what strategies help you stay grounded?**
   - This question addresses MBCT's focus on accepting discomfort rather than reacting impulsively.
6. **What emotions arise when you think about making this investment, and how do you manage them?**
   - This question encourages emotional regulation and awareness, aligning with MBCT principles.
7. **What past experiences shape your current perspective on this business challenge?**
   - MBCT promotes awareness of past experiences without becoming trapped by them.
8. **How does your team stay mindful and intentional when adapting to change?**
   - This question helps assess mindfulness practices in leadership and team dynamics.
9. **What small, incremental changes could make the biggest difference in achieving your goals?**
   - MBCT emphasizes gradual improvement over drastic shifts.
10. **How do you ensure your decisions align with your long-term vision rather than short-term pressures?**
    - This question promotes intentional, mindful decision-making.

15. Motivational Interviewing (MI)

In addition to the details shared below, there is a dedicated Motivational Interviewing section which further expands the relevance and importance of MI in the consultative sales process.

Overview: Motivational Interviewing (MI) is an approach that centers on guiding individuals through their internal conflicts, helping them to clarify their values and goals. It is based on the idea that motivation for change is most sustainable when it is self-generated rather than imposed. MI is used to support people in resolving ambivalence, building their confidence, and making decisions that align with their deeper aspirations. This method is particularly effective in contexts where individuals face resistance to change but possess the ability to move forward once their motivations are fully acknowledged and explored.[63]

Motivational Interviewing (MI) Client Indicators:

- Expresses ambivalence or resistance to change (e.g., I know I should, but…)
- Feels stuck in decision paralysis, torn between two options
- Seems defensive when discussing necessary changes
- Needs autonomy in their decision-making process and dislikes being sold to[64]

Sales Questions Using MI Principles:

1. **On a scale from 1 to 10, how much of a priority is solving this challenge for you, and what makes you say that?**
   - This aligns with MI by prompting self-evaluation and uncovering internal motivation, helping the client articulate their level of urgency.
2. **What are some of the biggest hesitations or concerns you have about making this change?**
   - By acknowledging ambivalence, this question provides space for the client to voice reservations, making it easier to address and resolve barriers to action.
3. **If you were to take the first step toward change, what would that look like?**
   - This encourages action-oriented thinking and reduces overwhelm by focusing on a single, manageable step forward.
4. **What are the potential benefits of maintaining the status quo versus embracing a new approach?**
   - This MI-based question helps the client weigh both perspectives, fostering deeper internal reflection and increasing buy-in for change.
5. **What has prevented you from taking action on this issue in the past?**
   - Exploring past obstacles brings awareness to patterns or limiting beliefs, allowing the client to develop strategies to overcome them.
6. **How do you think your team would react if they saw you leading the charge on this initiative?**
   - Tying motivation to social impact helps the client recognize their influence on others and strengthens their commitment to taking action.
7. **If you successfully implemented this change, how would it positively impact you and your business?**
   - This question reinforces motivation by encouraging visualization of a successful outcome, helping the client emotionally connect with the benefits of change.

8. **What personal or organizational values do you hold most important, and how does this decision align with them?**
   - By linking the decision to core values, this question enhances intrinsic motivation, making the change feel more meaningful.
9. **If nothing changes over the next six months, what challenges or risks might you face as a result?**
   - This MI technique creates a gentle sense of urgency by prompting the client to consider the consequences of inaction, increasing their drive to move forward.
10. **What strengths or past experiences have helped you successfully navigate similar transitions before?**
    - Reinforcing past successes builds confidence and self-efficacy, helping the client recognize their ability to overcome challenges and implement change.

16. Narrative Therapy

Overview: Narrative Therapy helps individuals reframe their personal stories to create a more empowering and constructive self-identity. It emphasizes separating individuals from their problems and rewriting limiting narratives. By externalizing issues and viewing them objectively, clients can redefine their experiences in ways that promote personal agency and resilience.[65]

Narrative Therapy Client Indicators:

- Uses self-limiting narratives (e.g., I've always been bad at this.)
- Expresses frustration with the way their professional story is unfolding
- Feels defined by past failures or challenges
- Seeks empowerment by reframing their professional identity[66]

Sales Questions Using Narrative Principles:

1. **If you had to describe your company's journey as a story, what would the main theme be?**
   - This question encourages storytelling to shape meaning.
2. **What challenges have defined your organization, and how do you view them in hindsight?**
   - This question helps reframe past struggles into learning experiences.
3. **What's the most empowering part of your company's story, and how does that influence your decisions today?**
   - This question highlights strengths within the narrative.

4. **If you could rewrite the story of how your team handles adversity, what would that new story be?**
    - This question promotes constructing a more empowering perspective.
5. **What labels or beliefs about your company's capabilities might be holding you back?**
    - This question challenges limiting beliefs embedded in narratives.
6. **How do you want your company's story to be remembered five years from now?**
    - This question helps craft a forward-looking, purposeful narrative.
7. **What aspects of your company's story do you feel are misunderstood by customers or the market?**
    - This question explores external perceptions and helps reshape the company's narrative for a stronger identity.
8. **If you had to highlight a pivotal moment in your organization's journey, what would it be, and how has it shaped your direction?**
    - This question encourages reflection on defining moments to reinforce resilience and growth.
9. **How do you ensure that new team members understand and contribute to your company's evolving story?**
    - This question emphasizes the collaborative nature of storytelling within an organization.
10. **In what ways do you celebrate and communicate the successes within your company's journey?**
    - This question reinforces positive narratives and helps build an empowering company culture.

17. Person-Centered Therapy (PCT)

Overview: Person-Centered Therapy is built on the foundation of empathy, unconditional positive regard, and authenticity. The therapist acts as a supportive guide, allowing the individual to explore their thoughts and feelings without judgment. This modality focuses on self-actualization and personal growth, making it particularly valuable in fostering strong, trusting relationships in sales.[67]

Person-Centered Therapy (PCT) Client Indicators:

- Values authenticity and meaningful relationships
- Prefers a consultative, rather than transactional, sales approach
- Struggles with self-confidence in decision-making

- Expresses the need to feel heard and understood[68]

Sales Questions Using PCT Principles:

1. **What's most important to you in a business partnership?**
    o This aligns with PCT's emphasis on personal values and authenticity, helping uncover deeper client motivations.
2. **When considering solutions, what factors make you feel truly heard and understood?**
    o PCT prioritizes empathy and deep listening, making this question valuable in strengthening client trust.
3. **How do you prefer to communicate when making major business decisions?**
    o Understanding the client's preferred communication style aligns with PCT's emphasis on respect for individuality.
4. **What past experiences have shaped your approach to problem-solving?**
    o PCT focuses on personal growth and self-awareness, making this question insightful for uncovering patterns.
5. **What does success look like for you, beyond financial metrics?**
    o This question encourages clients to think holistically about their goals, aligning with PCT's focus on self-actualization.
6. **What concerns do you have about making this decision, and how can I support you in addressing them?**
    o PCT's non-directive approach fosters trust by addressing concerns without pressure.
7. **What values guide your company's decision-making process?**
    o This question aligns with PCT's emphasis on authenticity and alignment with core beliefs.
8. **When working with vendors, what makes you feel most valued and respected?**
    o This question encourages reflection on positive experiences, fostering deeper client engagement.
9. **How do you ensure that your team feels heard and valued?**
    o PCT focuses on active listening and empathy, making this question relevant for leadership development.
10. **What would make this sales process feel as seamless and stress-free as possible for you?**
    o This question nurtures collaboration and client comfort, key principles of PCT.

18. Positive Psychology Therapy

Overview: Positive Psychology Therapy emphasizes personal strengths, well-being, and resilience rather than focusing solely on symptom reduction. It encourages individuals to cultivate positive emotions, gratitude, and a sense of purpose in life. By shifting focus toward flourishing, this therapy aims to enhance overall life satisfaction and promote a more meaningful existence, even in the face of challenges.[69]

Positive Psychology Therapy Client Indicators:

- Expresses frustration with focusing too much on problems rather than strengths
- Seeks greater engagement, energy, and passion in their work
- Struggles with recognizing and celebrating their achievements
- Wants to cultivate a more positive mindset but doesn't know how[70]

Sales Questions Using Positive Psychology Principles:

1. **What strengths have consistently helped your business thrive, and how can you further amplify them for continued success?**
   - This question emphasizes identifying key strengths, fostering a growth-oriented approach that capitalizes on what's working.
2. **In what areas of your business do you feel most energized and motivated to make a difference?**
   - This question taps into intrinsic motivation, encouraging reflection on moments that fuel passion and engagement in the business.
3. **If you could infuse more enthusiasm into your daily work, what minor adjustments could make the biggest impact?**
   - This question focuses on increasing well-being and satisfaction, prompting small, actionable steps to enhance the work experience.
4. **Which aspects of your business bring you the most sense of fulfillment and align with your deeper purpose?**
   - This question encourages identifying what brings meaning to work, driving a connection between business actions and personal values.
5. **How do you recognize and celebrate even the smallest victories, and how does that boost morale across your team?**
   - This question promotes positive reinforcement, emphasizing the importance of celebrating progress to maintain motivation and morale.

6. **What part of your business are you most thankful for, and how can you use that as a foundation to expand further?**
    - This question centers on cultivating gratitude by focusing on what's already working well, enhancing opportunities for growth.
7. **What does resilience look like in your business, and how do you encourage it within your team for long-term success?**
    - This question highlights the importance of resilience and how it contributes to navigating challenges while maintaining progress.
8. **How do you foster a work environment where appreciation and acknowledgment are integral to the culture?**
    - This question aligns with building a positive and appreciative atmosphere in the workplace, driving a supportive and motivating culture.
9. **What have been your most meaningful achievements, and how can you build on those experiences for even greater success?**
    - This question encourages reflection on positive moments and how they can be leveraged to enhance future growth and fulfillment.
10. **How do you ensure your business goals resonate with your core values, helping you find deeper purpose in your work?**
    - This question connects intrinsic motivation with professional aspirations, ensuring that business objectives align with personal fulfillment and purpose.

19. Psychodynamic Therapy

Overview: Psychodynamic Therapy explores unconscious processes, past experiences, and early relationships to understand present behaviors. It helps individuals gain insight into deep-seated patterns and emotional conflicts. By bringing hidden motivations and unresolved emotions to awareness, this approach fosters self-reflection and long-term psychological growth.[71]

Psychodynamic Therapy Client Indicators:

- Mentions recurring struggles without understanding the deeper cause
- Expresses difficulty in breaking unhelpful patterns of behavior
- Talks about unresolved conflicts from early career experiences
- Feels emotions tied to business decisions but doesn't know why[72]

Sales Questions Using Psychodynamic Principles:

1. **How have your past experiences with similar business decisions influenced your current approach?**
    - This question brings unconscious patterns to conscious awareness.
2. **What recurring challenges do you face in your business, and do you see a pattern in how they arise?**
    - This question aligns identifies unconscious cycles that may be repeating.
3. **Do you ever feel like past experiences are unconsciously shaping the way you evaluate opportunities today?**
    - This question aligns encourages introspection on unconscious motivations.
4. **How do you typically handle pressure, and does that approach trace back to earlier career experiences?**
    - This question connects past conditioning to present coping mechanisms.
5. **What emotions come up for you when thinking about making a big change?**
    - This question emphasizes exploring underlying emotions rather than just rational analysis.
6. **If you could reframe the way you approach challenges, how would you want to see yourself handling them?**
    - This question supports deep self-reflection and identity restructuring.
7. **Are there any deep-seated fears or anxieties that tend to surface when you face uncertainty in business?**
    - This question uncovers unconscious fears that drive behavior.
8. **How do you think your early career experiences shaped your current leadership or decision-making style?**
    - This question connects past experiences to present professional identity.
9. **Do you notice any emotional patterns in the way you react to business challenges or difficult conversations?**
    - This question explores recurring emotional responses that may be rooted in past experiences.
10. **If you could rewrite the internal narrative you tell yourself about risk and success, what would that new story sound like?**
    - This question encourages a shift in self-perception and deeper insight into personal narratives.

20. Rational Emotive Behavior Therapy (REBT)

Overview: REBT teaches individuals to identify and challenge irrational beliefs that contribute to emotional distress. By replacing these beliefs with rational thoughts, clients can develop healthier thinking patterns, improve emotional resilience, and respond more effectively to life's challenges. This approach emphasizes that emotional suffering often stems from rigid thought patterns, which can be reshaped through intentional cognitive restructuring.[73]

Rational Emotive Behavior Therapy (REBT) Client Indicators:

- Demonstrates irrational or exaggerated emotional reactions to obstacles
- Uses self-defeating language (e.g., I should be better at this.)
- Struggles with perfectionism or rigid personal rules
- Expresses frustration over their own thought patterns[74]

Sales Questions Using REBT Principles:

1. **What assumptions do you have about this business challenge, and how certain are you that they're true?**
   - This question challenges irrational beliefs.
2. **How do you differentiate between facts and emotions when making business decisions?**
   - This question promotes rational evaluation.
3. **What is the worst-case scenario you're imagining, and how realistic is it?**
   - This question helps counter catastrophizing.
4. **How often do you find yourself saying "I must' or "I should' in decision-making?**
   - This question challenges rigid thinking patterns.
5. **How would your perspective change if you reinterpreted this challenge as an opportunity?**
   - This question focuses on cognitive reframing.
6. **If you approached this issue from a purely logical standpoint, what would your next step be?**
   - This question separates logic from emotional distortion.
7. **How do you challenge your own assumptions when making business decisions?**
   - This question encourages questioning irrational beliefs and rethinking assumptions.

8. **What would it take for you to feel more confident about this business decision?**
   - This question focuses on changing irrational beliefs to create more constructive emotions.
9. **How would you handle this situation if you reframed it as a learning opportunity rather than a failure?**
   - This question encourages cognitive reframing to turn negative experiences into constructive ones.
10. **What beliefs about success are limiting your business potential, and how can you challenge them?**
    - This question confronts irrational beliefs and promotes a more flexible, realistic approach to business success.

21. Solution-Focused Brief Therapy (SFBT)

Overview: SFBT focuses on finding solutions rather than analyzing problems. It encourages clients to identify what is working and build on their existing strengths. By emphasizing small, achievable steps, this approach helps individuals create meaningful change without dwelling on past difficulties.[75]

Solution-Focused Brief Therapy (SFBT) Client Indicators:

- Appears action-oriented and seeks quick, pragmatic solutions
- Expresses frustration with overanalyzing and wants immediate next steps
- Uses language focused on future goals rather than past challenges
- Already has ideas about possible solutions but needs confirmation[76]

Sales Questions Using SFBT Principles:

1. **What past successes can you draw from to navigate this challenge?**
   - This question aligns with SFBT by prompting the client to reflect on past wins, reinforcing confidence and uncovering strategies that can be reapplied.
2. **If your ideal outcome was already in place, what would be different?**
   - This encourages forward-thinking by helping the client define success, making it easier to identify steps to get there.
3. **What's one immediate action you can take that moves you in the right direction?**
   - SFBT emphasizes small, manageable steps. This question shifts focus from barriers to solutions, making progress feel attainable.
4. **What's currently working well, and how can you expand on it?**
   - By reinforcing strengths rather than weaknesses, this question fosters a mindset geared toward leveraging what's already effective.

5. **What would be the first noticeable sign that things are improving?**
    - This question helps the client visualize success, creating a clearer path forward by identifying key indicators of progress.
6. **Who on your team demonstrates the skills needed to solve this problem, and how can you empower them?**
    - This taps into existing resources, encouraging the client to recognize and leverage internal strengths rather than seeking external fixes.
7. **What current strategies are yielding positive results, and how can you maximize them?**
    - This question keeps the client solution-focused by building on their own effective approaches instead of reinventing the wheel.
8. **When faced with similar challenges before, what worked best?**
    - SFBT prioritizes learning from experience. This question helps the client connect past problem-solving strategies to their current situation.
9. **If nothing was holding you back, what's the first step you'd take?**
    - By removing perceived limitations, this encourages creative thinking and a proactive mindset toward problem-solving.
10. **Once this issue is resolved, how will your day-to-day work improve?**
    - By focusing on the benefits of resolution, this question keeps motivation high and helps the client maintain a positive outlook.

22. Somatic Therapy

Overview: Somatic therapy focuses on the connection between the body and mind, using the body's physical responses to process and release emotional trauma. It incorporates techniques like breathwork, movement, and bodily awareness to help individuals become more attuned to the sensations within their bodies. By exploring how the body holds stress and emotional pain, this approach fosters healing and self-awareness, facilitating emotional release and promoting mental and physical well-being.[77]

Somatic Therapy Client Indicators:

- Describes physical symptoms of stress, such as tension or fatigue
- Uses body-oriented language (e.g., I feel it in my gut.)
- Expresses difficulty processing stress mentally but feels it physically
- Struggles with anxiety that seems to manifest in the body[78]

Sales Questions Using Somatic Therapy Principles:

1. **How does stress or pressure physically manifest for you when making high-stakes business decisions?**
   - This question encourages awareness of the body's response to stress.
2. **What physical cues tell you when something in your business feels right or wrong?**
   - This question promotes intuition through bodily awareness.
3. **How do you recover from stressful work situations—do you use movement, deep breathing, or another method?**
   - This question focuses on embodied regulation strategies.
4. **What patterns have you noticed in how your body reacts during challenging conversations or negotiations?**
   - This question encourages reflection on physical reactions.
5. **When you feel overwhelmed, how do you reconnect with a sense of control and presence?**
   - This question emphasizes grounding techniques.
6. **Have you considered how small shifts in your physical state might influence your confidence in business interactions?**
   - This question highlights the power of somatic adjustments.
7. **How do you maintain a sense of calm and focus when facing critical decisions under pressure?**
   - This question emphasizes maintaining physical and emotional equilibrium in stressful situations.
8. **What role does body language play in your leadership or client interactions?**
   - This question brings awareness to how physical cues can influence communication and decision-making.
9. **Have you ever considered how regular physical activity or mindfulness practices could affect your business decision-making?**
   - This question encourages integration of mind-body practices to enhance cognitive processes.
10. **In what ways do you notice your body reacting when you're excited or passionate about an idea?**
    - This question connects bodily sensations with emotional responses, emphasizing alignment between the body and mind.

23. Transactional Analysis (TA)

Overview: TA explores communication through three ego states: Parent, Adult, and Child. It helps individuals understand how these states influence their interactions and decisions, promoting healthier, more balanced communication and improved self-awareness. By recognizing and shifting between these states consciously, individuals can foster more constructive conversations and resolve conflicts more effectively. Professional sellers should evaluate which roles (Parent, Adult, Child) they, their leaders, peers, subordinates, partners, and their customers play within the sales process.[79]

Transactional Analysis (TA) Client Indicators:

- Shifts between parent, child, and adult modes in communication
- Struggles with power dynamics in workplace relationships
- Feels emotionally reactive in certain professional interactions
- Expresses difficulties setting boundaries or asserting themselves[80]

Sales Questions Using TA Principles:

1. **When making business decisions, do you rely more on past experiences, logical analysis, or instinct?**
   - This question identifies whether the client is operating from a Parent, Adult, or Child state.
2. **How do you respond when a team member challenges your decisions?**
   - This question reveals interaction patterns between different ego states.
3. **Have you noticed any recurring dynamics in how negotiations or conflicts unfold in your business?**
   - This question helps uncover transactional patterns.
4. **When faced with high-pressure situations, do you tend to default to authority, collaboration, or independent action?**
   - This question examines ego-state-driven decision-making.
5. **What role do you naturally take in group discussions—do you guide, analyze, or react emotionally?**
   - This question helps identify dominant ego states.
6. **What communication patterns have you found most effective for motivating your team?**
   - This question emphasizes transactional awareness.
7. **How do you ensure that your communication stays balanced between authority and collaboration in team interactions?**
   - This question focuses on balancing the Parent and Adult ego states to facilitate effective communication.
8. **When conflict arises with clients or colleagues, do you focus more on finding a solution or ensuring emotional satisfaction?**
   - This question examines how different ego states influence conflict resolution strategies.

9. **How do you navigate situations where team members may revert to a Child ego state during stressful times?**
    - This question explores strategies for managing situations where people shift into a Child-like response.
10. **What do you do to ensure that you are engaging with others from a place of rationality rather than emotion?**
    - This question helps clients move from emotional reactions (Child) to rational, adult-centered decisions.

✿ PERSONAL EXPLORATION ✿

It's now time for you to reflect on how therapeutic modalities enhance consultative sales conversations. The techniques and frameworks you've just read aren't theoretical exercises—they're tools designed to deepen trust, uncover true client needs, and guide meaningful conversations. Some of these ideas may have immediately resonated with you, while others may have challenged the way you've traditionally approached sales. That's a good thing. Growth happens when we question, experiment, and refine our approach.[81]

As you consider how to integrate these concepts into your real-world interactions, here are four questions to help you reflect, challenge your thinking, and commit to putting these strategies into practice:

1. Which therapeutic modality resonated most with you, and why? How do you see yourself applying its principles in your next client conversation?
2. What beliefs about sales conversations or client relationships were challenged by this section? How do you feel about those challenges, and what might they reveal about your current approach?
3. Where do you anticipate resistance—either from yourself or your clients—when applying these techniques? How might you address that resistance to ensure authenticity and effectiveness?
4. If you were to commit to practicing just one small shift in your sales conversations based on what you've learned here, what would it be, and how will you hold yourself accountable to making that change?

Let these questions guide your thinking as you move forward. The goal isn't perfection—it's progress. The more you apply these strategies, the more natural they'll become, and the deeper your client relationships will grow.

☙ YOUR FINAL THOUGHTS ❧

Use The Space Below To Capture Your Thoughts And Reflections On What You've Learned In This Section

_____
_____
_____
_____
_____

LEVERAGING MOTIVATIONAL INTERVIEWING

Motivational Interviewing (MI) is a collaborative, person-centered, empathy-focused approach that invites individuals to challenge and question their thoughts, concerns, and motivations for change. Rather than offering suggestions for possible solutions, MI leverages open-ended gentle-challenging questions and active listening to help people articulate reasons for making or not making changes in their behaviors, perspectives, beliefs, or decisions. Originally developed to support therapeutic clients on their addiction recovery journey, MI has evolved over time and has now been widely adopted across professional coaching, counseling, corporate, and leadership settings.[1]

In consultative sales, MI reframes conversations from persuasive selling to guided discovery. Rather than pushing solutions or listing product benefits, sales professionals can use MI techniques to help clients uncover what truly matters to them.[2] By fostering an open, non-judgmental dialogue, salespeople empower clients to examine their current situation, identify challenges, and consider new possibilities—ultimately leading them to their own informed decisions.[3] This approach not only builds trust but also strengthens relationships, resulting in deeper engagement and long-term business success.[4]

The questions in the next section are designed to spark client reflection, surface unspoken needs, and bridge the gap between where they are and where they want to be, guiding the conversation toward solutions that feel both relevant and valuable.[5]

Questions for Building Rapport and Trust

- **What's most important to your team when choosing a partner for Managed Services?**
    - This question uncovers priorities and sets a collaborative tone.
- **Can you share a bit about what's been working well with your current vendor or approach?**
    - This question allows the client to share positive experiences, which the salesperson can later build upon.

- **What initially drew you to your current solution, and do you feel those same benefits are still being delivered?**
  - This question encourages the client to reflect on whether their needs are still being met.
- **How do you usually measure the success of a service provider relationship?**
  - This question shows interest in the client's metrics and aligns the salesperson's proposal to the client's values.
- **What's been your experience working with external consultants or vendors in the past? What worked, and what didn't?**
  - This question creates an opportunity to highlight the solution's differentiation.

Questions for Uncovering Needs and Gaps

- **What are some of the biggest challenges your IT team is facing right now?**
  - This question opens the door to discussing pain points.
- **How do you see these challenges impacting your team's ability to meet business objectives in the next 6-12 months?**
  - This question encourages forward-thinking and reveals urgency.
- **Are there specific risks or inefficiencies in your current setup that you'd like to see addressed?**
  - This question gets the client thinking critically about gaps.
- **If you could change one or two aspects of your relationship with your primary vendors, what would those changes be?**
  - This question helps identify areas where the salesperson can out-maneuver and leapfrog competitors.
- **What's stopping you from addressing these challenges today?**
  - This question uncovers obstacles and prepares the salesperson to position their solution.

Questions for Exploring Solutions and Alternatives

- **What would an ideal solution look like for you?**
  - This question encourages the client to visualize success, creating alignment with the salesperson's offering.
- **Have you considered how shifting to a different model or provider could improve outcomes?**
  - This question gently introduces the idea of change.

- If you had access to additional resources or expertise, how would it impact your team's performance?
  - This question frames the salesperson's offering as the missing piece.
- What would be the risks of staying with your current approach for another year?
  - This question encourages reflection on the status quo.
- What do you think would happen if your organization doesn't address these challenges soon?
  - This question reinforces urgency.

Questions for Creating Alignment with Value

- What would make you feel confident that switching to a new partner is the right move?
  - This question helps the salesperson address specific concerns or hesitations.
- How do you see your team benefiting from a partner who could [insert your key differentiator, e.g., "streamline your operations while reducing downtime"]?
  - This question frames the salesperson's offering as a solution to the client's problem.
- What role do you see us playing in helping your team meet its goals?
  - This question invites the client to visualize a partnership.
- How would having a more proactive partner help you personally in your role?
  - This question connects the conversation to the client's personal stakes and success.
- If we were able to solve [specific challenge they mentioned], what would that mean for your team, your timeline, and your results?
  - This question summarizes the client's concerns and ties the salesperson's solution directly to the client's goals.

Why Motivational Interviewing (MI) Questions Works

These questions incorporate the following Motivational Interviewing principles:

- **Open-ended questioning** to encourage reflection.

- **Focus on evoking "change talk"** by highlighting discrepancies between the client's current state and desired outcomes.
- **Collaborative tone** to avoid pressure or confrontation.
- **Personal and organizational alignment** by tying the solution to the client's goals and challenges.[6]

ఌఌఌఌ

ಞ PERSONAL EXPLORATION ೞ

Now that you've explored how Motivational Interviewing (MI) can transform sales conversations from transactional to consultative, take a moment to reflect on how this approach aligns with your current sales style. MI isn't about persuasion; it's about guiding clients toward their own realizations, helping them articulate their needs, and fostering a sense of trust and collaboration. By integrating MI into your sales process, you'll need to shift your mindset, practice patience, and commit to active listening. This approach can create deeper, more meaningful client relationships, but it may challenge some of your existing habits. Before moving forward, take some time to critically examine how MI can enhance your approach, and consider where you can implement these techniques to create more authentic and impactful conversations.

Here are four questions to guide your reflection:

1. How does the shift from persuading a client to guiding them toward their own conclusions challenge the way you currently approach sales conversations?
2. Think about a past sales conversation where the client seemed hesitant or resistant. How might an MI approach have changed the outcome? What questions could you have asked differently?
3. In what ways do you see MI benefiting not just your sales outcomes, but also your relationships with clients? How could adopting this approach improve long-term trust and partnership?
4. Do you agree that helping a client articulate their own reasons for change is more effective than persuading them with benefits and features? Why or why not?

These questions are designed to push you beyond surface-level understanding and into real-world application. The more you engage with these ideas, the more natural MI will become in your sales approach.

☙ YOUR FINAL THOUGHTS ❧

Use The Space Below To Capture Your Thoughts And Reflections On What You've Learned In This Section

_____
_____
_____
_____
_____
_____

UNDERSTANDING AND ADDRESSING BIASES
ᘓᔧᓎᘓᔧᓎ

Biases are cognitive shortcuts or mental frameworks that shape the way we perceive, evaluate, and make decisions. While they often emerge automatically and unconsciously, biases can skew our judgment, leading us to make decisions based on incomplete or distorted information. In the context of sales and decision-making, biases can significantly inhibit a client's ability to choose the best solution for their needs, as they may overemphasize past experiences, external influences, or emotional triggers rather than considering the full range of data and options available.[1] For sales professionals, understanding and identifying these biases is crucial—not only to help clients recognize how their biases may be shaping their thinking, but also to guide them toward a more informed, balanced decision.[2] By assisting clients in confronting and mitigating biases, a consultative salesperson can create a space where decisions are made from a clearer, bias-free mindset, allowing clients to make choices based on real value, not distorted perceptions.[3] Such an approach not only enhances decision quality but also fosters a more transparent and trustworthy client relationship.[4] This chapter aims to shed light on the most common cognitive biases, explore their impact on decision-making, and provide strategies to help clients overcome them, leading to more thoughtful and beneficial business outcomes.

ᘓᔧᓎᘓᔧᓎ

Implicit Bias

Implicit biases are unconscious assumptions or stereotypes that influence our judgments and behaviors without us realizing it. Shaped by personal experiences, societal norms, and cultural influences, these biases can subtly and unknowingly impact decision-making, often leading to unintentional favoritism or exclusion.[5] Recognizing and addressing implicit biases is essential for making more objective and rational choices.[6]

- **Personal Example:** A person assumes that a quiet neighbor is unfriendly or unapproachable, even though they have never spoken to them, simply because they subconsciously associate silence with coldness.
- **Business Example:** A company consistently hires extroverted candidates for sales roles, assuming that outgoing personalities are always better at

sales, despite research showing that introverts can be equally or more effective in consultative sales.

How To Identify This Bias and What To Do About It

- **Obvious Signs:** Prefers familiar solutions or vendors without clear justification.
- **Subtle Signs:** Struggles to articulate why they are uncomfortable with an option.
- **Statements:** "I just have a gut feeling this won't work for us."
- **Sales Insight:** Ask clarifying questions to uncover underlying concerns and provide relatable examples to challenge assumptions.[7]

Consultative Sales Questions

- **When evaluating vendors or partners, what criteria do you use, and have you ever examined whether any unspoken assumptions might be influencing your decisions?**
    - This question prompts the client to reflect on whether subconscious biases are shaping their vendor choices, encouraging a more objective evaluation process.
- **Are there alternative solutions or perspectives that may not have been considered due to past experiences or industry norms?**
    - This question encourages the client to challenge ingrained industry habits and explore overlooked opportunities.
- **How do you ensure that your selection process for new technologies, services, or team members is based on measurable outcomes rather than past habits or familiarity?**
    - This question helps the client focus on data-driven decision-making rather than relying on implicit biases formed from past experiences.
- **Have you ever reconsidered a previously dismissed solution after seeing new data or a fresh perspective?**
    - This question encourages the client to reflect on whether their initial dismissal of an option was due to bias rather than factual evaluation.
- **How do you ensure that your hiring or vendor selection process includes diverse perspectives rather than defaulting to 'safe' or familiar choices?**
    - This helps the client recognize that implicit bias can lead to repeatedly choosing similar candidates or vendors without broader consideration.

- **Are you open to the idea that the most successful approach might not align with conventional wisdom or your personal instincts?**
  - This challenges the client to acknowledge that their implicit biases might be leading them toward certain solutions without conscious awareness.

Explicit Bias

Explicit biases are conscious beliefs and attitudes that individuals are fully aware of and can deliberately endorse. These biases are often rooted in personal experiences, societal influences, or cultural norms, and they can lead to intentional discrimination or preferential treatment based on race, gender, age, or other characteristics.[8] Unlike implicit biases, explicit biases are accessible to an individual's awareness, meaning they are more likely to be expressed openly or acted upon intentionally.[9] Addressing explicit biases is crucial for creating more equitable and inclusive environments, as these biases can directly shape decision-making processes, behaviors, and social interactions.[10]

- **Personal Example:** A homeowner refuses to hire a contractor from a particular neighborhood, believing—without evidence—that contractors from that area do lower-quality work.
- **Business Example:** A CEO refuses to explore remote work options because they believe employees who work from home are inherently less productive, despite studies and performance data proving otherwise.

How To Identify This Bias and What To Do About It

- **Obvious Signs:** Openly rejects certain options or people without objective reasoning.
- **Subtle Signs:** Uses generalizations or stereotypes to justify decisions.
- **Statements:** "We never work with vendors from that region because they don't understand our needs."
- **Sales Insight:** Present data and success stories that counter their bias while encouraging an open discussion.[11]

Consultative Sales Questions

- **What criteria are you using to exclude certain options or vendors? Are those criteria based on past experience, data, or personal belief?**
  - This question forces the client to evaluate whether their exclusions are based on objective facts or personal biases.

- **How do you balance long-held business preferences with evolving industry trends and new innovations?**
    - This question encourages the client to examine whether their explicit biases are preventing them from adapting to changing market conditions.
- **What would change your perspective on a solution you've previously ruled out? Have you seen any data or case studies that might challenge your current stance?**
    - This prompts the client to reconsider a previously dismissed idea and assess whether new information could shift their viewpoint.
- **Is your current stance on this solution/vendor based on evidence, or has it remained unchanged despite industry shifts?**
    - This question challenges the client to reflect on whether their belief is rooted in current realities or outdated biases.
- **Have you ever seen an assumption you strongly believed in turn out to be wrong? How did that change your approach to decision-making?**
    - This helps the client recognize that their explicit biases may not always be accurate and that adjusting beliefs based on new evidence is valuable.
- **What risks might your organization face by holding onto long-standing beliefs without reassessing them periodically?**
    - This question highlights the potential negative impact of explicit biases on innovation, competitiveness, and overall decision-making.

༺☙❧༻

32 Critical Biases

1. Anchoring Bias

Placing excessive importance on initial information when making decisions, which can skew judgment and influence subsequent choices. This can create a disproportionate focus on the first piece of data encountered, even if it is irrelevant or outdated, leading to distorted conclusions. Being aware of Anchoring Bias helps in reassessing initial information and considering it in the broader context.[12]

- **Personal Example:** The first impression of a person (good or bad) strongly influences all future interactions.
- **Business Example:** A salesperson sets an initially high price, making subsequent "discounts" seem like a great deal.

How To Identify This Bias and What To Do About It

- **Obvious Signs:** Refers to an initial piece of information or first offer, using it as the baseline for all subsequent decisions.
- **Subtle Signs:** Compares everything to the first price or idea, even if new data contradicts it.
- **Statements:** "That first price you gave me seemed fair, so I'm not sure why you're asking for more."
- **Sales Insight:** If a client fixates on the first price, reframe the conversation with new data or a better proposal.[13]

Consultative Sales Questions

- **What criteria did you use when you first selected your current IT provider, and how relevant are those criteria today?**
    - This question encourages the client to reassess whether their original decision-making factors still hold value or if they are clinging to outdated reasoning.
- **If cost weren't the first thing you discussed, how else would you evaluate the value of this solution?**
    - This question helps the client shift focus away from price as the primary decision factor and consider a broader value-based perspective.
- **Are there legacy systems or outdated pricing models anchoring your expectations about what's possible?**
    - This question encourages the client to recognize how past investments or outdated benchmarks might be limiting their current decision-making.
- **When evaluating vendors, how do you ensure you don't get overly anchored to the first quote or solution presented?**
    - This question helps the client recognize whether they are giving undue weight to an initial offer rather than considering a range of options.
- **Are there any initial impressions or offers that could be skewing your decision-making process?**
    - This question encourages the client to reflect on whether their first exposure to pricing, features, or vendors is distorting their judgment.
- **How can you reassess your choices to ensure they reflect your long-term priorities rather than being influenced by the first option presented?**
    - This question helps the client step back and assess whether their choices are driven by strategy or just by a prior reference point.

2. Attribution Bias

This bias leads us to judge others harshly, blaming their actions on character flaws while excusing our own missteps as circumstantial. If a colleague misses a deadline, we see carelessness—but when we do, it's due to workload or bad timing. This bias distorts fairness and limits empathy, making self-awareness key to overcoming it.[14]

- **Personal Example:** Someone assumes a friend's rudeness is because they are a "bad person" rather than considering they might be going through a tough time.
- **Business Example:** A manager blames an employee's failure on incompetence but justifies their own mistakes as a result of external pressures.

How To Identify This Bias and What To Do About It

- **Obvious Signs:** Attributes successes to their own abilities and failures to external factors.
- **Subtle Signs:** Takes credit for positive results while blaming others or circumstances for failures.
- **Statements:** "Our success was because of my leadership; the failure was due to bad luck."
- **Sales Insight:** Guide clients to recognize both internal and external factors in their business decisions to ensure a more accurate understanding of their performance.[15]

Consultative Sales Questions

- **When evaluating vendor performance, do you take into account potential external factors that might be influencing outcomes?**
    - This question encourages the client to consider external challenges vendors may be facing before making judgments.
- **How often do you separate situational factors from individual performance in your assessments?**
    - This question helps the client develop a more balanced approach to performance evaluation.
- **Are you accounting for both internal and external challenges when discussing your team's progress and decision-making?**
    - This question ensures that leadership decisions are fair and well-rounded.

- **What mechanisms do you use to avoid unfairly attributing failures to individual performance without considering situational factors?**
  - This question encourages the client to implement structured evaluation processes.
- **Have you ever had a situation where you misjudged a decision due to attribution bias? What did you learn from it?**
  - This question helps the client reflect on past experiences and adjust their approach moving forward.
- **How do you differentiate between genuine performance issues and external challenges beyond a vendor or employee's control?**
  - This question prompts the client to think critically before making judgments about performance.

3. Authority Bias

Overvaluing the opinions of perceived authority figures. This bias leads individuals to give undue weight to the opinions of those in positions of power, assuming that their knowledge or expertise is always correct. Overcoming Authority Bias involves questioning authority figures' recommendations and evaluating information independently, based on evidence rather than status.[16]

- **Personal Example:** Someone follows bad medical advice from a celebrity rather than a doctor.
- **Business Example:** Employees accept a flawed plan because it was suggested by a high-ranking executive.

How To Identify This Bias and What To Do About It

- **Obvious Signs:** Defers to an authority figure's opinion without questioning it.
- **Subtle Signs:** References a leader's viewpoint as justification rather than objective reasoning.
- **Statements:** "If our CEO thinks this is the best option, then it must be right."
- **Sales Insight:** Encourage critical thinking by asking how the decision aligns with their own goals and data.[17]

Consultative Sales Questions

- **Are you giving too much weight to recommendations from perceived authority figures without considering all available evidence?**
    - This question challenges the client to critically assess whether they are prioritizing expertise or simply deferring to hierarchy.
- **How do you ensure you're critically evaluating recommendations, even when they come from trusted sources?**
    - This statement encourages a systematic approach to decision-making rather than accepting advice blindly.
- **Are you consulting a range of experts to avoid being influenced by a single authority figure?**
    - This question reinforces the importance of cross-referencing different sources before making a final decision.
- **How do you ensure that all decisions, even those suggested by high-ranking individuals, are thoroughly evaluated from multiple perspectives?**
    - This question helps the client reflect on whether they have processes in place to challenge and validate leadership directives.
- **Are you relying too heavily on advice from one source, or have you explored alternative opinions?**
    - This question directly addresses the risk of overvaluing a single perspective and prompts the client to seek multiple viewpoints.
- **How do you validate the advice you're receiving from authority figures, especially when it contradicts other data?**
    - This statement introduces the idea of fact-checking and balancing intuition with empirical evidence.

4. Availability Heuristic

The Availability Heuristic occurs when people make decisions or judgments based on the most easily recalled information, rather than considering all relevant data. This often leads to skewed perspectives, where recent or emotionally charged events hold more weight than they should. As a result, individuals may make choices based on vivid memories or readily accessible examples, rather than conducting a thorough assessment of all options, potentially overlooking important factors.[18]

- **Personal Example:** Someone avoids flying due to fear of crashes, despite statistics showing it's safer than driving.
- **Business Example:** A manager refuses to implement remote work because they recall one failed instance, ignoring broader success data.

How To Identify This Bias and What To Do About It

- **Obvious Signs:** Relies heavily on readily available information or recent experiences.
- **Subtle Signs:** Leans on a few vivid or memorable examples rather than considering the broader picture.
- **Statements:** "I remember this happening once before, so I'm sure it'll happen again."
- **Sales Insight:** Clients might make decisions based on recent news or personal anecdotes; introduce a broader view to provide context.[19]

Consultative Sales Questions

- **Are you focusing on recent technology failures or successes rather than long-term trends?**
    - This question helps uncover if the client is basing decisions on recent, easily recalled events rather than long-term data.
- **What cybersecurity risks do you worry about the most? Are those the most statistically likely threats to your business?**
    - This question challenges whether the client's fears are driven by memorable events rather than actual risk probabilities.
- **Have you explored industry-wide best practices, or are you basing decisions on just a few recent experiences?**
    - This question encourages the client to look beyond their personal experiences and consider broader industry data.
- **Are there any recent IT challenges that are dominating your decision-making, even if they may not be the most critical long-term risks?**
    - This helps the client recognize if their focus is skewed toward easily recalled but less impactful events.
- **How do you differentiate between isolated incidents and recurring patterns when evaluating your technology investments?**
    - This prompts them to consider whether they are making decisions based on memorable exceptions rather than actual trends.
- **Have you analyzed data across multiple years, or are your technology decisions shaped mainly by recent experiences?**
    - This encourages them to step back and assess whether their perspective is too short-term.

5. Base Rate Fallacy

Ignoring general statistical probabilities in favor of specific anecdotes. This bias leads individuals to give more weight to individual stories or specific examples than to broader statistical data, which can distort their understanding of likelihoods and probabilities.[20] Overcoming the Base Rate Fallacy requires giving appropriate weight to the overall data rather than isolated incidents.[21]

- **Personal Example:** Someone avoids online dating because they heard one horror story, despite the success rates.
- **Business Example:** A hiring manager rejects a candidate based on a bad interview experience, ignoring their strong track record.

How To Identify This Bias and What To Do About It

- **Obvious Signs:** Focuses on a single anecdotal story while ignoring broader trends.
- **Subtle Signs:** Dismisses statistics or general data in favor of personal experiences.
- **Statements:** "I heard a story about someone who tried that and failed, so I don't think it's a good idea."
- **Sales Insight:** Gently redirect the conversation to include broader data and industry trends that support your solution.[22]

Consultative Sales Questions

- **Are you focusing too much on a single anecdote about a vendor or solution, rather than the broader industry trends?**
    - This question helps the client recognize when they may be relying on a dramatic outlier rather than comprehensive data.
- **How do you ensure you're considering statistical probabilities when evaluating a solution, rather than relying on isolated examples?**
    - This statement reinforces the importance of data-driven decision-making over emotional reactions to single incidents.
- **What steps can you take to ensure that your decisions are based on broader data and not specific anecdotes?**
    - This question encourages the client to put systems in place that rely on evidence rather than personal stories.
- **Are you allowing specific anecdotes or isolated incidents to override statistical trends in your decision-making?**
    - This statement prompts the client to examine whether they are making decisions based on exceptions rather than rules.

- **How often do you evaluate the broader context and base rates when assessing risk and reward in your strategy?**
    - This question highlights the importance of looking at patterns rather than just individual cases.
- **What data points do you use to ensure your decisions are based on broader patterns rather than outliers?**
    - This statement reinforces the need for structured, objective analysis rather than emotional reactions to singular experiences.

6. Choice-Supportive Bias

Choice-Supportive Bias occurs when individuals view their past decisions more positively than they actually were. After making a decision, people tend to focus on its benefits while downplaying or ignoring any negative aspects.[23] This bias is often a way to maintain a sense of self-consistency and avoid feelings of regret, but it can hinder objective reflection and prevent learning from past experiences.[24] By overvaluing their choices, individuals may overlook important lessons or misjudge future decisions.[25]

- **Personal Example:** Someone recalls a past relationship as "perfect," overlooking real issues they once wanted to escape.
- **Business Example:** A leader rationalizes a poor hiring decision instead of acknowledging they made a mistake.

How To Identify This Bias and What To Do About It

- **Obvious Signs:** Defends past decisions despite clear evidence of flaws.
- **Subtle Signs:** Selectively recalls only positive aspects of a past choice.
- **Statements:** "That solution worked great for us before, so I don't see why we need to change."
- **Sales Insight:** Gently challenge their recollection by introducing objective data or past pain points they may have overlooked.[26]

Consultative Sales Questions

- **How do you evaluate the success of past technology decisions, and do you think any of those decisions could be reconsidered today?**
    - This question encourages reflection on whether past choices are still relevant or need to be reassessed.
- **What lessons have you learned from previous investments in IT solutions?**
    - This question helps the client extract valuable insights rather than justifying past decisions.

- **Are you still holding onto any technology choices because you want to validate them, even if they may not be serving your current needs?**
    - This question challenges the client to consider whether they are clinging to decisions for emotional reasons.
- **If you were making this decision today with a fresh perspective, would you choose the same technology or provider?**
    - This question encourages the client to assess their current needs without bias from past justifications.
- **Have there been any cases where past IT investments didn't work out as expected? How did you address them?**
    - This question promotes an open discussion about learning from mistakes rather than justifying them.
- **What criteria do you use to determine whether a past decision was genuinely successful, beyond just reinforcing that it was the "right choice" at the time?**
    - This question pushes for objective analysis rather than emotional validation of previous choices.

7. Clustering Illusion

Seeing patterns in random events. This bias occurs when people mistakenly perceive a pattern or trend in a series of random or unrelated data points. It leads to the assumption that the future will mirror the perceived pattern, even though it is purely coincidental and lacks predictive value.[27]

- **Personal Example:** Someone believes that every time they wear a certain shirt, they have a great day.
- **Business Example:** A trader believes stock prices follow a predictable pattern, even when movements are random.

How To Identify This Bias and What To Do About It

- **Obvious Signs:** Sees patterns or trends where none exist, making decisions based on perceived connections.
- **Subtle Signs:** Relies on anecdotal experiences rather than data-driven insights.
- **Statements:** "Every time we launch a product in Q2, it performs better—so we have to stick with that timing."
- **Sales Insight:** Help them recognize randomness by emphasizing statistical analysis and broader market trends.[28]

Consultative Sales Questions

- **Do you find yourself seeing patterns in technology usage where there may be randomness?**
  - This question helps the client reflect on whether their perceived trends are actually supported by data or just coincidences.
- **How do you ensure that you're not misinterpreting isolated incidents as trends when making decisions?**
  - This question encourages the client to analyze patterns objectively and differentiate between meaningful trends and random occurrences.
- **What methods do you use to verify that patterns you observe in performance data are statistically valid?**
  - This question prompts the client to validate their observations with data analysis before making strategic decisions.
- **Have there been situations where you made decisions based on perceived trends that later turned out to be misleading?**
  - This question helps the client recognize past mistakes and improve their decision-making process.
- **What tools or processes do you use to separate random fluctuations from meaningful insights in your data?**
  - This question encourages the client to adopt more rigorous analytical methods to avoid cognitive bias.
- **How do you differentiate between correlation and causation when evaluating technology performance or business trends?**
  - This question ensures the client critically assesses whether an observed pattern truly reflects a cause-and-effect relationship.

8. Confirmation Bias

Tendency to seek out and favor information that confirms existing beliefs while ignoring contradictory evidence. This bias can limit one's ability to objectively assess new information and can reinforce preconceived notions, leading to a narrow understanding of situations. Overcoming Confirmation Bias involves actively seeking diverse perspectives and challenging personal assumptions.[29]

- **Personal Example:** Someone in a relationship overlooks clear warning signs because they believe their partner is perfect.
- **Business Example:** A hiring manager favors a candidate because they fit a preconceived ideal, ignoring red flags.

How To Identify This Bias and What To Do About It

- **Obvious Signs:** Rejects new ideas or evidence that contradicts their initial belief.
- **Subtle Signs:** Only references supporting sources or experiences, ignoring others.
- **Statements:** "I've always thought this way, and I've seen it work in the past."
- **Sales Insight:** Watch for clients who only mention positive aspects of past solutions while downplaying negatives.[30]

Consultative Sales Questions

- **What assumptions are you making about your current IT strategy that you haven't challenged in the past year?**
    - This question encourages the client to reflect on whether they are operating on unexamined beliefs instead of objective data.
- **Have you ever been surprised by a failed IT initiative that you were initially confident in? What led to that misjudgment?**
    - This question helps the client recognize past decisions where they ignored contradictory evidence in favor of their existing beliefs.
- **How do you ensure you're considering alternative viewpoints before finalizing a technology investment?**
    - This question encourages the client to actively seek out dissenting opinions instead of only reinforcing their existing views.
- **When evaluating new solutions, what steps do you take to actively seek out perspectives or data that challenge your current assumptions?**
    - This question encourages the client to reflect on whether they deliberately seek out opposing viewpoints or just confirm what they already believe.
- **Are there any vendors, technologies, or strategies you've dismissed in the past that might be worth reconsidering with fresh insights or new data?**
    - This question helps the client recognize that past rejections may have been based on bias rather than objective evaluation.
- **How do you differentiate between evidence that truly supports your decision versus information that simply aligns with what you already believe?**
    - This question encourages the client to critically assess whether they are objectively analyzing data or just validating pre-existing opinions.

9. Curse of Knowledge

Forgetting what it was like to not know something, making it hard to communicate with beginners. This bias occurs when individuals assume others have the same level of understanding as they do, leading to overly complex explanations or the assumption that everyone knows what they know.[31] Overcoming the Curse of Knowledge requires empathy and simplifying explanations to match the listener's level of understanding.[32]

- **Personal Example:** A skilled cook gets frustrated when their partner doesn't understand a recipe's techniques.
- **Business Example:** A senior engineer struggles to train new hires because they assume concepts are "obvious."

How To Identify This Bias and What To Do About It

- **Obvious Signs:** Assumes others understand complex concepts immediately, leading to confusion.
- **Subtle Signs:** Becomes impatient or frustrated when explaining basics or terms to others.
- **Statements:** "This is really basic, I'm surprised you don't get it."
- **Sales Insight:** Use simple, clear language and check in to ensure the client understands, even when discussing advanced topics.[33]

Consultative Sales Questions

- **How do you ensure that your IT strategy is communicated clearly to all stakeholders, regardless of their level of expertise?**
    - This question helps the client recognize the need for clear communication tailored to different audiences.
- **What steps can you take to make sure you're not assuming a high level of understanding when introducing new technologies?**
    - This question encourages the client to check for knowledge gaps and adjust their approach accordingly.
- **Are there any areas where you might need to simplify explanations to ensure your entire team is aligned?**
    - This question prompts the client to make technical discussions more accessible to a broader audience.
- **How do you determine whether your audience truly understands your message, rather than just assuming they do?**
    - This question helps the client implement feedback mechanisms to verify comprehension.

- What communication techniques do you use to bridge the gap between experts and non-experts in your organization?
  - This question encourages the client to adopt structured methods, such as analogies or step-by-step guides, to facilitate understanding.
- Have you received feedback indicating that some of your explanations may be too complex? How have you adjusted based on that feedback?
  - This question helps the client reflect on past communication challenges and refine their approach.

10. Dunning-Kruger Effect

People with low ability overestimate their competence, while experts underestimate theirs. This bias stems from a lack of awareness of one's own limitations and a false sense of mastery.[34] It can result in poor decision-making, as individuals with limited knowledge may make decisions with excessive confidence, while those with more expertise may doubt their abilities.[35]

- **Personal Example:** Someone gives unsolicited relationship advice despite having little experience themselves.
- **Business Example:** A new manager is overly confident in their leadership skills, failing to seek mentorship.

How To Identify This Bias and What To Do About It

- **Obvious Signs:** Overestimates their abilities or knowledge in a particular area.
- **Subtle Signs:** Demonstrates unwarranted confidence in tasks or situations where they have little experience.
- **Statements:** "I don't need to learn more; I already know everything I need to."
- **Sales Insight:** Offer educational support or additional resources to help clients realize the complexity of a problem they may be underestimating.[36]

Consultative Sales Questions

- How do you ensure you're not underestimating the complexity of managing cloud security?
  - This question helps the client recognize that cybersecurity is a nuanced field that requires deep expertise, potentially beyond their own knowledge.

- **Would an independent assessment validate your current approach to IT security and infrastructure?**
    - o   This question encourages the client to seek external validation rather than relying solely on their own confidence in their existing setup.
- **Are you relying on internal opinions, or are you bringing in subject matter experts to confirm your strategy?**
    - o   This question challenges the client to reflect on whether they are making decisions based on limited internal knowledge or seeking expert insights.
- **How do you differentiate between confidence in your team's expertise and overconfidence that could lead to blind spots?**
    - o   This question encourages the client to assess whether their confidence is justified or if they may be overlooking critical gaps in their knowledge.
- **Have you ever encountered a situation where a technology decision seemed simple at first but turned out to be more complex than expected?**
    - o   This question helps the client reflect on past experiences where initial overconfidence may have led to unexpected challenges, making them more open to expert guidance.
- **What strategies do you use to identify areas where you or your team might have knowledge gaps?**
    - o   This question encourages the client to proactively seek out areas where they may lack expertise and take steps to address those gaps through training or external support.

11. Endowment Effect

Overvaluing things simply because we own them. There are two types of the Endowment Effect. (1) Psychological Ownership Bias: The tendency to assign greater value to things simply because we own them, leading to resistance when faced with selling, replacing, or upgrading—even when logic suggests a better alternative.[37] (2) Emotional Attachment Distortion: A cognitive bias where personal connection to an asset, idea, or decision inflates its perceived worth, making it difficult to part with, even when objective measures suggest a different course of action.[38]

- **Personal Example:** Someone holds onto an old, broken-down car, refusing to sell it at fair market value because it "has sentimental value."
- **Business Example:** A business leader refuses to sell a struggling division at market price, believing it's worth more just because they built it.

How To Identify This Bias and What To Do About It

- **Obvious Signs:** Overvalues something simply because they own or are familiar with it.
- **Subtle Signs:** Exhibits reluctance to let go of a current product or service even when there are better alternatives available.
- **Statements:** "I've been using this software for years, and I'm not ready to change."
- **Sales Insight:** Help clients recognize the potential value in switching to a new solution by focusing on future benefits rather than past attachments.[39]

Consultative Sales Questions

- **How do you assess whether your current IT infrastructure is truly the best fit for your needs versus simply being familiar and comfortable?**
    - This question encourages the client to critically evaluate whether their current systems serve their future goals or if they are merely holding on out of habit.
- **Are there any legacy systems or processes you're holding onto because of past investments, even if they may not be the most efficient or cost-effective today?**
    - This question helps uncover emotional attachments to outdated solutions that may be limiting growth and efficiency.
- **If you were starting from scratch, would you make the same technology choices you have today, or would you consider different solutions?**
    - This question pushes the client to remove emotional bias and evaluate their current IT investments objectively.
- **What criteria do you use to determine when it's time to replace or upgrade a system, and are those criteria based on performance or attachment?**
    - This question challenges the client to examine whether their decision-making is rooted in measurable outcomes rather than sentimentality.
- **Have you considered the opportunity cost of keeping outdated technology instead of investing in more scalable, efficient solutions?**
    - This question highlights the potential losses in productivity and innovation due to clinging to legacy systems.

- **How do you ensure your decisions about maintaining existing technology are based on business impact rather than emotional attachment?**
    - This question prompts the client to implement structured evaluation methods rather than relying on personal bias.

12. False Consensus Effect

Overestimating how much others agree with our views. This bias leads to the belief that one's own opinions, preferences, or behaviors are more common and widely shared than they actually are.[40] It can cause misunderstandings and conflict, as individuals fail to recognize that others may have different perspectives or preferences.[41]

- **Personal Example:** Someone believes all their friends share their political views, failing to recognize differing opinions.
- **Business Example:** A team leader assumes everyone agrees with their strategy, leading to poor collaboration.

How To Identify This Bias and What To Do About It

- **Obvious Signs:** Assumes everyone agrees with their perspective without verifying.
- **Subtle Signs:** Dismisses differing viewpoints as outliers or uninformed.
- **Statements:** "Everyone I talk to thinks this is the best approach."
- **Sales Insight:** Present data or outside perspectives to gently challenge their assumption of universal agreement.[42]

Consultative Sales Questions

- **Are you assuming that your team or organization shares your perspective on this technology decision?**
    - This question challenges the decision-maker to reflect on whether they might be projecting their own beliefs onto their team, which could lead to blind spots in decision-making.
- **How do you make sure you're not overestimating agreement within your organization about technology needs?**
    - This statement encourages the leader to consider whether they are actively seeking dissenting opinions rather than assuming consensus.

- **What steps do you take to gather a diverse range of opinions before committing to a major IT change?**
    - This question prompts the client to think about whether they are engaging with different departments, perspectives, and levels of experience to validate their decision.
- **Have you gathered feedback from a diverse group of stakeholders when making IT decisions?**
    - This question ensures that the decision-maker is not just relying on a narrow set of voices, which can reinforce false consensus.
- **What steps are you taking to ensure you're not assuming everyone shares the same priorities or views?**
    - This question highlights the risk of assuming alignment without verifying if different stakeholders have conflicting needs or concerns.
- **How do you foster collaboration and avoid making decisions based solely on your perspective?**
    - This statement shifts the focus toward building a culture of open dialogue, where different opinions can surface before finalizing decisions.

13. Framing Effect

Decisions are influenced by how information is presented rather than the facts themselves. The way a situation or data is framed—whether in terms of gain or loss—can dramatically impact decision-making, even if the underlying facts remain unchanged.[43] Recognizing the Framing Effect allows individuals to assess information more critically and make decisions based on content rather than presentation.[44]

- **Personal Example:** A friend describes an event as "a disaster," shaping how others perceive it, even if it wasn't that bad.
- **Business Example:** A CEO supports a project when it's pitched as having a "90% success rate" but rejects it when framed as a "10% failure rate."

How To Identify This Bias and What To Do About It

- **Obvious Signs:** Reacts differently depending on how the information is presented, even if the content is the same.
- **Subtle Signs:** Shifts opinions based on how a proposal is framed as a gain or loss.
- **Statements:** "This offer saves us 10%, but what if the savings were presented as a potential loss?"

- **Sales Insight:** Be mindful of how you present numbers and options; framing a proposal positively can influence decisions.[45]

Consultative Sales Questions

- **If you framed this decision in terms of long-term ROI instead of short-term cost, how would your perspective shift?**
    - This question helps the client recognize how their decision-making might change if they focused on long-term value rather than immediate expenses.
- **Are you considering technology investments as expenses or as strategic enablers?**
    - This question encourages the client to reassess whether they see IT costs as a burden or an opportunity for growth.
- **Would viewing this as a competitive advantage instead of a necessary upgrade change how you evaluate it?**
    - This question helps shift the client's mindset from compliance-based decision-making to strategic differentiation.
- **How do you ensure that your team's decisions are based on the full set of facts and not just how information is framed or presented?**
    - This question encourages the client to evaluate whether their team critically assesses information or is swayed by presentation techniques.
- **Are there alternative ways of framing this decision that could lead to a different perspective or outcome?**
    - This question helps the client recognize that reframing the problem might reveal more effective solutions.
- **How do you make sure that your strategy isn't shaped more by external influences than by actual needs?**
    - This question encourages the client to focus on internal business requirements rather than being led by industry hype or persuasive sales tactics.

14. Groupthink

Desire for consensus overrides critical thinking. This bias leads individuals to conform to group opinions or decisions, even if they might be flawed or unwise, in order to maintain harmony or avoid conflict.[46] Groupthink can stifle creativity and critical thinking, making it important to encourage open dialogue and diverse perspectives in decision-making processes.[47]

- **Personal Example:** A group of friends decides to visit a restaurant even though most secretly dislike it, simply because no one wants to be the one to challenge the decision.
- **Business Example:** A leadership team approves a risky IT investment because no one wants to contradict the CFO, despite underlying concerns.

How To Identify This Bias and What To Do About It

- **Obvious Signs:** Everyone in the group agrees quickly without voicing concerns or dissent.
- **Subtle Signs:** Unspoken tension or hesitation in individual responses, but no one speaks up.
- **Statements:** "I think everyone else is on board, so I'll go with the flow."
- **Sales Insight:** Encourage independent feedback from each individual to uncover hidden concerns or unspoken issues.[48]

Consultative Sales Questions

- **Are you challenging internal assumptions, or are you defaulting to agreement to avoid friction?**
    - This question encourages critical thinking and ensures the client isn't passively agreeing just to maintain harmony.
- **Who in your organization plays the 'devil's advocate' when evaluating new technology decisions?**
    - By introducing the idea of a devil's advocate, this question highlights the need for diverse perspectives and healthy debate in decision-making.
- **Have you gathered diverse perspectives, or are you relying on a small, like-minded group?**
    - This question urges the client to consider whether they are hearing a full range of opinions or just reinforcing existing beliefs.
- **How do you ensure that you're getting a variety of perspectives when making critical IT or business decisions?**
    - This question helps the client reflect on their decision-making process and whether they are actively seeking out differing viewpoints.
- **Are you involving key stakeholders from different departments to avoid groupthink and make sure all viewpoints are heard?**
    - This ensures that decisions are made with input from multiple departments, preventing a small, homogeneous group from dominating the discussion.

- **What checks are in place to ensure that consensus-building doesn't result in a decision that lacks diverse input?**
    - This question encourages the client to put safeguards in place to prevent groupthink from leading to poorly thought-out decisions.

15. Halo Effect

Letting one positive trait influence overall judgment. This bias occurs when an individual's overall impression of someone or something is disproportionately influenced by one standout feature or characteristic, such as attractiveness, charm, or a single success.[49] The Halo Effect can lead to overly favorable judgments based on limited information.[50]

- **Personal Example:** Someone assumes a physically attractive person must also be kind and intelligent.
- **Business Example:** A charismatic job candidate gets hired despite lacking qualifications because they made a great first impression.

How To Identify This Bias and What To Do About It

- **Obvious Signs:** Judging someone's overall character based on one positive trait.
- **Subtle Signs:** One good experience with a person or company leads to an overall positive opinion, even in unrelated areas.
- **Statements:** "I love their brand, so I trust everything they offer."
- **Sales Insight:** Encourage clients to critically assess all aspects of a vendor's offering, not just the surface-level impression.[51]

Consultative Sales Questions

- **Are you assuming that a vendor's reputation in one area guarantees excellence in all areas?**
    - This question challenges the client to separate a vendor's strengths in one domain from their overall capabilities.
- **How do you separate brand perception from real-world performance?**
    - This question encourages the client to rely on objective data rather than just a company's marketing or reputation.
- **Are you evaluating each aspect of a solution independently?**
    - This question helps the client focus on granular performance metrics rather than general assumptions.

- **What criteria do you use to ensure you're making data-driven technology decisions rather than relying on brand recognition?**
    - This question prompts the client to incorporate structured evaluations instead of being swayed by a company's market presence.
- **Have you ever chosen a technology or partner based on reputation alone and later found that it didn't fully meet your needs?**
    - This question encourages reflection on past decisions where the Halo Effect may have led to suboptimal outcomes.
- **How do you ensure that a strong first impression doesn't overshadow a thorough evaluation of long-term reliability and support?**
    - This question reminds the client to balance initial impressions with a deeper assessment of ongoing performance.

16. Hindsight Bias

Believing past events were predictable after they've already happened. This bias creates the illusion that events were foreseeable, leading to a false sense of clarity or control over past decisions.[52] It can distort learning from mistakes, as individuals may believe they should have foreseen an outcome, even when it was not obvious at the time.[53]

- **Personal Example:** After a breakup, someone says, "I knew this was going to happen," despite not acting on any warning signs earlier.
- **Business Example:** A CIO claims they "always knew" a failed product launch would flop, despite supporting it beforehand.

How To Identify This Bias and What To Do About It

- **Obvious Signs:** Claims they "always knew" an outcome after the fact.
- **Subtle Signs:** Rewrites past decision-making to align with the final result.
- **Statements:** "I had a feeling this deal wouldn't work out from the start."
- **Sales Insight:** Challenge their hindsight perspective by asking what specific indicators led them to that conclusion before the outcome.[54]

Consultative Sales Questions

- **How can you ensure that your past experiences, while valuable, don't cloud your judgment when making future technology decisions?**
    - This question encourages the client to remain open-minded rather than relying too heavily on past experiences.

- **Are you analyzing past projects objectively, without convincing yourself that the outcome was obvious from the start?**
  - This question helps clients avoid revisionist thinking and ensures they learn accurate lessons from the past.
- **Are you making future IT decisions based on a selective or overly simplistic view of past experiences?**
  - This question challenges the tendency to oversimplify past events, which can lead to misguided decisions.
- **How do you ensure past project evaluations are based on complete and accurate data?**
  - This question encourages the client to rely on data rather than gut feelings or hindsight-influenced narratives.
- **Are you learning the right lessons from past technology investments?**
  - This question ensures that past experiences are used productively rather than reinforcing incorrect assumptions.
- **How can you ensure you don't fall into the trap of oversimplifying past events when planning for the future?**
  - This question encourages the client to critically evaluate their past interpretations and seek a well-rounded perspective.

17. Horn Effect

Letting one negative trait overshadow everything else. In contrast to the Halo Effect, the Horn Effect occurs when a single negative attribute causes an overall unfavorable judgment.[55] This bias can unfairly color perceptions of a person or situation, making it essential to take a more holistic view when evaluating others.[56]

- **Personal Example:** Someone dismisses a potential partner because of one awkward comment on the first date.
- **Business Example:** A manager overlooks an employee's strong performance because they once made a minor mistake.

How To Identify This Bias and What To Do About It

- **Obvious Signs:** Forms a negative opinion of someone based on one unfavorable trait or experience.
- **Subtle Signs:** One bad experience leads to generalized negative views about a person, company, or idea.
- **Statements:** "They messed up that one thing, so I can't trust anything they say."

- **Sales Insight:** Help clients separate isolated issues from the overall value and offer of a solution.[57]

Consultative Sales Questions

- **Are you overly focused on one negative aspect of a potential solution and allowing that to overshadow the rest of the benefits?**
    - This question encourages the client to take a step back and assess the full picture rather than letting one flaw dictate their decision.
- **Do any past vendor mistakes still influence your perception of similar providers in the market?**
    - This question challenges the client to consider whether they are holding onto past negative experiences that may not be relevant to their current situation.
- **How do you ensure you're not dismissing a solution based on one isolated issue?**
    - This question helps the client focus on the overall value of a solution rather than fixating on a single imperfection.
- **What steps do you take to separate past negative experiences from an objective evaluation of new opportunities?**
    - This question prompts the client to reflect on their approach to decision-making and whether they allow past biases to cloud their judgment.
- **Are there any solutions or providers you've previously dismissed that might be worth reevaluating with fresh criteria?**
    - This question encourages the client to reconsider past decisions that may have been influenced by the Horn Effect.
- **How do you balance weighing risks and negatives against the broader benefits a solution could bring?**
    - This question helps the client develop a structured way to assess trade-offs without letting a single flaw dominate their evaluation.

18. IKEA Effect

Overvaluing things we create ourselves. This bias occurs when individuals place a higher value on things they have assembled or created, even if the item is objectively of lower quality.[58] The sense of accomplishment and personal involvement inflates the perceived worth, making it difficult to objectively assess the value of one's work or creations.[59]

- **Personal Example:** Someone refuses to part with an ugly DIY home project because they built it themselves.

- **Business Example:** A COO insists on keeping a flawed company process because they designed it.

How To Identify This Bias and What To Do About It

- **Obvious signs:** Overvalues a personally developed solution despite clear flaws.
- **Subtle signs:** Resists alternative options, even when they're objectively better.
- **Statements:** "We built this process ourselves, so we know it works best for us."
- **Sales Insight:** Validate their efforts while subtly introducing improvements that build on their existing work.[60]

Consultative Sales Questions

- **Are you holding onto outdated technology because it's what you or your team created, even if it's no longer the best solution?**
    - This question forces an objective evaluation of whether legacy systems still add value.
- **Do you find it difficult to let go of a solution you implemented, even when newer options would provide better results?**
    - This question challenges emotional attachment to self-created solutions.
- **How do you ensure your attachment to previous systems doesn't limit innovation?**
    - This question encourages continuous improvement rather than clinging to past work.
- **Would a third-party solution bring more value than continuing to invest in your in-house processes?**
    - This question helps the client objectively compare internally built versus external solutions.
- **How do you balance internal pride with ensuring the best possible solutions for your business?**
    - This question encourages a focus on outcomes over ownership.
- **Are there areas in your IT infrastructure that you may be holding onto simply because they were built internally?**
    - This question pushes clients to reevaluate legacy systems.

19. Illusory Correlation

This bias happens when people believe that two unrelated events are connected, simply because they occurred together. The mind may mistakenly interpret the simultaneous occurrence of events as a causal link, leading to the false belief that one event influences the other. This can result in flawed decision-making, as it's easy to attribute outcomes or patterns to spurious relationships. Being mindful of this bias is crucial in making judgments based on actual data, rather than coincidental occurrences.[61]

- **Personal Example:** Someone believes their lucky charm helped them ace a test, ignoring their preparation.
- **Business Example:** A manager attributes a company's recent success to a new employee's arrival, even though the two are unrelated.

How To Identify This Bias and What To Do About It

- **Obvious Signs:** Draws conclusions based on coincidences rather than actual causation.
- **Subtle Signs:** Attributes outcomes to factors with no logical connection.
- **Statements:** "Ever since we switched vendors, our sales have increased—it must be because of them."
- **Sales Insight:** Redirect focus to measurable data and cause-and-effect reasoning to validate or challenge their assumption.[62]

Consultative Sales Questions

- **Have you observed patterns in your previous technology implementations that may not be as closely connected as you think?**
    - This question helps the client critically assess whether their perceived patterns are backed by real data or just coincidences.
- **Are there any common misconceptions influencing your choice of solutions, based on isolated events?**
    - This question encourages the client to recognize and challenge any assumptions they may have formed based on anecdotal evidence.
- **Do you find yourself attributing certain outcomes to specific factors without considering all possibilities?**
    - This question prompts the client to take a broader analytical approach rather than relying on instinctive but potentially misleading correlations.

- **What data or evidence do you use to confirm whether two factors are truly related or just coincidental?**
    - This question helps the client establish a more objective, data-driven approach to identifying real causal relationships.
- **Have past experiences led you to develop any assumptions about technology performance that might not hold up under deeper analysis?**
    - This question encourages the client to revisit past decisions and determine if they were based on valid reasoning or false correlations.
- **How do you ensure that strategic decisions are based on verified cause-and-effect relationships rather than perceived patterns?**
    - This question prompts the client to implement structured decision-making methods to avoid falling for illusory correlations.

20. Illusory Superiority

Illusory Superiority occurs when people overestimate their abilities, qualities, or knowledge relative to others, even in areas where they may not excel. This bias leads individuals to believe they are better or more skilled than the average person, often disregarding evidence to the contrary.[63] It can result in inflated self-confidence, poor decision-making, and a lack of awareness of areas that may require improvement or growth.[64]

- **Personal Example:** Someone believes they are a better driver than most, despite evidence that they have made unsafe driving decisions.
- **Business Example:** A company overestimates its market position, failing to account for the competition.

How To Identify This Bias and What To Do About It

- **Obvious Signs:** Dismisses advice or feedback, believing they already know best.
- **Subtle Signs:** Downplays competitors' strengths and overstates their own capabilities.
- **Statements:** "We don't need to change our strategy—our team is already the best in the industry."
- **Sales Insight:** Challenge their perception by presenting objective comparisons and industry benchmarks.[65]

Consultative Sales Questions

- **Are you overestimating your organization's readiness for the challenges ahead, or are you considering external factors that may shift your competitive edge?**
    - This question helps clients reflect on whether their confidence in their company's preparedness is justified or if they are underestimating risks and market shifts.
- **What areas of your business or team might benefit from a more realistic self-assessment of current capabilities?**
    - This question encourages a reality check, prompting the client to analyze where overconfidence may be leading to blind spots or missed opportunities for improvement.
- **How do you ensure you're not underestimating your competition by assuming you're more prepared than you actually are?**
    - This question challenges the assumption that their company is ahead of the competition, prompting them to consider whether they have objectively analyzed competitive threats.
- **How do you ensure your business is continuously improving rather than assuming it's already the best in class?**
    - This question forces introspection on whether the company is actively evolving or stagnating due to an inflated sense of superiority.
- **What competitive threats might you be underestimating due to overconfidence in your current strategy?**
    - This question makes the client consider whether overconfidence is leading them to ignore potential threats that could disrupt their market position.
- **How do you validate your team's expertise and decision-making against objective industry benchmarks rather than relying solely on internal confidence?**
    - This question challenges the client to assess whether their confidence in their team's capabilities is based on measurable, external standards or merely internal perceptions.

21. Loss Aversion

This is the tendency to fear losses more than valuing equivalent gains, leading to cautious decision-making. This can result in avoiding risks, resisting change, or holding onto failing investments to prevent loss, often at the expense of potential growth. Recognizing this bias helps in making more objective, forward-thinking choices.[66]

- **Personal Example:** Someone stays in a bad relationship because they fear being alone more than they value their happiness.
- **Business Example:** A company avoids a strategic shift because leadership fears short-term losses, even if long-term gains are likely.

How To Identify This Bias and What To Do About It

- **Obvious Signs:** Demonstrates stronger reactions to potential losses than equivalent gains.
- **Subtle Signs:** Sticks with an outdated or suboptimal solution because the thought of changing feels like a loss.
- **Statements:** "I'd rather not risk losing what we already have, even if it's not perfect."
- **Sales Insight:** Help clients see the potential long-term value of switching solutions to overcome the fear of loss.[67]

Consultative Sales Questions

- **Are you prioritizing avoiding losses over maximizing potential gains in your technology strategy?**
    - This question encourages the client to consider whether fear is driving decision-making rather than potential benefits.
- **What risks are you avoiding that might actually be opportunities?**
    - This question helps reframe risk as a chance for innovation rather than just something to be feared.
- **How do you balance fear of failure with the need for innovation?**
    - This question encourages the client to find a middle ground between caution and progress.
- **Have you calculated the cost of inaction versus the cost of making a change?**
    - This question helps highlight that inaction can also be costly, making the fear of loss less dominant.
- **Are there examples where competitors took risks that paid off, and how does that compare to your current approach?**
    - This question prompts the client to look at external success stories and reassess their risk tolerance.
- **What safeguards can you put in place to minimize the impact of potential losses while still moving forward?**
    - This question encourages clients to take calculated risks by implementing risk-mitigation strategies.

22. Mere Exposure Effect

Developing a preference for things simply because they are familiar, rather than because it is the best option. This bias leads individuals to favor options or ideas that they have been exposed to repeatedly, even if they are not the optimal choice.[68] Overcoming the Mere Exposure Effect requires actively considering new alternatives and challenging the comfort of familiarity.[69]

- **Personal Example:** Someone continues to watch the same TV show or movie because it's familiar, even though there are better options out there.
- **Business Example:** A client sticks with a suboptimal software solution just because they are used to it, even though better alternatives are available.

How To Identify This Bias and What To Do About It

- **Obvious Signs:** Continues to use outdated solutions or preferences without exploring new options.
- **Subtle Signs:** Resists considering new alternatives, even when presented with clear benefits.
- **Statements:** "I've always used this, so I don't see why I should change now."
- **Sales Insight:** Gently introduce new solutions by framing them as enhancements or improvements rather than complete replacements.[70]

Consultative Sales Questions

- **Are you sticking with the same technology or vendor simply because it's familiar, rather than exploring potentially better alternatives?**
    - This question helps the client recognize when comfort is driving their decisions rather than quality.
- **How do you ensure you're not holding on to outdated solutions because of comfort or familiarity?**
    - This question encourages the client to re-evaluate whether their choices are still optimal.
- **What steps can you take to evaluate new options and avoid the mere exposure effect from shaping your decisions?**
    - This question helps the client implement a structured process for exploring alternatives.

- **How often do you review your technology stack or vendor relationships to ensure they still align with your business needs?**
    - This question encourages regular assessments to prevent stagnation.
- **What factors, beyond familiarity, should be considered when deciding whether to maintain or change a business process?**
    - This question prompts the client to create an objective evaluation framework.
- **Have you ever hesitated to change a tool or system, only to later realize the new option was far superior? What did you learn from that experience?**
    - This question helps the client reflect on past instances where familiarity may have led to suboptimal decisions.

23. Optimism Bias

Overestimating the likelihood of positive outcomes while underestimating risks. This bias leads individuals to believe that things will turn out better than they realistically might, often underprepared for potential setbacks.[71] Recognizing optimism bias allows for more balanced planning and decision-making, factoring in both positive and negative possibilities.[72]

- **Personal Example:** Someone assumes they won't need health insurance because they "never get sick."
- **Business Example:** A startup founder assumes their business will succeed despite clear financial risks.

How To Identify This Bias and What To Do About It

- **Obvious Signs:** Downplays risks and assumes everything will work out positively.
- **Subtle Signs:** Ignores potential obstacles and avoids discussing contingency plans.
- **Statements:** "We don't need a backup plan—this initiative is guaranteed to succeed."
- **Sales Insight:** Introduce risk-mitigation strategies and case studies to encourage a balanced perspective.[73]

Consultative Sales Questions

- **Are you underestimating the potential challenges that could arise in the implementation of this new system?**
    - This question helps clients critically assess risks they may be overlooking in their enthusiasm for the new system.
- **What's your backup plan if this new IT initiative doesn't deliver as expected?**
    - This question encourages the client to think beyond best-case scenarios and develop contingency plans.
- **How do you assess risks realistically when you're focused on positive outcomes?**
    - This question helps the client evaluate whether they have an objective approach to risk assessment or if optimism is clouding their judgment.
- **Are you assuming best-case scenarios when planning IT budgets and resources?**
    - This question forces the client to consider whether they have budgeted realistically or are setting themselves up for financial strain.
- **Are you underestimating the likelihood of cybersecurity threats or system failures?**
    - This question highlights specific IT risks that optimism bias may cause them to downplay.
- **How do you plan for worst-case scenarios in your business operations?**
    - This question ensures that the client has a structured approach to preparing for potential disruptions.

24. Overconfidence Bias

This bias involves an inflated sense of one's skills, knowledge, or influence over outcomes. People affected by overconfidence tend to make overly positive assumptions about their abilities, leading to underestimation of potential risks and overlooking possible challenges. This can result in taking on tasks or projects without proper preparation, which can backfire when unforeseen issues arise. It is crucial for individuals to challenge their assumptions and gather external perspectives to avoid this bias.[74]

- **Personal Example:** Someone believes they can "fix" their partner despite clear, unchangeable incompatibilities.
- **Business Example:** An executive disregards market research, believing their intuition is enough to make a major decision.

How To Identify This Bias and What To Do About It

- **Obvious Signs:** Displays excessive certainty about the outcome of their decisions.
- **Subtle Signs:** Dismissing others' opinions or not considering risks because they believe their approach will succeed.
- **Statements:** "I'm sure this strategy will work because it always has."
- **Sales Insight:** If a client is overly confident in their own judgment, help them reflect on potential risks and unknowns.[75]

Consultative Sales Questions

- **What assumptions are you making about your ability to manage IT internally versus leveraging outside expertise?**
    - This question helps the client recognize whether they are overestimating their internal capabilities and overlooking the value of external expertise.
- **How often do you test or challenge your cybersecurity defenses instead of assuming they are sufficient?**
    - This question encourages the client to question whether their confidence in their security measures is based on actual testing or mere assumption.
- **If your competitor were making this decision, how might they approach it differently?**
    - This question helps the client step outside their own perspective and consider alternative strategies they may have overlooked due to overconfidence.
- **How do you ensure that your confidence in your current IT strategy is backed by data and expert input?**
    - This question encourages the client to validate their decisions with objective data rather than relying solely on personal conviction.
- **Are you confident in your ability to adapt to new technologies, or is there room for improvement in your knowledge and preparation?**
    - This question helps the client assess whether their confidence in adapting to change is justified or if they need to invest in further learning.
- **How do you manage overconfidence in decision-making, especially when working with complex projects or uncertain outcomes?**
    - This question encourages the client to reflect on their decision-making processes and consider safeguards against overconfidence-driven mistakes.

25. Pessimism Bias

Overestimating the likelihood of negative outcomes. In contrast to Optimism Bias, this bias leads individuals to expect the worst-case scenario, often overestimating risks and overlooking potential benefits. Overcoming Pessimism Bias involves balancing caution with a realistic evaluation of opportunities and outcomes.[76]

- **Personal Example:** Someone avoids dating because they assume all relationships will end badly.
- **Business Example:** A manager refuses to invest in a new strategy because they assume it will fail, despite market research suggesting success.

How To Identify This Bias and What To Do About It

- **Obvious signs:** Focuses heavily on potential failures and worst-case scenarios.
- **Subtle signs:** Resists innovation or change due to a belief that past failures will repeat.
- **Statements:** "We tried something similar before, and it failed—there's no point in trying again."
- **Sales Insight:** Provide data-driven success stories and gradual implementation strategies to ease their concerns.[77]

Consultative Sales Questions

- **Are you too focused on potential failures and missing opportunities for growth in your technology strategy?**
    - This question challenges the client to reassess whether a negative outlook is limiting innovation and growth.
- **How can you shift your mindset to recognize the positive outcomes that might be more likely than you think?**
    - This question prompts reflection on whether they are misjudging probabilities and missing viable opportunities.
- **Do you have an over-emphasis on the downsides of new technology adoption?**
    - This question encourages a balanced approach to evaluating risks versus benefits in adopting new solutions.

- **Are you avoiding certain technological investments because of a worst-case outlook, even though there's a strong potential for success?**
    - This question forces the client to challenge their assumptions and reconsider decisions driven by excessive caution.
- **How often do you explore opportunities to innovate when you feel the risk outweighs the reward?**
    - This question encourages the client to assess whether their mindset is stifling innovation.
- **Have you weighed the long-term potential of new technologies versus short-term fears?**
    - This question helps the client separate immediate concerns from long-term strategic benefits.

26. Planning Fallacy

Underestimating the time, effort, and costs required to complete a task. This bias leads individuals to be overly optimistic about how long projects will take or how much they will cost, often resulting in missed deadlines or budgets.[78] Overcoming the Planning Fallacy requires a more realistic assessment of the challenges involved and factoring in potential delays.[79]

- **Personal Example:** Someone starts a home renovation thinking it will take two weeks, but it drags on for months.
- **Business Example:** A project manager promises delivery in six months, but the project takes a year due to unforeseen obstacles.

How To Identify This Bias and What To Do About It

- **Obvious Signs:** Sets unrealistic timelines and cost expectations.
- **Subtle Signs:** Dismisses potential roadblocks as minor or unlikely.
- **Statements:** "This implementation should be quick and easy—let's aim for next month."
- **Sales Insight:** Use phased planning and historical data to help set more realistic expectations.[80]

Consultative Sales Questions

- **How do you build realistic timelines for new projects, especially when considering unforeseen challenges?**
    - This question ensures that clients consider potential roadblocks before committing to timelines.

- **Can you recall any past initiatives where you underestimated the time or resources required? What could have helped?**
  - This question encourages reflection on past mistakes to improve future planning.
- **What strategies do you employ to avoid being overly optimistic in project planning?**
  - This question helps clients evaluate whether they are taking steps to counteract the planning fallacy.
- **Are you accurately assessing the time and resources needed for IT implementations?**
  - This question challenges the client to review their resource allocation assumptions.
- **What past projects took longer than expected, and why?**
  - This question prompts analysis of past project delays to identify patterns and solutions.
- **How do you incorporate buffer time for delays in your planning process?**
  - This question ensures the client has a risk-mitigation strategy in place for timeline overruns.

27. Reactance Bias

Resisting suggestions or rules just because they feel like restrictions. This bias arises from a desire for autonomy and the belief that being told what to do limits one's freedom.[81] Reactance can hinder decision-making, as individuals may reject helpful advice or rules simply because they perceive them as constraints on their personal freedom.[82]

- **Personal Example:** A teenager rebels against their parents' advice, even when it's in their best interest.
- **Business Example:** Employees reject a new company policy simply because they don't like being told what to do.

How To Identify This Bias and What To Do About It

- **Obvious Signs:** Pushes back against recommendations solely due to perceived control.
- **Subtle Signs:** Frames objections emotionally rather than logically.
- **Statements:** "I don't like being told what to do—I'll decide on my own time."
- **Sales Insight:** Offer choices rather than directives to help them feel in control of the decision.[83]

Consultative Sales Questions

- **Are your team members resistant to new technology just because it's being imposed on them?**
    - o   This question gets the client to recognize whether the resistance is due to the change itself or the way it was introduced.
- **How do you address resistance to change and foster more openness to new solutions?**
    - o   This statement encourages the client to consider proactive change management strategies rather than forcing adoption.
- **What strategies do you use to reduce reactance in your organization when implementing new processes?**
    - o   This question challenges the client to think about whether they are introducing change in a way that respects employee autonomy.
- **When introducing new technology, how do you ensure that team members feel empowered rather than restricted?**
    - o   This question helps the client reframe technology adoption from something that is being "forced" onto employees to something that benefits them.
- **What steps do you take to gain buy-in from key stakeholders when changes are needed?**
    - o   This statement reinforces the idea that involvement and participation in decision-making can reduce pushback.
- **How do you ensure that policies or recommendations are framed in a way that minimizes resistance?**
    - o   This question highlights the power of framing and communication in reducing psychological reactance.

28. Recency Bias

Rather than considering the full picture, this bias gives greater importance to events simply because they occurred recently. Recent events or experiences are assigned more relevance and importance, historical data or long-term patterns are overlooked, which leads to decisions based on what is most immediately available in memory rather than a comprehensive evaluation of broader past experiences.[84]

- **Personal Example:** A person judges their whole relationship based on the last argument, ignoring years of happiness.
- **Business Example:** A leader promotes an employee based on their latest performance rather than long-term contributions.

How To Identify This Bias and What To Do About It

- **Obvious Signs:** Gives undue weight to the most recent information or events.
- **Subtle Signs:** Focuses more on recent successes or failures, forgetting historical patterns.
- **Statements:** "Our last project was a success, so I think we're on the right track."
- **Sales Insight:** Encourage clients to consider a more balanced view by revisiting past results and not over-emphasizing the latest outcomes.[85]

Consultative Sales Questions

- **What recent events have influenced your IT decision-making? Do they reflect long-term trends or just short-term issues?**
    - This question helps clients identify whether their decision is based on a single event or a broader pattern.
- **How do you ensure you're considering your IT needs holistically and not just reacting to the most recent challenges?**
    - This question encourages a long-term perspective rather than knee-jerk reactions to the latest issue.
- **Are there any past successes or long-term patterns in your technology that should be considered in this decision?**
    - This question prompts the client to factor in historical data and proven strategies.
- **How do you differentiate between a temporary issue and a fundamental challenge that requires strategic change?**
    - This question helps clients recognize whether their response is proportionate to the actual scope of the problem.
- **Have you reviewed past IT trends in your company to see if similar challenges have occurred before?**
    - This question encourages clients to look at historical patterns instead of assuming that recent events are unique.
- **What processes do you have in place to prevent short-term disruptions from dictating long-term strategy?**
    - This question helps clients establish safeguards against reactionary decision-making.

29. Reciprocity Bias

Feeling obligated to return favors, leading to suboptimal decisions. This bias occurs when individuals feel compelled to reciprocate favors, even if doing so is not in their best interest. It can result in decisions that prioritize maintaining social harmony over making rational, beneficial choices.[86]

- **Personal Example:** A person continues to lend money to a friend who never repays them because they once received help from that friend in the past.
- **Business Example:** A company continues purchasing from a long-time vendor despite declining service quality because the vendor once gave them a discount during a financial crunch.

How To Identify This Bias and What To Do About It

- **Obvious Signs:** Feels compelled to agree or accept offers due to past favors.
- **Subtle Signs:** Reluctantly continues relationships or deals due to a perceived obligation.
- **Statements:** "They helped me out before, so I feel like I should keep doing business with them."
- **Sales Insight:** Be mindful of past favors; ensure that decisions are being made based on value, not just a sense of obligation.[87]

Consultative Sales Questions

- **Are you maintaining vendor relationships based on performance, or because you feel loyal to past deals?**
    - This question helps the client assess whether their ongoing vendor relationships are based on current value or past obligations.
- **Would you choose this solution if there were no previous business relationship?**
    - This forces the client to evaluate the vendor's present-day capabilities rather than being influenced by historical partnerships.
- **Are you evaluating all vendors equally, or are past partnerships influencing your objectivity?**
    - This question challenges the client to consider whether emotional factors are affecting their vendor assessments, ensuring a fair comparison.

- **What criteria are you using to assess whether continuing with an existing vendor is truly in your best interest?**
    - This encourages the client to take a structured, criteria-based approach to vendor selection rather than making decisions based on feelings of obligation.
- **If this were a brand-new decision, would you choose the same vendor or partner today?**
    - This question prompts the client to take a fresh perspective and reassess whether the vendor still aligns with their needs.
- **How do you ensure past favors or incentives aren't preventing you from making the most strategic decisions for your business?**
    - This helps the client recognize whether past benefits are clouding their ability to make the best decision moving forward.

30. Status Quo Bias

Preferring things to stay the same rather than considering change. This bias arises from the comfort of familiarity and the perceived risks associated with change, which can hinder innovation and personal growth. Overcoming this bias requires embracing uncertainty and considering the long-term benefits of change over short-term comfort.[88]

- **Personal Example:** Someone stays in an unfulfilling relationship because change feels too difficult.
- **Business Example:** A company sticks with outdated technology because "it's always worked this way."

How To Identify This Bias and What To Do About It

- **Obvious Signs:** Dismisses new solutions in favor of existing ones without evaluation.
- **Subtle Signs:** Expresses discomfort with change but struggles to articulate why.
- **Statements:** "We've been doing it this way for years, and it works just fine."
- **Sales Insight:** Highlight risks of inaction and demonstrate how small, manageable changes can lead to significant improvements.[89]

Consultative Sales Questions

- **If you were starting from scratch today, would you design your IT infrastructure the same way? Why or why not?**
    - This question helps the client evaluate whether their current setup is truly optimal or just a result of inertia.
- **What risks do you see in changing your approach to technology, and what risks exist in staying the same?**
    - This question encourages the client to weigh the hidden risks of maintaining the status quo against the perceived risks of change.
- **Are you sticking with your current provider because they're the best fit, or because change feels overwhelming?**
    - This question helps the client recognize whether their loyalty is based on merit or simply resistance to change.
- **How do you evaluate whether your long-term strategy is evolving with the market or stuck in outdated practices?**
    - This question encourages the client to consider if they are proactively adapting or just maintaining old habits.
- **What would need to happen for you to feel comfortable making a significant change in your IT environment?**
    - This question helps uncover the specific barriers—whether emotional, logistical, or financial—that are keeping them from change.
- **Have you ever regretted not making a change sooner? What lessons did you take from that experience?**
    - This question helps the client reflect on past instances where delaying change had negative consequences, making them more open to reconsidering their current approach.

31. Sunk Cost Fallacy

Continuing an investment (time, money, effort) despite diminishing returns, just because something has already been invested. This bias leads individuals to throw good money after bad, refusing to cut losses or abandon a failing course of action.[90] Overcoming the Sunk Cost Fallacy requires focusing on future value rather than past investments and making decisions based on potential outcomes.[91]

- **Personal Example:** Someone stays in a toxic relationship because they've "been together for years."
- **Business Example:** A company keeps funding a failing project because they've already spent millions on it.

How To Identify This Bias and What To Do About It

- **Obvious Signs:** Sticks with a decision or investment because they've already committed time, money, or resources.
- **Subtle Signs:** Reluctance to abandon a failing initiative because of past investments.
- **Statements:** "We've already spent so much on this, so we need to see it through."
- **Sales Insight:** Encourage clients to think about future value rather than past investments; help them focus on the best possible outcome moving forward.[92]

Consultative Sales Questions

- **Are there technology investments you're maintaining simply because you've already spent money on them?**
    - This question helps the client recognize whether they are holding onto outdated or ineffective solutions solely due to past expenditures.
- **If you weren't already invested in your current solution, would you choose it today?**
    - This question encourages the client to assess their current technology based on present needs rather than past commitments.
- **How do you ensure you're making future-focused decisions rather than trying to justify past ones?**
    - This question helps the client shift their mindset from rationalizing past investments to focusing on what will drive future success.
- **Are you making decisions based on previous investments rather than focusing on the current value and potential of the opportunity?**
    - This question encourages the client to evaluate opportunities based on their current and future impact rather than sunk costs.
- **How do you evaluate whether a continuing commitment is yielding the desired results, or if it's time to shift focus?**
    - This question helps the client establish a framework for measuring the effectiveness of ongoing investments and whether they should be reconsidered.
- **What steps are you taking to minimize sunk cost bias in your investment and growth decisions?**
    - This question encourages the client to proactively implement strategies that prevent emotional attachment to past investments from clouding judgment.

32. Survivorship Bias

Focusing on success stories while ignoring failures. This bias leads to an overly optimistic view of outcomes, as the failures are hidden from view or overlooked. By only examining the successful cases, one fails to learn from the mistakes or challenges faced by those who did not succeed, leading to distorted decision-making.[93]

- **Personal Example:** Someone believes that long-distance relationships always work because they only hear success stories, ignoring the ones that failed.
- **Business Example:** A startup founder believes they'll succeed because they've read about successful entrepreneurs, ignoring the thousands of failed startups.

How To Identify This Bias and What To Do About It

- **Obvious Signs:** Cites only successful examples as proof of a strategy's effectiveness.
- **Subtle Signs:** Overlooks risks or dismisses failures as irrelevant.
- **Statements:** "We've seen companies thrive with this approach, so we know it works."
- **Sales Insight:** Provide a balanced view by including failure rates and emphasizing factors that differentiate success from failure.[94]

Consultative Sales Questions

- **How do you ensure that your decision-making is based on a broad range of outcomes, not just the success stories?**
    - This question encourages the client to consider a full spectrum of experiences, not just the most visible or desirable ones.
- **When considering your next big project, are you also learning from past challenges or failures, not just successes?**
    - This question pushes the client to integrate lessons from past setbacks into their future decision-making.
- **Are you taking the time to look at all available data, including failures, to create a more complete picture of your options?**
    - This question helps the client ensure they are making balanced, informed choices rather than selectively viewing information.

- **What processes do you have in place to track and analyze unsuccessful projects, and how do those insights shape your future strategies?**
    - This question encourages the client to develop structured learning from past missteps rather than focusing solely on wins.
- **Are you benchmarking your strategy against only top-performing competitors, or are you also analyzing companies that failed in similar circumstances?**
    - This question helps the client recognize the importance of understanding why others did not succeed.
- **How do you prevent optimism bias from leading you to ignore potential risks that past failures could have warned you about?**
    - This question challenges the client to balance confidence with critical thinking and risk management.

ೞ PERSONAL EXPLORATION ೞ

Now that you've examined how cognitive biases shape decision-making in consultative sales, take a step back and reflect on how these biases might be influencing your own conversations with clients. Biases aren't just something your clients experience—they affect you, too. They can cloud judgment, reinforce assumptions, and subtly guide interactions in ways you might not even realize. Recognizing and mitigating these biases isn't about removing human intuition; it's about sharpening your awareness and making more intentional, evidence-based decisions. This awareness can help you build deeper trust with clients, ask better questions, and guide them toward solutions that truly serve their needs. Before moving forward, take a moment to challenge yourself—where do these biases show up in your sales process, and how can you actively work to counter them?[95]

Here are four questions to guide your reflection:

1. Think about a recent sales conversation where a client's resistance surprised you. Could a cognitive bias—yours or theirs—have influenced that interaction? How might recognizing it in the moment have changed your approach?

2. Which cognitive bias do you think affects your sales process the most? How does it shape the way you gather information, present solutions, or respond to objections?

3. How can you tell the difference between a well-informed instinct and an assumption influenced by bias? What specific steps can you take to verify that your decisions are grounded in objective information rather than quick judgments?

4. Think about a time when you misunderstood a client's needs. In hindsight, do you think a bias played a role in your perception? What could you have done differently to gain a more accurate understanding of their situation?

These questions are meant to challenge your thinking and deepen your self-awareness. The more intentional you become about recognizing and addressing biases, the more effectively you'll navigate complex client conversations and drive meaningful, trust-based sales outcomes.

೧೮ YOUR FINAL THOUGHTS ೨೦

Use The Space Below To Capture Your Thoughts And Reflections On What You've Learned In This Section

_____
_____
_____
_____
_____
_____

PRESENTING YOUR SOLUTION

Successful consultative sales conversations don't happen by chance; they are the result of a well-structured approach, built on a foundation of thoughtful, intentional questioning.[1] Just as a skilled therapist guides a client toward self-awareness and change through carefully crafted inquiries, a consultative salesperson must ask the right questions at the right time to uncover a client's true needs, challenges, and decision-making processes.[2] Without a structured framework, sales conversations risk becoming reactive, generic, and ineffective, missing opportunities to build trust and drive meaningful engagement.[3]

Although a customer presentation centers around a salesperson sharing information about their products, services, or solutions—for which the seller needs to demonstrate a level of proficiency and expertise—if the seller does not prepare and ask curated questions in the client's preferred communication style, the effectiveness of the time with the client will be diminished.[4] A sales presentation should never be a one-way monologue from the seller about the offering's features, benefits, and values. Rather, time with the client should stimulate an open and honest dialogue between both parties and this is accomplished through effective questioning throughout the presentation.[5]

In this chapter, we explore how consultative sales professionals can leverage therapeutic questioning techniques to elevate their client interactions during a presentation. We will cover:

- A **Sales Questioning Framework**, modeled after therapeutic session structures, to provide a roadmap for effective questioning throughout the sales process.
- **Pre-, Mid-, and Post-Presentation Questioning Strategies**, ensuring that every stage of a sales conversation is guided by purposeful inquiry.
- **Connections to Key Therapeutic Modalities**, demonstrating how different questioning styles—rooted in modalities like Cognitive Behavioral Therapy (CBT), Motivational Interviewing (MI), and Gestalt Therapy—can enhance client discovery and engagement.
- **Bias Mitigation Strategies**, equipping salespeople with techniques to ask better questions while reducing cognitive distortions that impact decision-making.

Let's begin with the **Sales Questioning Framework**—a step-by-step guide designed to help sales professionals navigate client presentations with precision, insight, and adaptability.

Sales Questioning Framework: A Step-by-Step Guide

A successful sales conversation mirrors an effective therapy session: intentional, goal-oriented, and responsive to the client's needs. Consultative sales professionals don't just present information; they engage in dynamic, client-focused conversations before, during, and after their presentations. Just as a therapist tailors their approach based on a client's responses, an effective salesperson strategically integrates modality-specific questions throughout their interactions to uncover insights, address concerns, and guide decision-making.[6]

This structured questioning framework aligns with therapeutic methodologies, ensuring sales professionals lead conversations with precision, insight, and adaptability. It is divided into three key stages:

1. **Pre-Presentation:** Establishing credibility, uncovering client priorities, and setting the stage for a meaningful discussion.
2. **Mid-Presentation:** Ensuring engagement, adapting to client reactions, and validating alignment with their needs.
3. **Post-Presentation:** Addressing objections, reinforcing key takeaways, and securing next steps.

By integrating intentional, research-backed questions in the client's preferred style at each stage, sales professionals transform presentations from passive information transfers into collaborative, results-driven conversations.

Pre-Presentation: Establishing Credibility & Psychological Safety (Person-Centered Therapy, Interpersonal Therapy)

Before diving into business discussions, a salesperson must create a space of trust and openness, much like a therapist ensures a client feels seen, heard, and understood. Constructing and positioning strategic questions that align to therapeutic modalities like Person-Centered Therapy and Interpersonal Therapy enables the salesperson to foster trust, create psychological safety, and deepen client engagement before presenting a solution.[7] A consultative seller earns credibility by demonstrating deep research and asking insightful, strategic questions that reflect an understanding of the client's business. Generic inquiries such as, *"Can you tell me what your top three goals are this year?"* signal a lack of preparation and do not warrant the gift of the client's time.

Instead, effective sales professionals ask questions that immediately show respect, engagement, and value.[8]

Example Questions:

- "I saw in your latest 10-K report that your company is investing heavily in AI-driven automation. How is that initiative progressing, and what impact are you seeing on your team's workflows?"
- "Your CEO recently posted on LinkedIn about a renewed focus on customer experience. From your perspective, what internal changes are happening to support that shift?"
- "Your company had a strong presence at [Industry Conference]. What were your biggest takeaways, and did you see any emerging trends that could impact your strategy?"

Why It Works

These questions demonstrate thorough research, establishing credibility and showing the seller understands the client's strategic priorities. They shift the conversation away from a generic pitch and toward a meaningful discussion about real challenges and opportunities. By doing so, the seller fosters psychological safety, encouraging open dialogue and deeper engagement from the start.[9]

೧೩೮೦೮೦೧೩೮೦೧೩೮೦

Mid-Presentation: Identifying Core Needs and Ensuring Engagement Through Strategic Questioning (Solution-Focused Brief Therapy, CBT, Adlerian Therapy)

Once rapport is established, the next step in the consultative sales process is uncovering the client's core needs and ensuring the conversation remains dynamic. Drawing on therapeutic techniques such as Solution-Focused Brief Therapy (SFBT), Cognitive Behavioral Therapy (CBT), and Adlerian Therapy, strategic questioning allows the salesperson to understand the client's challenges, reinforce alignment, and adjust the message accordingly.[10]

By asking the right questions both early in the conversation and during the presentation, sales professionals can stay aligned with the client's evolving needs, ensuring the conversation is collaborative and responsive, not one-sided.[11]

Example Questions:

- "Earlier, you mentioned scalability is a major focus for your team. Based on what we've covered so far, do you see alignment between your needs and the solutions we're discussing?"
- "I noticed several of your competitors have recently adopted [new technology/strategy]. How do you see that trend impacting your business, and what challenges does it present for your team?"
- "Given the shift toward [relevant industry trend], how are you balancing the need for innovation with operational efficiency? Are there any constraints holding you back?"

Why It Works

These questions effectively uncover latent pain points while allowing for ongoing engagement. They position the salesperson as a thought partner by integrating both market intelligence and client feedback into the conversation. By asking dynamic, open-ended questions, the salesperson ensures that the conversation stays responsive, adjusting messaging as needed while reinforcing the client's voice. This approach creates stronger alignment, deeper insights, and greater investment in the proposed solution.[12]

Post-Presentation: Exploring Future Possibilities and Securing Next Steps (Motivational Interviewing, Narrative Therapy, Logotherapy)

In consultative sales, the focus isn't just on diagnosing problems—it's about helping clients envision a better future. This is akin to therapeutic techniques like Motivational Interviewing, Narrative Therapy, and Logotherapy, which guide individuals toward goal-setting, personal transformation, and finding purpose in their challenges.[13] Great salespeople act as visionaries, helping clients see the potential path forward and identifying the steps that will lead to success.[14]

By exploring future possibilities, the salesperson positions themselves as a strategic partner who understands the client's ultimate goals and can help them navigate potential obstacles. Post-presentation questions should build on this vision, addressing any lingering hesitations and reinforcing the path forward to secure the next steps.[15]

Example Questions:

- "If additional budget was allocated to solve [identified challenge], what would your ideal solution look like?"

- "I noticed that [industry leader] recently made a bold move in this space. If you could implement a similar strategy, how do you think it would impact your long-term growth?"
- "You've shared valuable insights into your team's priorities. Based on what we've discussed, what aspects of our approach resonate most with your current initiatives?"

Why It Works

These questions encourage forward-thinking by prompting the client to visualize a positive future state, helping them align their goals with the proposed solution. They reinforce the salesperson as a strategic advisor who can help the client overcome potential roadblocks and turn their vision into reality. By tying the conversation back to the client's priorities and decision-making framework, these questions address any remaining hesitations, making it easier to secure a clear path forward and maintain momentum in the sales process.[16]

◌☙◌☙◌☙◌☙

Mastering Consultative Sales Questioning: A Strategic, Client-Centric Approach

Mastering consultative sales questioning requires more than just asking good questions—it demands a structured framework that balances psychological insight with business acumen. By leveraging therapeutic modalities, sales professionals can guide conversations with purpose, uncover deeper client needs, and foster meaningful engagement. A well-structured pre-, mid-, and post-presentation questioning strategy ensures sales professionals lead, rather than react to, client conversations. Research-backed questions establish credibility, deepen engagement, and uncover the client's true priorities, turning presentations into consultative, trust-building experiences.[17]

However, this approach is not one-size-fits-all. The most effective sales professionals tailor their questioning styles to align with the client's business landscape, industry trends, and decision-making process. More importantly, these methods must feel natural, authentic, and flexible to each client's unique personality and needs. The best consultative sellers are those who remain intentional in their approach—always ensuring that each conversation is a step toward long-term partnership and success, ultimately driving stronger relationships and better outcomes.[18]

Connections to Key Therapeutic Modalities

In consultative sales, the ability to empathetically facilitate and guide a client's decision-making process is what separates top performers from transactional sellers.[19] This book has explored numerous therapeutic modalities, each offering unique ways to foster trust, uncover insights, and help clients move toward meaningful action. In this section, we focus on five key therapeutic modalities—Motivational Interviewing, Cognitive Behavioral Therapy, Solution-Focused Brief Therapy, Gestalt Therapy, and Adlerian Therapy—as examples of how psychological frameworks can be applied to sales conversations throughout a customer presentation. However, it's important to recognize that all of the therapeutic modalities presented in this book are equally valid and have their own distinct merits. The key is not to rigidly adhere to one approach but rather to understand the overarching framework and adapt the modality and questioning style to what best aligns with the client's preferences and decision-making process.

The five key therapeutic modalities explored here and their direct application in consultative sales are:

1. **Motivational Interviewing (MI)** – Eliciting change through guided discovery.
2. **Cognitive Behavioral Therapy (CBT)** – Restructuring limiting beliefs and biases.
3. **Solution-Focused Brief Therapy (SFBT)** – Steering conversations toward actionable solutions.
4. **Gestalt Therapy** – Deepening client awareness and ownership of decisions.
5. **Adlerian Therapy** – Aligning solutions with the client's broader organizational goals and values.

By integrating these approaches, sales professionals gain a structured, research-backed framework for influencing decision-makers in a way that feels authentic, consultative, and trust-driven.

1. Motivational Interviewing (MI): Eliciting Change Through Guided Discovery

What It Is

Motivational Interviewing (MI) is a therapeutic modality that helps clients on their journey toward a mentally healthier existence explore their unique and personal motivations for change as opposed to feeling pressured by others into making decisions and taking actions for which they are not yet ready.[20] The practitioner that uses MI leverages open-ended questions, reflective listening, and guiding—not forcing—clients toward solutions.[21]

Application in Sales:

- Instead of pushing a product or solution during a client presentation, MI-based selling leverages a questioning style that helps clients verbalize their own pain points, challenges, and goals, increasing their internal commitment to change.
- This approach is particularly effective with skeptical or resistant clients who may not initially see the need for a new solution.[22]

Example Sales Questioning Using MI:

- "I know your company has been operating with its current infrastructure for over a decade. What's been working well, and what challenges have started to emerge as your business scales?"
- "Many leaders in your industry have shared concerns about cybersecurity risks increasing with hybrid work models. How does your team currently evaluate risk exposure, and what strategies have been most effective so far?"
- "If your team were to implement a solution like this, what impact do you think it would have on your day-to-day operations six months from now?"

Why It Works

By allowing the client to articulate their own pain points and desired future state, the salesperson becomes a trusted facilitator rather than an aggressive persuader. This style of selling throughout a sales presentation results in a meeting that is void of high-pressure sales tactics and turns the time together with a client into a meaningful collaborative discussion about possibilities.

2. Cognitive Behavioral Therapy (CBT): Restructuring Limiting Beliefs and Biases

What It Is

CBT helps individuals recognize and challenge cognitive distortions—faulty patterns of thinking that lead to poor decision- making.[23] In sales—especially during a presentation—these distortions often appear as status quo bias, sunk cost fallacy, or overgeneralization ("We tried something like this before, and it didn't work").

Application in Sales:

- Sales professionals using CBT techniques help clients identify and reconsider rigid, unexamined beliefs that may be preventing progress.
- This is especially useful when clients resist change due to past failures or unfounded assumptions.

Example Sales Questioning Using CBT:

- "I understand that a previous vendor partnership didn't deliver the expected results. What specifically didn't work, and what aspects were successful?"
- "You mentioned concerns about the complexity of switching solutions. What aspects feel most overwhelming, and are there specific ways we can make the transition easier for your team?"
- "Many companies we work with initially hesitate to invest in automation due to cost concerns, yet they later find the ROI to be significantly higher than expected. What metrics would be most helpful for you in evaluating whether a solution like this makes financial sense?"

Why It Works

By challenging cognitive distortions, the seller creates an opening for new possibilities and reduces resistance to change.

3. Solution-Focused Brief Therapy (SFBT): Steering Conversations Toward Actionable Solutions

What It Is

SFBT is a forward-focused approach that helps individuals shift from problem-focused thinking to solution-oriented decision- making.[24] Instead of dwelling on obstacles, SFBT encourages envisioning a preferred future and identifying small steps to get there. The solution-oriented focus, with reasonable and attainable short term goals are critical elements of a client presentation because they demonstrate your understanding and awareness of the complexities that implementing any solution entails. The more the seller helps the customer clearly see the steps to reach the solution during the presentation, the less ambiguity exists, and the more likely the customer will leave the meeting with enough information to make a decision.[25]

Application in Sales:

- Many sales conversations stall because clients become fixated on why a problem exists rather than how to solve it. Customer presentations are not just for sharing the solution. The salesperson delivering the presentation should articulate the solution steps needed to reach the desired outcome.
- SFBT-driven sales questioning helps clients imagine the benefits of change and focus on the next actionable steps.

Example Sales Questioning Using SFBT:

- "If you had a solution in place today that completely resolved [challenge], what would your team's day-to-day look like?"
- "If we fast-forward a year and your company successfully rolled out a new infrastructure, what would be the first signs that it was a success?"
- "What's one small step your team could take right now to begin moving in this direction?"

Why It Works

By keeping the conversation solution-oriented, SFBT techniques reduce decision paralysis and increase client confidence in taking action.

4. Gestalt Therapy: Deepening Client Awareness and Ownership of Decisions

What It Is

Gestalt therapy emphasizes awareness, present-moment thinking, and taking full ownership of decisions. In sales, this means helping clients recognize their own role in driving change rather than externalizing responsibility.[26]

Application in Sales:

- Clients sometimes shift blame to external factors ("We'd love to make this change, but leadership won't approve the budget").
- Gestalt techniques encourage clients to take ownership of their choices and recognize their own influence over decision- making.[27]

Example Sales Questioning Using Gestalt Techniques:

- "I hear that budget approvals are a challenge. What steps have been successful in getting leadership buy-in for past initiatives?"
- "Your team is clearly committed to solving this issue. What decision-making criteria do you personally find most compelling?"
- "It sounds like there's strong momentum for this change. What role do you see yourself playing in moving this initiative forward?"

Why It Works

This shifts the locus of control back to the client, reinforcing their ability to drive progress rather than feeling stuck.

5. Adlerian Therapy: Aligning Solutions with Broader Organizational Goals and Values

What It Is

Adlerian therapy focuses on how individuals and groups strive for belonging, meaning, and achievement. In sales, this means helping clients connect solutions to their company's overarching mission, vision, and values.[28] Making a connection like this while executive leadership is in the room during the presentation will set the seller apart from others who are simply attempting to close a sale. When sales presentations connect the dots from the proposed offering to the customer's stated mission, vision, culture, values, and goals, the seller is one step closer to being viewed by the customer as a trusted advisor as opposed to simply another vendor.[29]

Application in Sales:

- Decision-makers often think beyond short-term solutions—they want investments that align with long-term strategic objectives.
- Adlerian techniques help sellers frame solutions not just as tactical fixes but as meaningful contributions to the company's larger goals.

Example Sales Questioning Using Adlerian Principles:

- "Your company has made sustainability a core part of its mission. How do you see technology investments playing a role in furthering that commitment?"
- "I saw that your CEO recently emphasized innovation in your annual report. How does your team measure success in driving forward new initiatives?"
- "Your company has a strong culture of customer-centricity. How do you ensure that internal technology investments also enhance the end-user experience?"

Why It Works

By aligning solutions with higher-level organizational values, the seller increases emotional and strategic buy-in from decision-makers and this is a critical element of a successful sales presentation.

While this chapter highlights just five therapeutic modalities in action, they are by no means the only ones that can elevate consultative sales conversations during a presentation. Throughout this book, we have examined multiple psychological frameworks, each offering valuable insights into client behavior, motivation, and decision-making. The most effective sales professionals do not rely on a single approach but instead develop the ability to recognize their client's communication style, cognitive biases, and preferred way of processing information.[30] By mastering this framework and flexibly applying the right modality at the right time, sellers can engage in deeper, more meaningful conversations—ones that build trust, challenge assumptions, and ultimately guide clients toward confident, well-informed decisions; which is one of the most important and desired outcomes of a customer presentation.[31]

ஜ௫ஜ௫ஜ௫ஜ

Bias Mitigation Strategies – How to Structure Questions to Counter Cognitive Biases that Interfere with Decision-Making

Cognitive biases shape how people interpret information, assess risks, and make decisions—often in ways that are irrational yet predictable.[32] In consultative sales, especially during a client presentation when agreement to move forward is sought after, failing to recognize and address a client's biases can lead to stalled deals, resistance to change, or decisions that go against their best interests.[33] Throughout this book, we have explored a many biases that influence the way customer's think, react, and respond during a sale conversation, from confirmation bias to loss aversion to status quo bias and the sunk cost fallacy. In this section, we'll focus on a select few cognitive biases and provide strategies to structure questions that help counter them. However, it's important to note that these are just examples—effective sellers must first diagnose which biases are at play and then tailor their approach accordingly. Mastering this skill allows sales professionals to guide clients toward clearer, more objective decision-making, ensuring that choices are based on logic and long-term value rather than mental shortcuts or emotional reactions. If a client reaches that conclusion at the end of the meeting, the seller has accomplished one of the primary goals of any sales presentation.

1. Countering Status Quo Bias – Overcoming Fear of Change

Status Quo Bias makes clients resistant to change, even when a better alternative exists. They may feel that their current setup is "good enough" or fear that switching solutions will cause disruption.[34]

- **How to Mitigate:** Structure questions that challenge the assumption that staying the same is risk-free and help the client reframe change as an opportunity.[35]
- **Example Questions:**
    - "I noticed in my research that your competitors have adopted [new strategy or tool]. What do you think would happen if they gained an efficiency advantage while your team continued with the current approach?"
    - "You mentioned that things are 'working fine.' If we fast-forward a year, what potential problems do you see if nothing changes?"
    - "What improvements have you considered but put on hold? What's the impact of delaying those changes?"

Why It Works

These questions subtly shift the client's perception, helping them see that maintaining the status quo also carries risk—the risk of falling behind, missing opportunities, or ignoring inefficiencies. Deeper conversations during a customer presentation that uncover answers to the questions above will help the salesperson stand apart from the crowd of transactional sellers.[36]

2. Addressing Confirmation Bias – Expanding Perspective

Confirmation Bias leads clients to seek information that supports their existing beliefs while ignoring contradictory evidence. This can make them dismiss potential solutions before fully exploring them.[37] A presentation that encounters this bias and fails to address it head-on will usually fall short of the salesperson's goals.

- **How to Mitigate:** Encourage clients to consider alternative viewpoints and challenge assumptions by asking open-ended, reflective questions.[38]
- **Example Questions:**
    - "I see that you've successfully used [current solution] for five years. What's one aspect of your process that could be improved but hasn't been challenged yet?"
    - "If you were starting from scratch today, would you design your current setup the same way? Why or why not?"
    - "What would it take for you to consider an alternative approach? What would have to be true for that to be a viable option?"

Why It Works

These questions encourage the client to broaden their thinking, challenge their own assumptions, and re-evaluate whether their current belief system is serving them optimally. This is an ideal situation for any client presentation.[39]

3. Reducing Loss Aversion – Shifting the Focus from Fear to Opportunity

Loss Aversion means that clients fear losing something they already have more than they desire potential gains. This can cause them to hesitate when making a switch, even when the upside is clear.[40]

- **How to Mitigate:** Frame the conversation in a way that highlights the risk of inaction and the potential gains from change.[41]
- **Example Questions:**
    - "I saw that your team is already investing significant resources into [current solution]. What's the hidden cost of maintaining this approach versus modernizing it?"
    - "How do you think your competitors view this kind of change? Are they waiting or moving forward?"
    - "What's the potential downside of staying where you are? What would happen if you wait another 12 months before making a decision?"

Why It Works

By shifting the focus from "what they might lose" to "what they risk by standing still", the seller helps the client reframe their fear and consider the bigger picture. Again, a consultative salesperson that helps open the client's eye when they suffer from a Loss Aversion bias will be viewed as a true partner, not just a seller.[42]

4. Overcoming the Sunk Cost Fallacy – Helping Clients Let Go of Past Investments

The Sunk Cost Fallacy makes clients reluctant to abandon past investments, even when a new solution would clearly be more effective. They may say, *"We've already spent so much money on this—we can't afford to change now."*[43]

- **How to Mitigate:** Help clients separate past decisions from future opportunities by focusing on what's best moving forward rather than what's already been spent.[44]
- **Example Questions:**
    - "Since you've already invested in [existing solution], what's your expectation for its ROI over the next five years? Does that align with what you're seeing?"
    - "If another company in your position were evaluating this today, without any previous investment, what choice do you think they would make?"
    - "Knowing what you know now, if you could go back, would you make the same investment again? If not, what would you do differently?"

Why It Works

These questions allow the client to acknowledge their investment without feeling like they've made a mistake, while shifting their focus toward making the best decision for the future.[45]

5. Neutralizing the Authority Bias – Encouraging Independent Thinking

Clients often defer to senior leadership opinions or popular industry practices, assuming that if others are doing it, it must be right (Authority Bias). This can prevent them from exploring more innovative or tailored solutions.[46]

- **How to Mitigate:** Ask questions that empower independent thinking and challenge assumptions based on authority rather than objective evaluation.[47]
- **Example Questions:**
    - "I noticed that your leadership prefers [current solution]. What additional insights or perspectives might they need to consider an alternative?"
    - "What criteria do you personally find most important in making this decision, regardless of what others have done?"
    - "What would it take for leadership to feel confident in exploring a different approach?"

Why It Works

These questions validate the influence of leadership while encouraging the client to think critically and consider what truly serves their needs best. One important point to make here is that if the salesperson is attempting to help a client move beyond their Authority Bias AND the executives they ascribe the authority to are also in the room, the salesperson must proceed with an abundance of respect and humility so as to not insult or embarrass anyone in the room during the presentation.[48]

Cognitive biases are powerful forces that influence every decision we make—often without conscious awareness. By integrating bias-mitigating questioning techniques during a presentation, consultative sales professionals can help clients challenge flawed assumptions, reduce emotional decision-making, and consider alternative perspectives. While this section has explored only a handful of modalities, approaches, and biases in depth, this book has covered many more, each with unique implications for sales conversations. As mentioned before, the true skill lies in recognizing which biases are influencing a particular client and adapting your questioning style to guide them toward a well-reasoned, confident decision. A consultative sales professional who understands what their client thinks and why they think it will always stand out amongst their peers, earning the client's trust and driving long-term success.[49]

Reflections

This chapter has provided a framework and structured approach to presenting solutions with intention and focus, and breaking down pre-, mid-, and post-presentation strategies that align with beneficial therapeutic modalities. We've explored how varying the questioning style, and aligning it to the client's preferred method of communication can influence client engagement and how biases have the tendency to shape and distort the conversation during a customer presentation. An important takeaway is to understand that effective solution presentations are never just about pitching a product's or solution's value—they're about helping clients discover it for themselves. When you intentionally shift your approach from convincing to uncovering and from pitching to guiding, the result is that you create an environment for the foundation of trust and rapport to flourish. This adds to your credibility, and to your long-term client relationships which extend well beyond a single transaction.

॰ PERSONAL EXPLORATION ॰

Now that you've explored the art of presenting solutions through a consultative, therapy-informed approach, take a moment to reflect on how these concepts might shift your mindset in sales conversations. The questions you ask—before, during, and after your presentation—aren't just a means to an end; they shape how your client experiences the discussion, how open they are to your insights, and ultimately, how they perceive you and your value. Effective sales professionals don't just deliver solutions; they create an environment where clients feel heard, understood, and empowered to make decisions with confidence.

Here are four questions to guide your reflection:

1. How does your current approach to presenting solutions compare to the frameworks discussed in this chapter? Where do you see opportunities to adjust your questioning strategy for greater impact?
2. Think about a recent sales conversation where a client disengaged or resisted your recommendations. In hindsight, do you think your questioning style played a role? What might you do differently next time?
3. What biases—yours or the client's—could be influencing the way your solutions are received? How can you proactively address these biases to create a more open and productive conversation?
4. Consultative sales is as much about guiding as it is about listening. How can you ensure that your questioning approach encourages dialogue rather than feeling like an interrogation?

These questions are designed to not only challenge your thinking, but also to help you recognize and understand connection opportunities, and help you improve your ability to present solutions to important clients in a way that feels—to you and to the client—authentic, honest, engaging, empathetic, and client-centric. The more intentional you are about implementing these techniques into your daily sales meetings, the more effective your sales conversations will become.

❧ YOUR FINAL THOUGHTS ❧

Use The Space Below To Capture Your Thoughts And Reflections On What You've Learned In This Section

_____
_____
_____
_____
_____
_____

MOVING THROUGH OBJECTIONS

Objections in sales are often viewed as barriers to overcome, but a deeper understanding reveals that they are expressions of underlying emotions—fear, uncertainty, the desire for control, or the need to protect one's status, reputation, or job security.[1] From a therapeutic perspective, objections are not just logical concerns but are deeply tied to cognitive biases, past experiences, and personal stakes in the decision.[2] People resist change because it introduces uncertainty, and with uncertainty comes risk.[3]

Therapists do not move past, over, or around objections. Instead, they help clients move through them. And it is navigating through discomfort—which often accompanies objections—where discoveries can be made and change can be implemented.[4] The same principle applies to consultative sales: effective sales professionals do not dismiss objections or confront them with data alone. Instead, they approach objections with curiosity, empathy, and non-judgmental questioning that allows the client to explore their own concerns.[5] Traditional sales objection handling often focuses on disproving the client's concern, which can create resistance and defensiveness. In contrast, a therapy-inspired approach to sales acknowledges the emotional weight behind objections and seeks to guide clients toward self-discovery.[6]

In therapy, confrontation is never aggressive, judgmental, or condescending. Instead, it is person-centered and empathetic.[7] The same must be true in sales. Asking 'why' questions can trigger defensiveness because they make people feel judged or put on the spot to justify their stance. Instead, using open-ended 'how,' 'what,' 'when,' and 'where' questions allows clients to process their concerns without feeling attacked.[8] The key is to help the client uncover insights that make them comfortable moving forward rather than feeling forced into a decision.[9] Timing and setting also matter—clients are less likely to be introspective in a group setting where admitting uncertainty could make them feel vulnerable. A private, one-on-one conversation often provides the best opportunity for deeper reflection.[10]

Therapeutic Questioning: Moving Through Objections with Empathy

Below are five categories of therapeutic sales questions designed to address different emotional and psychological barriers to commitment. Each set of five questions targets a specific root cause of objections.

1. Fear of Uncertainty and Change

Clients worry about making the wrong choice, leading to risk aversion.

- **What would need to happen for you to feel more confident in moving forward?**
    - Helps the client articulate specific concerns and conditions for progress.
- **How have you successfully navigated similar decisions in the past?**
    - Encourages reflection on past successes to build self-trust.
- **What aspects of this decision feel most uncertain to you?**
    - Identifies the root of their hesitation so it can be addressed collaboratively.
- **Where do you see the biggest potential impact—positive or negative—on your role?**
    - Uncovers personal stakes in the decision-making process.
- **How could we work together to create more certainty around this?**
    - Positions the conversation as a joint effort rather than a persuasion battle.

Why It Works

These questions help clients examine their fears without feeling pressured, making space for them to identify potential positive outcomes alongside perceived risks.[11]

2. Desire to Retain Control and Power

Clients may resist being 'sold to' because they want to feel in control of the process.

- **What aspects of this solution do you feel most in control of?**
    - Reinforces autonomy and reduces the sense of being pressured.
- **How does this align with the direction you see for your team/company?**
    - Ensures alignment with the client's vision and strategic priorities.
- **What would make this decision feel like it's truly yours to own?**
    - Empowers them to take psychological ownership of the choice.
- **Where do you feel you need more input or influence in this process?**
    - Identifies areas where they may feel sidelined or undervalued.

- **What role do you see me playing in helping you navigate this decision?**
  - Positions the salesperson as a trusted advisor rather than an external force.

Why It Works

These questions acknowledge the client's need for control and shift the conversation from resistance to empowerment.[12]

3. Risk to Job, Status, or Reputation

Clients worry about how the decision reflects on them professionally.

- **What factors do you think your peers or leadership team would weigh most heavily in this decision?**
  - Frames the decision in terms of broader organizational perception.
- **How do you think this choice will reflect on you and your leadership?**
  - Brings hidden concerns about professional credibility into the open.
- **What safeguards or assurances would make you feel more secure?**
  - Addresses the need for risk mitigation.
- **How does this decision compare to others you've had to champion internally?**
  - Allows for benchmarking against previous successful (or challenging) experiences.
- **What conversations would be helpful to have before finalizing your decision?**
  - Identifies key influencers in the process.

Why It Works

These questions help the client shift from fear to envisioning success and align the decision with their career aspirations.[13]

4. Bias-Based and Emotional Resistance

Clients may have preconceived notions or negative past experiences.

- **What prior experiences have shaped how you view this type of solution?**
    - Surfaces past biases that may be influencing the objection.
- **How do you see this solution differing from what you've encountered before?**
    - Creates space to separate past experiences from present reality.
- **What would need to be different for you to feel comfortable re-evaluating?**
    - Invites a mindset shift without forcing one.
- **Where have you seen similar strategies succeed or fail?**
    - Encourages analytical rather than emotional reasoning.
- **What would it look like to explore this with fresh eyes?**
    - Encourages open-mindedness and curiosity.

Why It Works

These questions help clients separate past experiences from present opportunities, allowing them to reframe their perspectives.[14]

5. Organizational and Stakeholder Influence

Clients may object because of internal politics, competing priorities, or stakeholder resistance.

- **How does this align with the broader goals of your organization?**
    - Ensures the solution supports company-wide objectives, increasing its strategic relevance.
- **Who else would need to be on board for this to move forward smoothly?**
    - Identifies key decision-makers and influencers who could impact the approval process.
- **What internal discussions need to happen to gain alignment?**
    - Uncovers potential roadblocks and the steps needed to secure stakeholder buy-in.
- **How have similar initiatives been received internally?**
    - Provides insight into past organizational responses, helping to anticipate potential resistance.

- **What are the key concerns from others that we should anticipate and prepare for?**
    - Equips the salesperson to proactively address objections and mitigate risks before they arise.

Why It Works

These questions encourage the client to think about the broader picture and proactively address internal hurdles.[15]

Blending Therapeutic Modalities for Maximum Impact

Therapeutic sales questioning while navigating objections can be enhanced by blending different counseling techniques. For example:

- **Motivational Interviewing** – Guiding clients toward self-driven conclusions through open-ended, exploratory questions.
- **Cognitive Behavioral Therapy (CBT)** – Helping clients challenge cognitive distortions or limiting beliefs.
- **Solution-Focused Brief Therapy (SFBT)** – Encouraging clients to identify and focus on solutions rather than problems.
- **Gestalt Therapy** – Encouraging clients to take ownership of their perspectives and decisions.

The key take away from the concept of therapeutic modality blending is to always ensure that you feel authentic in its application AND that the chosen modalities do not just serve you, but are also aligned to the customer's preferred communication style.[16]

Real-World Application: Mini Case Study

Scenario: A CIO objects to adopting a new technology due to past implementation failures.

Salesperson: "What lessons did your team learn from past implementations that should guide this decision?"

CIO: "We experienced major delays and cost overruns."

Salesperson: "What safeguards would give you confidence that this time would be different?"

CIO: "More transparency and a stronger partner."

Salesperson: "How can we structure our engagement to provide that level of transparency and partnership?"

Closing the Loop: Converting Objections into Commitments

While this chapter focuses on moving through objections, ultimately, objections must transition into commitments. This process involves aligning solutions with client needs and creating a path forward without pressure. A full chapter on closing the sale will explore this further, but for now, the key takeaway is that the best commitments arise when clients feel understood and empowered, not coerced.[17]

PERSONAL EXPLORATION

This approach reframes objection handling, positioning sales professionals as facilitators of insight rather than enforcers of persuasion. By using modality-specific therapeutic questions rooted in empathy, curiosity, and strategic inquiry, salespeople create an environment where clients feel heard, understood, and empowered to arrive at their own conclusions—decisions that are both logically sound and emotionally aligned with their true priorities.

- What objections do you encounter most frequently, and what underlying fears or concerns might they stem from?
- How can you adjust your questioning style to foster more introspection rather than defensiveness?
- What past objections have you successfully moved through, and what worked?
- How can you create a safe space for clients to explore their objections privately before making a decision?

HOMEWORK CHALLENGE

In your next sales conversation, identify an objection and use one of the therapeutic questioning techniques discussed in this chapter. Reflect on the client's response and how it changed the dynamic of the conversation. You may want to identify a recurring objection you hear in your sales role and use 3-5 questions from this chapter in your next conversation. Consider taking time to journal about a time when someone helped you reframe a hesitation or resistance and reflect on what made their approach effective?

☙ YOUR FINAL THOUGHTS ❧

Use The Space Below To Capture Your Thoughts And Reflections On What You've Learned In This Section

_____
_____
_____
_____
_____
_____

CLOSING THE SALE

Closing a sale should feel as natural and seamless as a therapist guiding a client toward an actionable decision. It is not an isolated, pressure-filled moment but the inevitable outcome of a well-structured, trust-driven conversation. When done correctly, closing doesn't require persuasion or force; instead, it emerges organically when the client has gained clarity, resolved internal hesitations, and feels ready to take action.[1] However, as any sales professional will tell you, even if all roads lead to the logical conclusion desired by the seller—the customer to agree to purchase—a buying decision is rarely made in a vacuum and often involves decision makers across multiple areas of the business. So despite all efforts, even if the plan was followed with precision, a buyer may still decide to not move forward with the purchase. And that is ok. Professional salespeople know that they cannot be everything for everybody and that not ever buyer will say yes. The most a seller should do is proceed with integrity, empathy, humility, intentionality, a bit of hunger to succeed, and a willingness to embrace the challenges within this noble profession.

Traditional sales methodologies often frame closing as a high-pressure maneuver—a set of scripted techniques designed to push a hesitant buyer over the edge. But this approach is fundamentally flawed. When clients feel coerced, they instinctively resist, even if the solution is right for them.[2] Trust erodes, skepticism rises, and the decision-making process becomes strained. In contrast, an empathy-based, consultative approach delivered in the client's preferred communication style establishes rapport and fosters trust, making the customer's decision to move forward feel like a natural next step rather than a hard sell. No one wants to be backed into a corner with the only way out being agreement to buy. This approach may succeed in the moment but certainly does not lay the foundation for a long-term buying relationship, and should be avoided by consultative sellers.

This shift in mindset for the professional salesperson is critical: Closing is not an event. It is the culmination of a meaningful, client-centered dialogue.[3] When the salesperson has done their job well—by asking the right questions, in the right way, helping the client process their concerns, and aligning the solution with their true needs—closing becomes a formality rather than a battle.

Direct Connection Between Therapy and Sales Closing

As shared in the Foreword, therapists and sales professionals share a fundamental goal: guiding someone through an internal process of discovery and commitment to action. In therapy, a client may struggle with uncertainty, fear, or limiting beliefs before making a life-altering decision. Similarly, in sales, a client may hesitate due to risk aversion, status quo bias, or unclear value perception.[4] The role of the therapist—and the sales professional—is to create an environment where the client can work through these hesitations and confidently choose their next step.

Much like therapists use motivational interviewing and other therapeutic techniques to help clients articulate their own reasons for change, sales professionals should use open-ended questioning, reflective listening, and strategic reframing to guide clients toward their own buying decisions.[5] The key is to facilitate clarity rather than impose direction—helping the client discover their path on their own in their own way rather than pushing them down one.

Just as a therapist would never say, "You must change your behavior today," a consultative salesperson should never say, "You need to buy this now." Instead, the conversation should naturally lead to the client recognizing that moving forward is in their best interest. When clients—therapy or sales—feel ownership of the decision, they are more likely to commit fully and proceed with clarity and confidence.

Step-by-Step Process Mirroring Therapeutic Commitment Models

Therapists help clients commit to action using structured approaches that can be adapted for sales. Below is a modified therapeutic commitment model that has been adapted to and aligns with a consultative, trust-based closing process:

1. Establish Emotional Readiness (Acceptance & Commitment Therapy - ACT)

- **Therapy:** A therapist helps a client acknowledge internal struggles and accept them rather than resist change.

- **Sales:** A salesperson ensures the client has addressed any underlying fears, hesitations, or biases before moving forward.
- **Key Question:** "What, if anything, is still holding you back from feeling confident about this decision?"

2. Challenge Limiting Beliefs (Cognitive Behavioral Therapy - CBT)

- **Therapy:** A therapist guides clients in identifying negative thought patterns and reshaping them into healthier, more productive perspectives.
- **Sales:** A salesperson identifies misconceptions or cognitive biases that may be preventing the client from seeing the true value of the solution.
- **Key Question:** "You mentioned concerns about X—how do you see that playing out if you don't make a change?"

3. Create Meaning and Motivation (Logotherapy & Motivational Interviewing - MI)

- **Therapy:** Clients explore how a decision aligns with their values and long-term goals.
- **Sales:** Clients connect the solution to their business priorities and personal motivations.
- **Key Question:** "How does implementing this solution align with the long-term goals you've shared?"

4. Shift from Discussion to Action (Reality Therapy & Solution-Focused Brief Therapy - SFBT)

- **Therapy:** The therapist encourages small, actionable steps toward progress.
- **Sales:** The salesperson provides a clear, low-resistance path to next steps.
- **Key Question:** "What's the first step we should take together to make this happen?"

By following this structured approach, closing becomes a guided commitment rather than a forced transaction. When clients feel psychologically, intellectually, and emotionally ready, understand the decision fully, and see the connection between the solution and their goals, signing the contract is not a point of pressure—it's a moment of clarity.

Closing Techniques Aligned with NLP Predicates

Closing a sale is about securing commitment, and the most effective way to do so is by speaking in the client's preferred language. When we mirror a client's Neuro-Linguistic Programming (NLP) predicate—how they naturally process and express information—we increase their comfort level and create a seamless decision-making experience.[6] Below are closing techniques tailored to each NLP predicate style.

1. Visual (Seeing, Imagining, Perceiving)

Clients with a visual processing style need clarity, structure, and the ability to envision success. Use language that paints a picture of the outcome.[7]

Closing Questions & Statements:

- "Can you see how this solution fits into your strategy?"
- "Let's bring the vision into focus—what stands out as the best next step?"
- "If you picture your team using this, does it align with your expectations?"
- "This will give you a clear roadmap for success. Does that look good to you?"

2. Auditory (Hearing, Listening, Discussing)

Auditory clients rely on verbal clarity and rhythm in conversations. They engage best when they can talk through ideas and hear a logical flow.[8]

Closing Questions & Statements:

- "Does this sound like the right approach for your team?"
- "I hear your priorities, and this solution echoes them perfectly. Shall we move forward?"
- "Let's tune into what matters most—do you feel we're in harmony on this?"
- "I'd love to hear your final thoughts—what resonates most with you?"

3. Kinesthetic (Feeling, Sensing, Experiencing)

Kinesthetic clients need to feel confident and connected to the solution. They process through emotion, experience, and gut instinct.[9]

Closing Questions & Statements:

- "Does this feel like the right decision for your company?"
- "I want to make sure this sits well with you—what are your thoughts?"
- "You'll notice the difference as soon as you start using it. Are you ready to take the first step?"
- "This approach provides a strong foundation—does that give you a sense of security moving forward?"

4. Olfactory (Smelling, Sensing Intuition)

Olfactory clients make decisions based on instinct and environmental cues. Their language revolves around freshness, intuition, and filtering information.[10]

Closing Questions & Statements:

- "Does this solution pass the sniff test for you?"
- "I sense that this direction feels right—do you agree?"
- "Let's clear the air on any lingering concerns—what's holding you back?"
- "This approach has the scent of success. Are you ready to go with it?"

5. Gustatory (Tasting, Digesting Information)

Gustatory clients process information through taste, nourishment, and digestion. They prefer decisions that are satisfying and easy to absorb.[11]

Closing Questions & Statements:

- "Does this proposal leave a good taste in your mouth?"
- "Let's chew on this a little more—what else do you need to feel good about moving forward?"
- "This is designed to be easy to digest—does it feel like the right fit?"
- "You don't want a deal that's hard to swallow. Does this feel palatable to you?"

6. Auditory Digital (Logical, Analytical Processing)

Auditory digital clients rely on logic, structure, and step-by-step reasoning. They want a rational and well-organized justification for their decision.[12]

Closing Questions & Statements:

- "Does this logically align with your business objectives?"
- "The data supports this move—do the numbers make sense to you?"
- "Structurally, this plan is sound. Are you comfortable proceeding?"
- "Let's go step by step—do all the components add up to a yes?"

7. Temporal (Time-Oriented Decision Making)

Temporal clients evaluate decisions based on timing, sequencing, and future implications. They prefer solutions that fit within their long-term vision.[13]

Closing Questions & Statements:

- "Does this timing align with your business goals?"
- "Looking ahead, can you see how this will position you for long-term success?"
- "If we fast-forward six months, how do you see this impacting your workflow?"
- "This is the right step at the right time—are you ready to move forward?"

Applying NLP Predicates to Closing Conversations

By actively listening to your client's language patterns and aligning your closing approach accordingly, you create a more natural, comfortable, and persuasive buying experience. When the language of the close mirrors how the client thinks, they are more likely to feel comfortable making a commitment free of uncertainty. This method transforms traditional closing tactics into a personalized, psychology-driven approach that fosters trust and long-term relationships.

☙❧☙❧

Breaking Down Closing by Categories

1. Categorizing Objections

To effectively navigate objections during closing, we categorize them into four primary types:

- **Fear-Based Objections**
    - Rooted in risk aversion, uncertainty, or reluctance to change.
    - **Example:** "What if this doesn't work out for us?"

- o **Approach:** Reassure with evidence, success stories, and risk-mitigation strategies.
- o **Recommended Therapeutic Modalities:**
  - Cognitive Behavioral Therapy (CBT): Challenge catastrophic thinking and introduce alternative, evidence-based perspectives.[14]
  - Motivational Interviewing (MI): Help clients uncover their intrinsic motivation for overcoming uncertainty.[15]
  - Mindfulness-Based Cognitive Therapy (MBCT): Guide clients to detach from fear-driven thoughts and focus on present realities.[16]
- **Power/Control Objections**
  - o Clients may resist being "sold to" or feel they lack ownership in the decision.
  - o **Example:** "I need to be the one driving this decision, not pressured into it."
  - o **Approach:** Use collaborative language and let the client steer the conversation.
  - o **Recommended Therapeutic Modalities:**
    - Adlerian Therapy: Encourage clients to take ownership of the decision-making process, reinforcing their autonomy.[17]
    - Gestalt Therapy: Use present-moment awareness to address resistance and foster self-directed choices.[18]
    - Transactional Analysis (TA): Identify power dynamics in communication and shift interactions to a more collaborative style.[19]
- **Budget/Resource Objections**
  - o Perceived misalignment between cost and value.
  - o **Example:** "This seems expensive compared to what we currently do."
  - o **Approach:** Reframe cost as investment and highlight ROI.
  - o **Recommended Therapeutic Modalities:**
    - Solution-Focused Brief Therapy (SFBT): Shift the conversation toward solutions and long-term value rather than short-term costs.[20]
    - Rational Emotive Behavior Therapy (REBT): Identify and reframe irrational beliefs about cost and investment.[21]
    - Positive Psychology Therapy: Reinforce optimism and highlight small wins to showcase ROI.[22]

- **Timing Objections**
  - The belief that now is not the right time.
  - **Example:** "Let's revisit this next quarter."
  - **Approach:** Address underlying concerns and show the cost of inaction.
  - **Recommended Therapeutic Modalities:**
    - Motivational Interviewing (MI): Explore ambivalence and guide clients toward their own reasons for taking action now.[23]
    - Existential Therapy: Help clients reflect on the bigger picture and the long-term impact of delaying decisions.[24]
    - Acceptance and Commitment Therapy (ACT): Encourage clients to acknowledge internal resistance while committing to meaningful action.[25]

2. Bias Mitigation in Closing Questions

Before closing, ensure that cognitive biases are addressed. If biases still exist, the client may:

- Purchase without full understanding, leading to regret and trust breakdown.
- Reject the purchase based on flawed reasoning rather than logical evaluation.

Key Principle: If biases persist, it is not the right time to close.

- **Status Quo Bias:** Client prefers to do nothing because change feels risky.
  - **Response:** "What risks do you see in staying where you are today?"
  - **Recommended Therapeutic Modalities:**
    - Motivational Interviewing (MI): Guide the client to explore their ambivalence and uncover their own reasons for change.[26]
    - Existential Therapy: Help the client reflect on the broader impact of inaction and the responsibility they have in shaping their future.[27]
    - Solution-Focused Brief Therapy (SFBT): Shift focus toward small, achievable steps that make change feel more manageable.[28]

- **Loss Aversion:** Fear of making the wrong decision outweighs potential benefits.
    - **Response:** "What specific concerns are holding you back from moving forward?"
    - **Recommended Therapeutic Modalities:**
        - Cognitive Behavioral Therapy (CBT): Challenge distorted thinking about risk and reframe the decision as an opportunity rather than a threat.[29]
        - Acceptance and Commitment Therapy (ACT): Encourage the client to acknowledge fear while committing to value-driven action.[30]
        - Positive Psychology Therapy: Reinforce optimism and focus on past successful decisions to build confidence.[31]
- **Confirmation Bias:** Client filters information to reinforce doubts.
    - **Response:** "What new perspectives have emerged in our discussions that challenge your initial concerns?"
    - **Recommended Therapeutic Modalities:**
        - Rational Emotive Behavior Therapy (REBT): Help the client identify and reframe irrational beliefs that reinforce their doubts.[32]
        - Gestalt Therapy: Use present-moment awareness to challenge rigid thinking and encourage a fresh perspective.[33]
        - Constructivist Therapy: Guide the client in developing a new, more balanced framework for evaluating the decision.[34]

For a more in-depth exploration of biases and how to address them with therapeutic modality-specific approaches, please refer back to the chapter on biases.

3. Therapeutic Modalities for Closing

Closing requires action and there are some therapeutic modalities that lend themselves more naturally to the closing stage of the sales process. Although the following therapeutic modalities encourage forward movement from the customer, the list that follows is far from exhaustive and should be taken only as a recommendation for where to start your exploration. As shared many times before in this book, the critical point to always remember is that whichever approach the salesperson uses must feel natural to them AND align to the client's preferred way of experiencing and expressing.

Acceptance and Commitment Therapy (ACT)

- **Why It Works:** It helps clients accept internal struggles and take action aligned with their values.[35]
- **Question Example:** "What aspect of this decision best aligns with your long-term goals and values?"

Cognitive Behavioral Therapy (CBT)

- **Why It Works:** It challenges unhelpful thought patterns and introduces alternative perspectives.[36]
- **Question Example:** "What assumptions might be influencing your hesitation, and how can we challenge them?"

Logotherapy

- **Why It Works** Helps clients find meaning in their current challenges and future goals.[37]
- **Question Example:** "How does resolving and overcoming the complexities of this difficult situation contribute to the overall picture of what you hope and intend to achieve?"

Motivational Interviewing (MI)

- **Why It Works** Guides clients to uncover their intrinsic motivation for change.[38]
- **Question Example:** "On a scale of 1-10, how important is solving this challenge now? Why that number and not lower?"

Reality Therapy

- **Why It Works:** It focuses on personal responsibility and actionable steps.[39]
- **Question Example:** "What's one step you're willing to take today to move toward a solution?"

Solution-Focused Brief Therapy (SFBT)

- **Why It Works:** It encourages rapid solutions and future-focused thinking.[40]
- **Question Example:** "If we fast-forward six months and this solution has worked, what changes would you notice?"

Like therapy, sales is built on trust. If biases remain, the sale should not proceed until the client fully understands and is comfortable with their decision. Closing should feel like a natural progression, not a forced conclusion. **Always prioritize the trusted relationship over the transaction.** And always strive to communicate within the modality that most aligns to the customer's preferred style.

☙❧☙❧

Common Closing Mistakes and the Therapy Parallel

Just as in therapy, where a counselor must be attuned to the client's emotional and psychological state before introducing deeper work, a sales professional must be equally present and aware when closing a deal. Closing isn't about forcing a decision; it's about ensuring the client is mentally and emotionally ready to take action.

Here are common mistakes sales professionals make when closing, along with their therapeutic parallels:

- **Over-talking instead of listening**
    - **Mistake:** Talking too much in an effort to "convince" the client rather than allowing them space to process their own decision-making.
    - **Therapy Parallel:** A therapist knows that silence is a powerful tool. Clients often need time to reflect, and too much verbal input can crowd their thinking. Likewise, sales professionals must embrace strategic pauses and give the client space to process.[41]
- **Pressuring instead of guiding**
    - **Mistake:** Using high-pressure tactics that trigger resistance instead of guiding the client through a natural decision-making process.
    - **Therapy Parallel:** In Motivational Interviewing, the goal is to guide clients toward their own intrinsic motivation for change. Pushing too hard creates resistance. Instead of "convincing" the client, a sales professional should guide them to recognize their own reasons for saying yes.[42]
- **Asking for the close too soon**
    - **Mistake:** Attempting to close the deal before the client is psychologically ready, leading to objections, hesitation, or buyer's remorse.
    - **Therapy Parallel:** A therapist wouldn't ask a client to confront a deep-seated trauma before they've built enough trust and coping

mechanisms. Similarly, a sales professional must ensure that all psychological barriers (biases, fears, uncertainties) have been addressed before asking for a commitment. If biases still exist, the client may make a decision without fully understanding what they're buying—or worse, resist making a decision at all.[43] Timing is critical.

- **Failing to adjust based on the client's state of mind**
  - **Mistake:** Using a one-size-fits-all approach to closing rather than adapting to where the client is in their journey.
  - **Therapy Parallel:** A skilled therapist knows when to push a client toward progress and when to ease off to avoid overwhelming them. Similarly, a sales professional must read the client's verbal and nonverbal cues to determine whether they need reassurance, clarification, or a gentle nudge forward.[44]

Ultimately, closing a sale should feel like a natural next step, not an aggressive push. The key for the consultative salesperson is to remain present, listen actively, and ensure the client is psychologically and emotionally prepared to move forward. Just as trust is the foundation of an effective therapeutic relationship, trust is the foundation of a successful sales close. Rushing to close without this foundation can damage credibility and erode the relationship, making long-term success unlikely.[45]

Reflections

Closing a sale is not about forcing a decision—it's about facilitating one. When done effectively, closing is the natural outcome of a well-guided, trust-based conversation where the client feels seen, heard, and fully aligned with their choice. By integrating therapeutic principles, we ensure that closing is not about pressure but about clarity. If biases remain, if doubts linger, or if the client feels disconnected from their own decision, the sale is not truly closed—it is merely postponed or, worse, forced under false pretenses. The strongest sales professionals recognize that closing is not an isolated step but the culmination of a process rooted in trust, insight, and mutual discovery. By applying therapeutic modalities such as Motivational Interviewing, Cognitive Behavioral Therapy, and Solution-Focused Brief Therapy, sales professionals can guide clients through their hesitations with integrity. Closing, in its highest form, is not about getting a contract signed—it's about ensuring that the client is fully committed, fully informed, and fully empowered to take the next step with confidence.[46]

❧ PERSONAL EXPLORATION ☙

Now that you've explored the psychology behind closing, take a step back and consider how these principles align with your current sales approach. Closing is not a transactional moment—it's a reflection of the relationship you've built, the clarity you've provided, and the intellectual, psychological and emotional readiness of your client. The best sales professionals don't rush to the finish line; they ensure their clients are emotionally and logically prepared to take action.[47]

Here are four questions to guide your reflection:

1. **Think about a past sale that stalled or fell through.** What psychological barriers—such as fear, control, or bias—may have played a role? In retrospect, what therapeutic questioning strategies could have helped move the client toward resolution?
2. **How do you personally feel about the act of closing?** Do you see it as a high-pressure moment, or as a natural next step in a trusted relationship? What mindset shifts might help you approach closing with more ease and authenticity?
3. **Consider the last time a client hesitated before making a decision.** How did you respond? Did you create space for introspection, or did you default to persuasion? How might you refine your approach to align with the client's emotional state?
4. **What's one specific closing question or technique from this chapter that you want to experiment with?** How will you integrate it into your next sales conversation in a way that feels natural and client-centered?

HOMEWORK CHALLENGE

In your next client meeting, pay close attention to the psychological readiness of your client. Before attempting to close, ask yourself: "Have I addressed their biases?" "Have I guided them through their hesitations?" "Have I built enough trust that closing feels like the next logical step, rather than a pressured moment?" Use one of the therapeutic closing techniques from this chapter and observe how it impacts the conversation. Reflect on what worked, what didn't, and what adjustments you might make in the future.

By treating closing as a natural extension of a meaningful conversation rather than a pressured finish line, you'll transform the way clients experience the sales process—and in doing so, you'll build deeper trust, stronger relationships, and lasting success.

YOUR FINAL THOUGHTS

Use The Space Below To Capture Your Thoughts And Reflections On What You've Learned In This Section

_____
_____
_____
_____
_____

MID-PROJECT CHECK-IN

A therapist's role is not just to guide a client through their journey but to consistently check in, creating a space for reflection, insights, and course correction. These check-ins are essential for ensuring that the client feels supported, aligned with their therapeutic goals, and confident in their progress. Similarly, in consultative sales, mid-project check-ins are critical to fortifying trust, validating the client's decision, and addressing any emerging concerns before they become obstacles.[1]

While this chapter provides a structured framework for these check-ins, as mentioned before, it is important to note that no single approach fits all clients. The most effective sales professionals tailor their check-in questions to align with the customer's preferred communication style, cognitive biases, and psychological tendencies. Just as a therapist adapts their approach to meet a client's needs, a consultative salesperson must do the same to ensure a meaningful and constructive conversation. This is never more important than in the middle of an ongoing delivery engagement. These client check-ins send the clear message that the salesperson is committed to the successful outcome of the solution and invested in the long-term strategic relationship with the customer.[2]

The Psychology of Post-Purchase Perception

Once a sale is made, clients often experience a mix of emotions—excitement, uncertainty, validation, and even regret. Understanding the psychological and emotional factors at play is crucial for structuring productive check-in conversations. Key cognitive biases that influence post-purchase perception include:

- **Confirmation Bias:** Clients may seek evidence that supports their belief that they made the right decision—or ignore signs that suggest otherwise.[3]
- **Loss Aversion:** Fear of potential failure or missed opportunities can cause unnecessary doubt about the purchase.[4]
- **Sunk Cost Fallacy:** Clients may continue with a solution simply because they've already invested time and resources, even if doubts arise.[5]
- **Status Quo Bias:** Hesitation to embrace change may lead them to question whether the purchase was necessary.[6]

- **Overconfidence Bias:** Some clients may initially overestimate how seamlessly the solution will integrate into their workflow, leading to frustration if there are unforeseen challenges.[7]

By recognizing these biases, a salesperson can structure check-in questions that guide the client toward a balanced, rational evaluation of their experience while reinforcing trust in the decision-making process.[8]

The Therapeutic Approach to Sales Check-Ins

Just as therapists use different modalities to facilitate progress, sales professionals must adapt their check-in approach to match the client's psychological and communication style. Although not a complete and exhaustive list, below are five therapeutic modalities particularly relevant to mid-project check-ins:

1. **Motivational Interviewing (MI):** Encourages open dialogue by exploring the client's intrinsic motivations and concerns.[9]
2. **Cognitive Behavioral Therapy (CBT):** Challenges unhelpful thought patterns by helping clients reframe their perspectives.[10]
3. **Person-Centered Therapy:** Focuses on deep listening, empathy, and unconditional positive regard to reinforce trust.[11]
4. **Solution-Focused Brief Therapy (SFBT):** Guides clients toward future-focused solutions rather than dwelling on problems.[12]
5. **Gestalt Therapy:** Encourages present-moment awareness to help clients articulate real-time concerns without overanalyzing past or future scenarios.[13]

Using elements from these modalities, a salesperson can craft questions that align with the client's thought process and ensure they feel heard, valued, and supported.

Structuring Effective Check-In Conversations

1. Creating Psychological Safety

Example Questions:

- Now that we're mid-project, how are you feeling about the progress so far?
    - Person-Centered Therapy
- Have there been any unexpected surprises—good or bad—that we should discuss?
    - Gestalt Therapy
- When you think about your original goals for this project, how do you feel we are tracking?
    - Motivational Interviewing

2. Addressing Hidden Concerns and Biases

Example Questions:

- Have you noticed any challenges that weren't immediately apparent at the beginning?
    - Cognitive Behavioral Therapy
- Sometimes, projects of this nature uncover new needs along the way. Are there any aspects you'd like to explore further?
    - Solution-Focused Therapy
- What is working exactly as you expected? What's different from what you anticipated?
    - CBT/MI hybrid

3. Reinforcing the Client's Decision with Strategic Framing

Example Questions:

- Reflecting on the decision-making process, what factors still make you feel confident about moving forward with this solution?
    - Confirmation Bias awareness
- If we could improve one specific aspect of your experience so far, what would it be?
    - Motivational Interviewing

- **What would success look like for you by the time we fully complete implementation?**
    - Solution-Focused Therapy

ଔଔଔଔ

The Art of Delivery: Ensuring Natural, Authentic Engagement

A well-structured question is only as effective as its delivery. Sales professionals must ensure that their check-ins feel natural and non-intrusive. This requires:

- **Adapting to the Client's Communication Style:** Analytical clients may appreciate structured, data-driven conversations, while relational clients may need emotional reassurance and dialogue.[14]
- **Practicing Conversational Authenticity:** Salespeople should integrate these questions seamlessly into discussions rather than making them feel like a formal review.[15]
- **Listening Deeply and Mirroring Thought Processes:** By mirroring the client's verbal and non-verbal cues, as well as speaking in the client's primary NLP predicate language, a salesperson can foster deeper trust and connection.[16]

ଔଔଔଔ

Reflections

Mid-project check-ins are not just an administrative touchpoint; they are a crucial opportunity to reinforce trust, address emerging concerns, and ensure client satisfaction. Just as a therapist continuously assesses and adapts their approach to best serve their client's needs, sales professionals must tailor their check-in style to align with each customer's cognitive and emotional style.[17]

This chapter offers a sample of the many ways check-ins can be structured, but ultimately, the most effective approach is the one that resonates most with the client. By prioritizing psychological safety, uncovering hidden concerns, and delivering questions in an authentic, adaptive manner, sales professionals can elevate the client relationship beyond a transaction—creating a partnership built on mutual trust and shared success.[18]

ॐ PERSONAL EXPLORATION ☙

Effective consultative sales professionals recognize that self-awareness is key to building genuine, trust-based client relationships. Similar to how therapists help clients navigate self-discovery for personal growth, sales professionals must continuously reflect on their own approach, challenge their biases, and strengthen their ability to connect authentically with customers.[19]

Sales is not just about transactions; it is about transformation. The most impactful sales professionals consistently evaluate their own thought processes, communication styles, and decision-making tendencies. By doing so, they can ensure they are serving clients in a way that aligns with both their own values and the client's needs. This requires honest self-reflection, a willingness to adapt, and the ability to recognize internal patterns that may unconsciously shape sales interactions.[20]

A core element of this exploration is understanding how cognitive biases, emotional triggers, and habitual communication styles influence behavior. Just as clients experience biases that affect their decision-making, sales professionals also carry biases that can impact the way they present solutions, interpret client concerns, and respond to objections. Awareness of these factors allows for a more intentional and strategic approach to client interactions.[21]

Therapeutic modalities can play a key role in personal sales exploration. For example:

- **Cognitive Behavioral Therapy (CBT):** Encourages the identification of negative thought patterns that may lead to self-doubt or misinterpretation of client feedback.[22]
- **Motivational Interviewing (MI):** Helps sales professionals refine their ability to ask open-ended, client-focused questions rather than making assumptions.[23]
- **Gestalt Therapy:** Promotes present-moment awareness, enabling sellers to stay fully engaged with the client rather than being preoccupied with their own agenda.[24]
- **Solution-Focused Brief Therapy (SFBT):** Reinforces a forward-thinking approach, allowing sales professionals to focus on actionable next steps rather than dwelling on past setbacks.[25]
- **Person-Centered Therapy:** Encourages deep listening and authenticity, ensuring that the client feels truly heard and valued.[26]

By embracing these principles, sales professionals can fine-tune their emotional intelligence, enhance their communication skills, and foster stronger client relationships. The reason why these details are presented in the Mid-Project Check-In chapter is to remind the seller that they must remain present and ever-attuned to how they engage their customer after the close of a sale. In the time between the closing of one sale and the start of a follow-on sales journey, the consultative seller must be intentional with how they relate to and communicate with the customer. This helps reaffirm that the customer's purchase decision was logical, sound, and beneficial. Self-Reflection for the professional seller at this point in the relationship journey is an essential part of sales.[27]

Mid-project check-ins are far more than an administrative obligation or formality—they are a strategic tool for deepening trust, reinforcing the client's decision, and ensuring long-term partnership and success. By integrating principles from therapy-based questioning techniques, sales professionals can move beyond surface-level conversations and create meaningful dialogues that guide clients through their post-purchase journey. The key to mastering this lies in self-awareness, adaptability, and the willingness to challenge both the client's and your own thought patterns.[28]

As you reflect on your own approach, consider how well you adapt to your clients' psychological needs, communication preferences, and cognitive biases. The following questions will help you examine your ability to lead meaningful check-ins that create value beyond the sale.

1. How do you currently approach mid-project check-ins, and do you tailor your questions based on the client's psychological and emotional state?
2. What cognitive biases might be influencing your client's perception of the solution, and how can you frame your check-in questions to address them?
3. Are you actively listening and adjusting your approach based on real-time client feedback, or are you following a rigid check-in script?
4. How often do you self-reflect on your own communication style and emotional intelligence during client interactions?

The additional questions below are designed to push you beyond a single moment of reflection. Growth comes from making self-reflection a habit. Top consultative sellers consistently evaluate their mid-project check-in practices, staying open to learning and refining their approach. Lasting success is built on continuous improvement, self-awareness, and a dedication to strengthening client relationships.

1. What internal biases or assumptions might I bring into sales conversations, and how do they influence my interactions with clients?
2. How do I typically respond to client objections or concerns, and does my approach align with my client's communication style and emotional needs?
3. What aspects of my sales approach feel most authentic to me, and where do I feel resistance or discomfort?
4. How do I ensure that I remain present, adaptable, and client-focused throughout the sales process rather than reverting to autopilot or relying on scripts?

HOMEWORK CHALLENGE

To reinforce the importance of mid-project check-ins, below are suggested exercises for you to implement into your weekly routine:

1. **Review a Past Client Check-In:**
    - Look back at a recent mid-project check-in you conducted. Identify what worked well and what could have been improved. Did you address cognitive biases? Did you deepen rapport with your client? Write down one thing you would do differently next time.
2. **Customize a Check-In Framework:**
    - Using the therapeutic modalities discussed in this chapter, create three tailored check-in questions for a current client. Ensure they align with their communication style and potential post-purchase emotions.
3. **Record and Analyze a Client Conversation:**
    - With permission, record a mid-project check-in (or take detailed notes). Listen carefully to how the client responds and assess whether your approach fostered an open, constructive discussion. Identify one adjustment you can make for future check-ins.

Completing these exercises will sharpen your awareness of how you conduct mid-project check-ins and enhance your ability to foster meaningful, trust-driven conversations and relationships with your clients.

YOUR FINAL THOUGHTS

Use The Space Below To Capture Your Thoughts And Reflections On What You've Learned In This Section

_____
_____
_____
_____
_____
_____

POST-SOLUTION DEBRIEF

In mental health counseling, a key part of the client's journey is reflecting on how therapeutic interventions have impacted their life. Looking back on where they started versus where they are now provides valuable insight into their growth and helps shape their next steps toward stability, confidence, and lasting change.[1] To guide this process, therapists use structured, modality-aligned questions to help clients explore their progress, uncover new insights, and refine their path forward.

Just as therapists facilitate this self-discovery, they also document each session with SOAP notes—a structured approach to clinical reflection that ensures consistency and clarity. SOAP stands for:

- **Subjective** – The client's personal experience, emotions, and self-reported perceptions.
- **Objective** – The therapist's observations, factual data, and measurable elements of the session.
- **Assessment** – The therapist's clinical interpretation of the client's progress based on the Subjective and Objective details.
- **Plan** – The next steps for the client, including interventions, referrals, or follow-up actions.[2]

SOAP notes are a gold standard in the helping professions, and the same structured approach can elevate the post-solution customer-facing debrief in consultative sales. A well-executed debrief ensures the customer feels heard, valued, and understood, while also creating opportunities for future collaboration. In this chapter, we'll explore how to apply SOAP notes to sales conversations—both with customers and with internal stakeholders in two separate motions. As you read through the examples, consider how you can tailor these questions to match your customer's communication style and decision-making process—a recommendation that has been made throughout this book. The more aligned your approach, the stronger your foundation for future business.

SOAP-Structured Customer Debrief Questions

Each section below includes six strategic questions designed to help your customer reflect on the delivered solution. Details about which specific therapeutic modalities are in play, along with insights into the NLP predicates contained in the questions are provided throughout this section to provide deeper understanding.

Subjective (Customer's Experience & Perception)

Goal: Gather the customer's personal thoughts, emotions, and experiences regarding the solution.

1. **Now that the solution is fully implemented, how does it feel compared to what you originally envisioned?**
    - **Why It Works:** Taps into Gestalt therapy, encouraging the client to compare expectations with reality.
    - **NLP Predicate:** "Feel" aligns with kinesthetic learners who process through sensations.
2. **What aspects of the solution stand out the most to you now that you've had time to experience it?**
    - **Why It Works:** Uses Cognitive Behavior Therapy (CBT) to focus attention on the client's thoughts about key elements of the solution.
    - **NLP Predicate:** "Stand out" appeals to visual processors who recall images or key details.
3. **Can you walk me through how this solution has impacted your daily workflow?**
    - **Why It Works:** Solution-Focused Brief Therapy (SFBT) approach—centers on how the intervention has shifted routine behaviors.
    - **NLP Predicate:** "Walk me through" supports kinesthetic and sequential thinkers.
4. **If you had to describe this solution in just three words, what would they be?**
    - **Why It Works:** Taps into Motivational Interviewing (MI) by prompting concise reflection.
    - **NLP Predicate:** "Describe" engages auditory processors who think in words and verbal expressions.

5. **What emotions have surfaced as you've worked with this solution?**
   - **Why It Works:** Aligns with Person-Centered Therapy by validating emotional experience.
   - **NLP Predicate:** "Emotions" appeals to kinesthetic processors who process experiences through feelings.
6. **Looking back at our initial discussions, what surprised you the most about how this turned out?**
   - **Why It Works:** Uses Adlerian psychology—exploring mismatches between expectation and reality to create insight.
   - **NLP Predicate:** "Looking back" resonates with visual processors who recall past experiences as mental images.

Objective (Observations & Measurable Feedback)

Goal: Capture factual, observable customer feedback about solution performance.

1. **What specific outcomes have you noticed since implementing this solution?**
   - **Why It Works:** Uses Cognitive Behavioral Therapy by anchoring discussions in measurable results.
   - **NLP Predicate:** "Noticed" appeals to visual processors who recall observed details and changes.
2. **How have your teams been interacting with the new system/process since go-live?**
   - **Why It Works:** Taps into Transactional Analysis (TA), focusing on group dynamics.
   - **NLP Predicate:** "Interacting" engages kinesthetic processors who focus on actions and experiences.
3. **What patterns or trends have emerged since this went live?**
   - **Why It Works:** Encourages Cognitive Behavioral Therapy (CBT) thinking—recognizing patterns in experience.
   - **NLP Predicate:** "Patterns or trends" resonates with visual processors who recognize and interpret structured information.
4. **What feedback have you received from your internal stakeholders?**
   - **Why It Works:** Encourages a collaborative evaluation rooted in real-world experiences.
   - **NLP Predicate:** "Feedback" connects with auditory processors who process information through verbal input.

5. **From your perspective, what are the strongest and weakest elements of the solution so far?**
   - **Why It Works:** Draws from Rational Emotive Behavior Therapy (REBT) by isolating rational vs. emotional judgments.
   - **NLP Predicate:** "Perspective" appeals to visual processors who frame thoughts through mental imagery.
6. **Have you observed any unintended benefits or unexpected challenges?**
   - **Why It Works:** Helps uncover hidden value and potential areas for refinement.
   - **NLP Predicate:** "Observed" aligns with visual processors who rely on sight-based recognition.

Assessment (Interpretation & Insights)

Goal: Encourage deep reflection and analysis of the solution's effectiveness.

1. **Based on everything so far, how would you rate the overall success of this solution?**
   - **Why It Works:** Encourages Reality Therapy—allowing the customer to take ownership of their assessment.
   - **NLP Predicate:** "Rate" appeals to auditory-digital processors who assess and quantify experiences logically.
2. **If we were to do this again, what would you want to do differently?**
   - **Why It Works:** Leverages Gestalt Therapy, focusing on iterative learning.
   - **NLP Predicate:** "Do differently" resonates with kinesthetic learners who think through actions and adjustments.
3. **What new opportunities or challenges has this solution uncovered?**
   - **Why It Works:** Encourages Narrative Therapy, helping the client see their business as an evolving story.
   - **NLP Predicate:** "Uncovered" aligns with visual processors who conceptualize discovery and insight.
4. **What elements of this solution do you see as essential for future initiatives?**
   - **Why It Works:** Applies Adlerian Psychology, guiding forward-thinking reflection.
   - **NLP Predicate:** "See as essential" appeals to visual thinkers who prioritize based on mental imagery.

5. **From your perspective, how does this solution compare to others you've used?**
   - **Why It Works:** Encourages Cognitive Behavior Therapy (CBT) to refine decision-making.
   - **NLP Predicate:** "Compare" engages visual and analytical processors who evaluate side-by-side distinctions.
6. **How aligned was our implementation process with your company's internal way of working?**
   - **Why It Works:** Uses Person-Centered Approach by centering the conversation on alignment.
   - **NLP Predicate:** "Aligned" resonates with kinesthetic processors who assess fit and integration.

Plan (Future Steps & Next Opportunities)

Goal: Guide the conversation toward next steps, reinforcing partnership and future sales opportunities.

1. **What's the next challenge we can help solve together?**
   - **Why It Works:** Uses Motivational Interviewing (MI) to prompt future collaboration.
   - **NLP Predicate:** "Challenge" appeals to kinesthetic learners who process through problem-solving and engagement.
2. **What would a perfect next-phase solution look like for you?**
   - **Why It Work:** Encourages Solution-Focused Brief Therapy (SFBT) thinking.
   - **NLP Predicate:** "Look like" engages visual processors who conceptualize ideal solutions in images.
3. **How can we continue supporting your team beyond this phase?**
   - **Why It Works:** Uses Client-Centered Therapy, reinforcing ongoing partnership.
   - **NLP Predicate:** "Supporting" aligns with kinesthetic learners who value action and hands-on assistance.
4. **Are there other teams or departments that might benefit from a similar solution?**
   - **Why It Works:** Uses Family Systems Therapy to help explore workplace relationships.
   - **NLP Predicate:** "Benefit" appeals to kinesthetic processors who focus on value and experiential gains.

5. **If you had unlimited budget and resources, what would you implement next?**
    - **Why It Works:** Encourages Gestalt's Big-Picture Thinking to uncover deeper needs.
    - **NLP Predicate:** "Implement" resonates with kinesthetic learners who focus on execution and action.
6. **What's the best way for us to stay connected as you continue using this solution?**
    - **Why It Works:** Reinforces Relationship-Based Selling, keeping engagement active.
    - **NLP Predicate:** "Stay connected" appeals to auditory and kinesthetic processors who focus on communication and relationships.

As stated, the post-solution debrief isn't just about checking a box—it's about reinforcing trust, gathering insights, and setting the stage for future opportunities. By structuring your conversation using the SOAP framework, you create a thoughtful, guided dialogue that makes the customer feel heard, valued, and supported. When done well, this approach transforms your role from a vendor into a trusted advisor—someone the client actively seeks out when new challenges arise. A well-executed debrief leads naturally into the next sale—because it proves that you're invested in their long-term success, not just closing a deal.

☙❧☙❧

SOAP-Structured Internal Debrief Questions

A successful sales career isn't just about closing deals—it's about continuous growth. Just as we tailor our communication to match a customer's style, we must apply the same self-awareness to our own performance evaluation. Engaging in structured self-reflection—whether alone or with a mentor, supervisor, or peer—allows us to identify strengths, uncover blind spots, and refine our approach for future success.[3]

The SOAP framework offers a structured method for this self-assessment, helping sales professionals analyze what worked, what didn't, and how to improve. This process isn't about self-criticism; it's about intentional, strategic growth. The following questions will guide you through a thoughtful post-sales reflection, incorporating therapeutic questioning techniques, NLP predicates, and cognitive bias insights to deepen your understanding. Whether you're conducting this review alone or with a trusted advisor, these questions will help you develop a sharper, more adaptable sales approach—one that fosters long-term success.

SOAP-Structured Self-Evaluation Questions

Each section below provides six high-impact reflection questions, along with explanations of how they enhance self-awareness, improve sales effectiveness, and drive career advancement.

1. Subjective (Personal Experience & Emotional Reflection)

Goal: Uncover personal insights about your emotions, mindset, and expectations during the sales process.

1. **What emotions surfaced before, during, and after this sales engagement?**
   - **Why It Works:** Uses Cognitive Behavioral Therapy (CBT) to connect emotions with performance, identifying confidence gaps or stress triggers.
   - **NLP Predicate:** "Surfaced" appeals to kinesthetic learners who focus on internal emotional experiences.
2. **How aligned did I feel with the customer throughout the process?**
   - **Why It Works:** Draws from Person-Centered Therapy to assess rapport and emotional alignment.
   - **NLP Predicate:** "Aligned" resonates with kinesthetic processors who assess emotional and relational fit.
3. **At what point in the process did I feel the most confident? When did I feel the least confident?**
   - **Why It Works:** Uses Gestalt Therapy, highlighting peak moments to analyze personal strengths and growth areas.
   - **NLP Predicate:** "Feel" strongly engages kinesthetic thinkers who evaluate experiences through bodily sensations.
4. **Did I feel more reactive or proactive in this conversation? Why?**
   - **Why It Works:** Identifies whether emotional responses drove the engagement rather than strategic intent.
   - **NLP Predicate:** "Reactive or proactive" appeals to kinesthetic and auditory-digital learners analyzing behavioral patterns.
5. **How would I describe my tone, pacing, and body language during this interaction?**
   - **Why It Works:** Uses NLP principles to enhance self-awareness in verbal and non-verbal communication.
   - **NLP Predicate:** "Describe" engages auditory-digital processors who verbalize their self-assessment.

6. **If I had been in the customer's position, how would I have perceived my approach?**
    - **Why It Works:** Uses Reality Therapy or Family Systems which encourages Perspective-Taking to refine empathy and communication style.
    - **NLP Predicate:** "Perceived" resonates with visual learners who process experiences through mental imagery.

2. Objective (Tangible Performance & Observations)

Goal: Analyze measurable behaviors, sales tactics, and customer reactions during the sales process.

1. **Did I effectively uncover the customer's true pain points, or did I stay too surface-level?**
    - **Why It Works:** Uses Motivational Interviewing (MI) to assess deep discovery questioning.
    - **NLP Predicate:** "Uncover" appeals to visual and kinesthetic thinkers focused on discovery.
2. **What specific objections arose, and how did I navigate them?**
    - **Why It Works:** Encourages review of Objection Handling Strategies, ensuring adaptive responses.
    - **NLP Predicate:** "Arose" resonates with kinesthetic learners who track interactions through emotional shifts.
3. **Which parts of my pitch or proposal resonated most with the customer?**
    - **Why It Works:** Applies Pattern Recognition from Cognitive Behavioral Therapy (CBT) to identify high-impact messaging.
    - **NLP Predicate:** "Resonated" engages kinesthetic thinkers who gauge impact through emotional and experiential cues.
4. **What specific buying signals did I observe, and how did I respond?**
    - **Why It Works:** Reinforces Sales Psychology, training the brain to recognize customer intent cues.
    - **NLP Predicate:** "Observe" appeals to visual learners who process information through sight-based cues.
5. **Did I clearly differentiate our solution from competitors? How?**
    - **Why It Works:** Uses Comparative Analysis from Cognitive Bias awareness to ensure value differentiation.
    - **NLP Predicate:** "Differentiate" aligns with visual and analytical processors who compare solutions mentally.

6. **Did I control the conversation, or did I let the customer dictate the flow? Was this intentional?**
    - **Why It Works:** Evaluates the balance between Consultative Sales Control and Customer-Led Discovery.
    - **NLP Predicate:** "Control" engages kinesthetic learners who assess dominance and responsiveness in conversations.

3. Assessment (Interpretation & Key Learnings)

Goal: Extract meaningful insights from the sales engagement to refine future performance.

1. **What was the single biggest factor that influenced the customer's decision-making?**
    - **Why It Works:** Encourages Root-Cause Analysis, ensuring strategic adjustments for future deals.
    - **NLP Predicate:** "Influenced" appeals to kinesthetic and auditory-digital learners analyzing cause-and-effect dynamics.
2. **Did I adapt my communication style to match the customer's personality and decision-making process?**
    - **Why It Works:** Uses NLP Calibration, improving rapport-building techniques.
    - **NLP Predicate:** "Adapt" resonates with kinesthetic learners who focus on real-time behavioral adjustments.
3. **Where did I experience resistance and what could I have done differently to ease it?**
    - **Why It Works:** Applies Cognitive Reframing, helping navigate future objections with ease.
    - **NLP Predicate:** "Experience" and "ease" appeal to kinesthetic thinkers who recall emotions tied to resistance
4. **Which cognitive biases may have influenced my assumptions about this deal?**
    - **Why It Works:** Helps combat Confirmation Bias, Anchoring Bias, and Overconfidence Bias.
    - **NLP Predicate:** "Influenced" (biases) engages auditory-digital processors assessing logical decision errors.
5. **What elements of my approach worked well, and how can I replicate them consistently?**
    - **Why It Works:** Uses Positive Psychology Therapy because it emphasizes optimism, strengths, and small wins, which align closely with the concept of reinforcing successful behaviors.
    - **NLP Predicate:** "Worked well" resonates with kinesthetic and visual learners tracking past successes.

6. **What's one small adjustment I could make that would have the biggest impact on my sales success?**
    - **Why It Works:** Uses Solution-Focused Brief Therapy (SFBT) because it focuses on identifying what works and doing more of it.
    - **NLP Predicate:** "Adjustment" appeals to kinesthetic learners focusing on continuous improvement.

4. Plan (Future Growth & Career Development)

Goal: Set actionable goals and define next steps for improvement.

1. **What specific skill or technique will I focus on improving before my next sales engagement?**
    - **Why It Works:** Uses Adlerian Therapy and encourages self-efficacy and ownership.
    - **NLP Predicate:** "Focus on improving" engages auditory-digital processors tracking structured development.
2. **How can I incorporate customer feedback into my future approach?**
    - **Why It Works:** Leverages Cognitive Behavioral Therapy (CBT) by reinforcing adaptability by integrating new perspectives.
    - **NLP Predicate:** "Incorporate" appeals to kinesthetic thinkers who integrate feedback through action.
3. **Who in my network or organization can I learn from to refine my skills?**
    - **Why It Works:** Promotes mentorship as a source of belonging and purpose, a key aspect of Adlerian Therapy.
    - **NLP Predicate:** "Learn from" resonates with auditory learners who absorb insights through discussion.
4. **What steps will I take to ensure I stay in touch with this customer and nurture the relationship?**
    - **Why It Works:** Leverages aspects of Interpersonal Therapy which strengthens interpersonal connections through mindful engagement.
    - **NLP Predicate:** "Stay in touch" appeals to auditory and kinesthetic processors who value relationship continuity.
5. **What will I do differently in my next sales cycle to increase my close rate?**
    - **Why It Works:** Uses Reality Therapy's goal-driven adjustments for practical change.
    - **NLP Predicate:** "Do differently" engages kinesthetic learners who refine approaches through action.

6. **If I were coaching someone else through this same sales process, what advice would I give them?**
    - **Why It Works:** Uses Solution-Focused Brief Therapy (SFBT) to enhance self-reflection and structured problem-solving.
    - **NLP Predicate:** "Coaching" resonates with auditory-digital learners who process concepts through structured guidance.

※※※

Why Self-Evaluation is Essential for Sales Success

The most successful sales professionals aren't just skilled at selling—they're experts in self-reflection. High-performance sales is a craft, not a script—one that requires constant refinement, adaptability, and self-awareness. By using the SOAP notes framework from the helping professions, sales professionals move beyond gut feelings and into structured, evidence-based self-evaluation. This process helps them:

- **Recognize and reinforce strengths** that drive success.
- **Identify areas for improvement** before they become career-limiting habits.
- **Enhance self-awareness**, refining communication and rapport-building techniques.
- **Uncover hidden biases** that may be affecting sales performance.
- **Develop a continuous improvement mindset**, ensuring long-term career growth.[4]

The key takeaway? Sales isn't just about what happens during the conversation—it's about how you process, learn, and evolve afterward. By systematically evaluating each sales engagement through the SOAP notes framework, you transform every deal—won or lost—into a teachable moment and a stepping stone toward greater success.

※※※

❦ PERSONAL EXPLORATION ❧

Every successful salesperson understands that the sale doesn't end when the solution is delivered—it ends when both the customer and the salesperson have taken the time to reflect, evaluate, and extract key lessons from the experience. A structured debrief, both with the customer and internally, ensures that insights are captured, relationships are strengthened, and future opportunities are identified.[5]

The SOAP framework provides a structured and intentional way to navigate these post-solution discussions. By guiding the customer through a debrief, you demonstrate that their experience matters, their feedback is valued, and their future needs are already on your radar. This not only reinforces trust and credibility but also lays the groundwork for future sales conversations.[6]

However, external feedback alone is not enough. A salesperson's ability to self-reflect—to critically examine their own performance, recognize strengths and weaknesses, and refine their approach—is what separates transactional sellers from strategic, consultative professionals. The SOAP framework, when turned inward, helps salespeople process each engagement through a lens of continuous improvement, ensuring that every deal—won or lost—becomes a stepping stone toward mastery.[7] The SOAP notes are an essential client and personal tool for all therapists and the value it brings to salespeople is profound and necessary.

Below are four personal exploration questions designed to help you internalize the importance of both customer and self-debriefing, ensuring that you fully harness the power of reflection in your sales journey.

1. **What was the most valuable insight I gained from my customer's feedback, and how can I use it to strengthen future sales conversations?**
    - **Homework:** Review your most recent customer debrief. Identify one piece of feedback—whether positive or constructive—that surprised you or made you think differently about your sales approach. Write down how you will integrate this lesson into your next sales conversation.
2. **When I reflect on my own performance, what is one specific moment where I could have handled the conversation more effectively?**
    - **Homework:** Choose one part of your sales process—discovery, objection handling, closing, follow-up—and pinpoint a specific moment where you felt uncertain, hesitant, or reactive. Analyze what caused that moment and outline an alternative response that aligns with a more strategic, confident, client-centric or consultative approach.
3. **How well did I align my communication to the customer's preferred style, and where can I improve?**
    - **Homework:** Think back to the language, tone, and approach you used during your last customer interaction. Did you adapt to their communication preferences (e.g., data-driven vs. storytelling, big-picture vs. details)? Identify one way you could adjust your style

more effectively in future conversations to improve connection and trust.
4. **If I were coaching another salesperson on how to run a post-solution debrief, what three key principles would I emphasize?**
    - **Homework:** Imagine mentoring a new sales professional. Write down the three most critical lessons you've learned about conducting an effective customer debrief and self-reflection. Then, challenge yourself: Are you consistently applying these lessons to your own process? If not, commit to integrating them into your next sales cycle.

Sales is a continuous evolution, and the most successful professionals are those who actively learn from every experience. Whether through customer conversations or personal reflection, the SOAP framework offers a powerful way to turn every sale into an opportunity to learn and grow. By mastering the art of structured debriefing, you don't just close deals—you open doors to deeper relationships, greater self-awareness, and long-term sales success.

YOUR FINAL THOUGHTS

Use The Space Below To Capture Your Thoughts And Reflections On What You've Learned In This Section

_____
_____
_____
_____
_____
_____
_____

ROLE PLAY EXERCISES

Therapists dedicate significant time to role-playing exercises during their education and supervision because they understand that mastery comes from practice, not theory alone. These simulated conversations refine their ability to connect, interpret, and respond effectively to clients in real-world situations.[1] The same principle applies to professional sales. Successful salespeople are those who embrace the challenge and periodic awkwardness of role-playing, but actively seek out opportunities to explore in a safe space with their coaches, mentors, and peers.[2]

Practicing new approaches for the first time in a live sales conversation is risky. Without prior rehearsal, uncertainty and anxiety can surface, leading to missed opportunities and misaligned messaging—both of which damage client rapport and diminishes the trust a salesperson needs to sustain a long-term advisory relationship.[3] By practicing in a controlled, supportive environment, sellers develop confidence, refine their questioning techniques, and internalize the consultative skills they've learned throughout this book.[4]

The following role-play exercises provide an opportunity to apply everything you've explored—from recognizing cognitive biases and NLP language patterns to using therapeutic questioning and mirroring techniques. Each scenario presents a real-world sales conversation where you'll analyze client statements, identify psychological cues, and practice your responses. To maximize your growth, speak your responses aloud and write them down in the spaces provided. The more you practice, the more naturally these techniques will flow in actual sales conversations.[5]

Role-Playing Scenarios

Scenario 1: Overcoming an Objection in IT Security

Customer Role: CIO

Solution Being Sold: Next-generation cybersecurity platform

Relationship-Building Question: "Many IT leaders I speak with tell me that security is a constant balancing act between risk, cost, and ease of implementation. What's been your experience in maintaining that balance?"

Customer Statement (Includes NLP Predicate & Bias):

"We've been using our current security framework for years, and while it's not perfect, it hasn't let us down yet. I just don't see the need to fix something that isn't broken, especially when every new solution out there looks the same to me."

Reader's Response:

_____
_____
_____

Analysis & Insights:

- **Bias Identified:** Status Quo Bias (customer prefers to keep things as they are rather than change).
- **NLP Predicate:** Visual ("looks the same to me").
- **Mirroring Strategy:** Respond using a visual-based approach.

Suggested Seller Reply:

"I completely see where you're coming from. At first glance, many security solutions do seem identical. What might help is for me to show you a side-by-side comparison of your current framework versus the latest advancements, so you can get a clearer picture of any gaps you may not have noticed."

Scenario 2: Addressing Hesitation in Finance

Customer Role: CFO

Solution Being Sold: Cloud-based financial automation software

Relationship-Building Question: "Finance teams are under constant pressure to do more with less. How have you been managing the balance between efficiency and cost savings?"

Customer Statement (Includes NLP Predicate & Bias):

"I hear what you're saying about automation, but we've already invested heavily in our current system. The thought of switching makes me uneasy because if something goes wrong, I'll be the one left holding the bag."

Reader's Response:

_____
_____
_____

Analysis & Insights:

- **Bias Identified:** Loss Aversion (fear of losing what they already have).
- **NLP Predicate:** Auditory ("I hear what you're saying").
- **Mirroring Strategy:** Use auditory-based language.

Suggested Seller Reply:

"I completely understand, and I wouldn't expect you to make a change without having a solid plan in place. What if we sound this out together and walk through some real-world examples of companies like yours that transitioned smoothly, so you can hear firsthand how they minimized risk?"

Scenario 3: Navigating the Bias in Operations

Customer Role: VP of Operations

Solution Being Sold: AI-driven supply chain optimization software

Relationship-Building Question: "Many operations leaders I work with tell me they're under pressure to keep everything running smoothly while also adapting to market changes. How has that been playing out in your world?"

Customer Statement (Includes NLP Predicate & Bias):

"Look, I don't like being told we have to change just because AI is the latest shiny thing. Every vendor tries to push new technology on us, but I can't see how it would actually fit into our existing process."

Reader's Response:

_____
_____
_____

Analysis & Insights:

- **Bias Identified:** Reactance Bias (resistance to being told what to do).
- **NLP Predicate:** Visual ("I can't see how it would fit").
- **Mirroring Strategy:** Use visual-based language and provide autonomy.

Suggested Seller Reply:

"I get it—no one wants to be forced into change, especially when it's not clear how it fits into your world. What if I walk you through a visual representation of how similar companies have adapted AI without disrupting their current workflows? That way, you can determine for yourself if it's worth exploring further."

Scenario 4: Identifying the Objection in HR

Customer Role: CHRO

Solution Being Sold: Employee engagement and retention platform

Relationship-Building Question: "Retention is top of mind for many HR leaders today. What strategies have been working well for you in keeping employees engaged?"

Customer Statement (Includes NLP Predicate & Bias):

"The last time we invested in an engagement tool, it promised the moon but ended up being a black hole for time and resources. I have no appetite for another disappointment."

Reader's Response:

_____
_____
_____

Analysis & Insights:

- **Bias Identified:** Framing Effect (previous negative experience frames perception).
- **NLP Predicate:** Gustatory ("I have no appetite").
- **Mirroring Strategy:** Use gustatory-based language.

Suggested Seller Reply:

"I completely understand your hesitation. No one wants to take another bite of something that left a bad taste before. What if I share how our platform has been designed specifically to be easy to implement and digest, so it's more of a fresh start rather than a repeat of your past experience?"

Scenario 5: Countering Resistance and Bias in Marketing

Customer Role: CMO

Solution Being Sold: AI-powered customer analytics platform

Relationship-Building Question: "Many Marketing teams today have an overwhelming amount of data at their fingertips. How have you been navigating that challenge to ensure your insights lead to real action?"

Customer Statement (Includes NLP Predicate & Bias):

"We already have a pretty solid analytics process in place. I know all these AI solutions claim to offer something revolutionary, but I just don't see how they'd be any better than what we're already doing."

Reader's Response:

_____
_____
_____

Analysis & Insights:

- **Bias Identified:** Illusory Superiority Bias (overestimation of current capabilities).
- **NLP Predicate:** Visual ("I just don't see how").
- **Mirroring Strategy:** Use visual-based language.

Suggested Seller Reply:

"That makes sense—if you've built a strong process, it can be tough to envision how something new would add value. What if I show you a direct comparison of your current analytics workflow versus how AI enhances it, so you can see for yourself where it might create new opportunities?"

The Power of Continued Role-Play Practice in Consultative Sales

Therapists engage in weekly meetings with their clinical supervisor to receive guidance, insight, and coaching. They also participate in regular group supervision, where peer collaboration fosters shared learning and professional development.[6] A key component of these sessions is role-playing—a powerful technique used to refine skills and progress toward mastery in their field.[7]

The same commitment to continuous growth and development applies to the sales profession. While role-playing exercises may feel uncomfortable—often due to the vulnerability required to demonstrate skills in front of peers—embracing this challenge is essential for improvement.[8] As therapists often say, awareness, growth, and transformation occur by navigating through discomfort, not by avoiding it.[9]

With that in mind, here are five additional role-play scenarios to enhance your skills and elevate your performance.

Role-Play Scenario 6: Executive Leadership Concerned About Visibility

Customer Role: CIO of a mid-sized financial services company

Solution Being Sold: A cloud-based data analytics platform

Opening Relationship-Building Question: "I'd love to hear about your vision for how data can drive strategic decisions in your organization. What's most important to you when selecting a solution?"

Customer Statement:

"We've looked at analytics platforms before, but none have been able to show us the full picture. Every time we implement something new, it feels like we're looking through a foggy lens—just fragments of data that don't provide a clear roadmap. I doubt you'll be able to help me visualize how this will integrate with our current system."

Reader's Response:

_____
_____
_____

Analysis & Insights:

- **NLP Predicate:** Visual ("full picture," "looking through a foggy lens," "visualize")
- **Cognitive Bias:** Status Quo Bias (reluctance to change due to previous negative experiences)
- **Mirroring Opportunity:** Use visual language in response

Suggested Seller Response:

"I see what you mean—it's frustrating when a tool only gives you a blurry snapshot rather than a clear and complete view. Let me paint a picture of how our platform brings everything into focus by integrating seamlessly with your existing systems. Imagine a dashboard where all your critical data is displayed in one clear, interactive view—how would that impact your decision-making?"

Role-Play Scenario 7: Operations Leader Concerned About Change Management

Customer Role: VP of Operations at a logistics company

Solution Being Sold: AI-driven workflow automation tool

Opening Relationship-Building Question: "What are some of the biggest roadblocks your team faces when it comes to improving efficiency?"

Customer Statement (Includes NLP Predicate & Bias):

"Every time we try to improve our workflows, it sounds good on paper, but when it's time to implement, everything falls apart. I hear what you're saying about automation, but my team is already overwhelmed, and they don't have the bandwidth to listen to another solution that disrupts their operations."

Reader's Response:

_____
_____
_____

Analysis & Insights:

- **NLP Predicate:** Auditory ("sounds good on paper," "I hear what you're saying," "listen")
- **Cognitive Bias:** Loss Aversion (fear of disrupting current processes)
- **Mirroring Opportunity:** Use auditory language in response

Suggested Seller Response:

"I hear you—when new solutions sound great in theory but don't translate into real-world success, it can be frustrating. Let's tune into what's working and what's not with your current processes so we can ensure any changes harmonize with your team's existing workflows. What would need to change for this to sound like a win for them?"

Role-Play Scenario 8: CFO Concerned About ROI

Customer Role: CFO of a healthcare technology firm

Solution Being Sold: Cybersecurity risk assessment service

Opening Relationship-Building Question: "From your perspective, what's the most critical factor when evaluating cybersecurity investments?"

Customer Statement:

"We've invested in security tools before, and frankly, they've left a bad taste in my mouth. The costs keep piling up, and we don't always see the return. My gut tells me that unless you can prove otherwise, this will just be another expense that's hard to swallow."

Reader's Response:

_____
_____
_____

Analysis & Insights:

- **NLP Predicate:** Gustatory ("bad taste in my mouth," "hard to swallow")
- **Cognitive Bias:** Sunk Cost Fallacy (previous investments influencing future decisions)
- **Mirroring Opportunity:** Use gustatory language in response

Suggested Seller Response:

"I completely understand why past experiences might leave a sour taste. Our approach is designed to be digestible and results-driven, ensuring you're not just consuming another cost but actually gaining a measurable return. What would make this feel like a satisfying investment for you?"

Role-Play Scenario 9: IT Director Concerned About Compatibility

Customer Role: CFO of a healthcare technology firm

Solution Being Sold: Cybersecurity risk assessment service

Opening Relationship-Building Question: "From your perspective, what's the most critical factor when evaluating cybersecurity investments?"

Customer Statement:

"We've tried new systems before, but nothing ever fits right. We always end up trying to jam a square peg into a round hole. It just doesn't feel right. My team isn't eager for more change—we need something that actually integrates seamlessly."

Reader's Response:

_____
_____
_____

Analysis & Insights:

- **NLP Predicate:** Kinesthetic ("fits right," "feels right," "eager for change")
- **Cognitive Bias:** Confirmation Bias (expecting past failures to repeat)
- **Mirroring Opportunity:** Use kinesthetic language in response

Suggested Seller Response:

"I get why past experiences might make this feel like a poor fit. Our approach is designed to mold seamlessly into your existing workflows so that it feels natural, not forced. What would need to happen for this solution to sit well with your team?"

Role-Play Scenario 10: COO Focused on Employee Buy-In

Customer Role: Chief Operating Officer of a manufacturing company

Solution Being Sold: Employee engagement and retention software

Opening Relationship-Building Question: "What's been your experience with getting employees to adopt new workplace tools?"

Customer Statement:

"Honestly, our past attempts at engagement programs have fallen on deaf ears. We roll them out, and the team just tunes out. If this solution doesn't strike a chord with them, we'll just be wasting our time and money."

Reader's Response:

_____
_____
_____

Analysis & Insights:

- **NLP Predicate:** Auditory ("fallen on deaf ears," "tunes out," "strike a chord")
- **Cognitive Bias:** Status Quo Bias (resistance to change)
- **Mirroring Opportunity:** Use auditory language in response

Suggested Seller Response:

"I hear you—if a solution doesn't resonate with employees, it's just noise. Our approach ensures the program speaks directly to their needs. What would make this sound like a meaningful change to your team?"

෧෮෮෮෧෮෧෮

Role-Play, Role-Play, Role-Play, and then Role-Play Some More!

The continuation of this chapter is intentional, emphasizing the importance of continuous learning. Consistent practice enhances proficiency in applying these techniques and principles to consultative sales conversations. Sales professionals striving for mastery should fully engage with the next set of role-play scenarios.

To make these exercises as effective as possible, sellers should:

- **Work in pairs or small groups** to practice role-play scenarios.
- **Use real client accounts** (when possible) to tailor role-play sessions.
- **Record and review** (with permission, of course) practice conversations for improvement.
- **Get feedback** from peers, mentors, or sales coaches.
- **Experiment with different therapeutic modalities** to see what feels most natural and effective.

Each of the following real-world sales scenarios will include:

1. **The Sales Situation** – Context and background of the scenario.
2. **Challenges to Overcome** – The cognitive biases, objections, or psychological barriers at play.
3. **Role-Play Setup** – Suggested roles and structure for the exercise.
4. **Guided Questions & Sales Approach** – Key questioning techniques and tactics to apply.
5. **Debrief & Takeaways** – Reflection points for improvement.

Scenario 1: Convincing a Risk-Averse CFO to Modernize IT Infrastructure

The Sales Situation:

You are meeting with a Chief Financial Officer (CFO) of a mid-sized company that has relied on legacy IT infrastructure for over a decade. They acknowledge inefficiencies but fear the risks associated with migrating to a modern solution. Their primary concern is cost and potential operational disruptions.

Challenges to Overcome:

- **Loss Aversion Bias** – The CFO is more focused on the potential risk of change than the long-term benefits.
- **Status Quo Bias** – They believe that since the system is still functioning, there's no urgent need for change.
- **Sunk Cost Fallacy** – They hesitate to abandon past investments, even if they are outdated.

Role-Play Setup:

- One person plays the seller and another plays the CFO.
- The CFO should push back strongly, focusing on concerns about cost, risk, and past investments.
- The seller must apply bias mitigation strategies and use therapeutic questioning techniques to shift the CFO's perspective.

Suggested Guided Questions & Sales Approach:

- "I understand that your current system has served you well. Given the pace of technological change, what challenges do you foresee in the next two to three years if nothing changes?" (Status Quo Bias Reframe)
- "If we looked at the numbers together and found that your competitors were cutting operational costs by 20% with modern solutions, how would that impact your view on upgrading?" (Loss Aversion Shift – Showing the cost of inaction)
- "If another company in your industry were evaluating this decision today, without any previous investment, what choice do you think they would make?" (Sunk Cost Reframe – Encouraging a fresh perspective)
- Create your own questions now.

Debrief & Takeaways:

- Did the seller effectively shift the CFO's mindset?
- What additional concerns did the CFO raise, and how well were they addressed?
- How did therapeutic questioning change the tone of the conversation?

Scenario 2: Overcoming a CTO's Confirmation Bias About an Existing Vendor

The Sales Situation:

You are meeting with a Chief Technology Officer (CTO) who has worked with the same IT services provider for years. They believe this vendor is the "best fit" because of familiarity, even though they have had service issues and hidden costs. You need to help them see the value of exploring alternatives.

Challenges to Overcome:

- **Confirmation Bias** – The CTO only acknowledges evidence that supports their loyalty to the current vendor.
- **Authority Bias** – They defer to past executive decisions and resist questioning them.
- **Loss Aversion Bias** – Fear that switching vendors will lead to unexpected failures.

Role-Play Setup:

- One person plays the seller, another plays the CTO.
- The CTO should be firmly convinced that their current vendor is the best choice and challenge the seller at every turn.
- The seller must ask thought-provoking questions to get the CTO to rethink their position.

Suggested Guided Questions & Sales Approach:

- "What specific aspects of your current provider's performance make them the best fit? Are there any areas where you've had challenges?" (Confirmation Bias – Encouraging self-discovery of issues)
- "If we could demonstrate a way to achieve better service at a lower cost, what would be your criteria for considering a switch?" (Authority Bias – Encouraging independent evaluation)

- "If you had to start from scratch today with no existing vendor relationships, what factors would influence your choice?" (Loss Aversion Reframe – Helping them look at the decision objectively)
- Create your own questions now.

Debrief & Takeaways:

- Did the CTO start to recognize limitations of the current vendor?
- Did the seller avoid direct confrontation and instead guide the conversation with questioning?
- What additional information would have strengthened the case for change?

Scenario 3: Gaining Buy-In from a Skeptical COO Who Prefers In-House Solutions

The Sales Situation:

You are meeting with a Chief Operating Officer (COO) who is skeptical of outsourcing. They believe in keeping everything in-house despite increasing inefficiencies and costs. You need to position your managed services as a scalable, cost-effective solution.

Challenges to Overcome:

- **Overconfidence Bias** – The COO overestimates the company's ability to manage everything internally.
- **Reactance Bias** – They resist outside influence and dislike feeling "sold to".
- **Status Quo Bias** – They assume internal management is inherently safer than outsourcing.

Role-Play Setup:

- One person plays the seller, another plays the COO.
- The COO should push back by defending in-house management and resisting external solutions.
- The seller must use collaborative, consultative questioning to shift the COO's perspective.

Suggested Guided Questions & Sales Approach:

- "What factors make keeping everything in-house the best option for you today?" (Illusion of Control – Encouraging reflection on hidden inefficiencies)
- "What's your biggest challenge in scaling internal operations efficiently?" (Reactance Bias – Creating a collaborative problem-solving conversation)
- "Have you ever tested an outsourced solution to compare results? If not, what's holding you back from experimenting with one area?" (Status Quo Bias – Making change feel like a low-risk test rather than a commitment)
- Create your own questions now.

Debrief & Takeaways:

- Did the COO express openness to at least testing an alternative?
- Did the seller avoid pushing too hard and instead use an advisory approach?
- What objections were raised, and how effectively were they addressed?

☙❧☙❧

Turning Practice into Mastery

Role-play exercises like these provide a safe environment to refine questioning skills, experiment with different therapeutic modalities, and learn how to navigate real client objections without the pressure of a live sales call.[10] The key to success is not simply through consistent practice. The professional sales person must always approach the Role-Play exercises and every client conversation with genuine curiosity and authentic empathy.[11] Over time, sellers who incorporate bias mitigation, psychological insights, and strategic questioning will set themselves apart—not just as salespeople, but as trusted advisors who guide clients toward optimal decisions.[12]

Own Your Role-Playing Journey

Just as a therapy client must take responsibility for their progress, you too must own your journey in mastering therapeutic questioning for consultative sales. This isn't merely about practicing techniques—it's about integrating these skills into every conversation, refining your approach, and consistently challenging yourself to grow.[13] To accelerate your development, consider the following strategies:

- **Schedule a biweekly "Role Play Hour"** on your calendar. Invite mentors or peers, come prepared with potential client scenarios, or reenact recent interactions. Use this time for open, collaborative discussions to explore and refine how you apply these principles in future customer engagements.
- **Seamlessly integrate techniques into everyday interactions.** Practice applying the methods from this book in casual social conversations with friends and family, and observe how these strategies enhance rapport and understanding.
- **Record and review your role plays.** Capture your practice sessions on video (with permission from all participants). Take time to thoughtfully and critically reflect on your skills delivery, identify deficiencies that need to be addressed, and adjust your approach based on feedback and self-assessment.
- **Seek diverse feedback.** Regularly engage with a mentor or trusted colleague to review your role-playing sessions. Diverse perspectives can uncover blind spots and help you fine-tune your delivery for different client personalities and situations.[14]

Taking ownership of your role-playing journey is key to transforming your sales interactions. Consistent practice, honest reflection, and continuous feedback will not only boost your confidence but also ensure that you are always prepared to connect authentically and effectively with your customers.[15]

Engage with Like-Minded Professionals

Join our community at Ask Like a Therapist, Sell Like a Pro, where innovative sales professionals integrate therapeutic techniques into their careers. This platform offers a space to share ideas, exchange best practices, and provide guidance on leveraging these approaches to enhance sales performance. Visit www.asklikeatherapist.com to connect, collaborate, and elevate your professional journey.[16]

ೞ PERSONAL EXPLORATION ೞ

In the dynamic field of consultative sales, role-playing is not merely a rehearsal—it's a transformative tool for self-improvement. By simulating real-world interactions, you can hone your ability to connect authentically, adapt to diverse client needs, and refine your communication strategies.[17] Just as therapists train tirelessly to perfect their skills, the most successful sales professionals use role-playing to challenge their assumptions, uncover hidden biases, and build confidence in their consultative approach.[18] Incorporating regular role-playing exercises into your self-improvement journey ensures that you continually learn from each interaction, turning every practice session into a stepping stone toward mastery.[19]

1. **What specific moments during role-playing have revealed unexpected challenges in your communication style, and how can you address these areas for improvement?**
   Consider instances where your intended message wasn't clearly conveyed. Reflect on the feedback you received and think about how you might adjust your tone, pace, or language to better resonate with your audience.
2. **How do you adapt your role-playing scenarios to reflect the unique needs and communication styles of different client personalities?**
   Analyze how variations in client behavior—such as a preference for data-driven insights versus a need for emotional connection—influence your approach. What changes do you make in your questioning techniques or delivery to match these differences?
3. **In what ways have role-playing exercises helped you recognize and mitigate your own cognitive biases during sales interactions?**
   Reflect on the patterns you've noticed, such as overconfidence or confirmation bias, and consider how role-playing has illuminated these tendencies. How can you further adjust your approach to ensure you remain objective and client-focused?
4. **What feedback from peers or mentors during role-playing sessions has been most impactful, and how will you integrate that feedback into your future sales conversations?**
   Think about constructive critiques that have led to measurable improvements. Identify specific strategies you plan to implement and monitor how they change your interactions over time.

Reflections

Role-playing is a powerful avenue for personal and professional growth in consultative sales. By actively engaging in reflective exercises and embracing feedback, you not only enhance your communication skills but also build the resilience and adaptability needed for long-term success.[20] Remember, every role-play session is an opportunity to refine your approach, overcome internal barriers, and ultimately, become a more effective, trusted advisor to your clients.[21]

૭ૐ YOUR FINAL THOUGHTS ૪૭

Use The Space Below To Capture Your Thoughts And Reflections On What You've Learned In This Section

_____
_____
_____
_____
_____
_____
_____

CLOSING THOUGHTS
ಣಲಣಲಣಲ

Sales is not about closing deals; it's about opening and nurturing relationships. It is truly about engaging your customer with genuine curiosity and authentic empathy. Throughout this book, we've explored how the principles of therapy—active listening, meaningful questioning, mirroring, bias awareness, and much more—can elevate consultative sales from transactional to transformational. By applying therapeutic modalities to sales conversations, we move beyond persuasion and into true partnership, guiding clients toward solutions that align with their deepest needs and aspirations in a manner that unconsciously resonates with how they naturally think, feel, communicate, and function.

Consider the power of this shift: When clients feel genuinely understood, they respond with trust, openness, and long-term loyalty.[1] When we replace rehearsed pitches with thoughtful inquiry, we foster real dialogue that uncovers what truly matters. When we challenge assumptions with care and insight, we empower customers to make the best decisions for their businesses and their futures. These are not just sales techniques—they are career-defining skills that will forever change how you engage, connect, and lead.

The most successful sales professionals are not merely dealmakers; they are trusted advisors, problem solvers, and relationship architects.[2] By adopting the mindset of a therapist, you are not just improving your ability to sell—you are redefining the way you serve, influence, and create value. The strategies in this book are not quick tricks; they are foundational principles that, when practiced consistently, will compound into mastery.

The future of sales belongs to those who listen with intent, communicate with empathy, and guide with integrity.[3] You now have the tools to transform your consultative sales approach, leveraging the wisdom of therapy to build deeper, more meaningful, and more successful client relationships. The question is no longer, *"How do I sell?"* but rather, *"How do I help?"* When you embrace that mindset fully, sales success is no longer something you chase—it becomes the natural byproduct of the trust and impact you create.

❦ PERSONAL EXPLORATION ❧

Now that you've finished this book, I encourage you to take some time to read and answer the few questions below. They are similar to the questions you first answered before you began. I suggest that you write down your answers to document your thoughts and perspectives now that you've completed this journey. After answering these questions below, I encourage you to flip back to the beginning and read your original answers to give you perspective on your newfound understanding of this meaningful sales approach. How changed are you? What do you now believe to be true?

How do you now approach sales conversations, and what do you recognize as your greatest strength in building client relationships? How has this changed from when you started?

_____
_____
_____

Think back to a recent sales conversation where you felt deeply connected to a client. What specific techniques or mindset shifts from this book contributed to that connection?

_____
_____
_____

What was the most surprising or impactful lesson you learned from this book, and how has it influenced the way you engage with clients?

_____
_____
_____

On a scale of 1-10, how confident are you now that integrating therapeutic techniques into sales enhances your success? How does this compare to your confidence level before reading the book?

_____
_____
_____

Looking at how you engage with clients today, what is the most significant transformation you've experienced, and what impact has it had on your sales results and professional fulfillment?

❧ YOUR FINAL THOUGHTS ☙

Use The Space Below To Capture Your Thoughts And Reflections On What You've Learned In This Section and Throughout This Book

BONUS TECHNIQUE: THE MIRACLE QUESTION
ଔଌଔଌଔଌଔଌ

The Miracle Question from Solution-Focused Brief Therapy (SFTB) is a transformative tool that helps clients envision their lives without their current problems. This question encourages clients to focus on possibilities and goals by retrospectively examining a changed reality.[1] The Miracle Question is: *"Suppose tonight, while you are asleep, a miracle happens. The problem that brought you here is solved. However, because you were asleep, you don't know that the miracle has happened. When you wake up tomorrow morning, what will be different that will tell you a miracle has happened?"*[2]

This retrospective approach helps clients bypass limiting beliefs, allowing them to identify evidence of change rather than imagining an unattainable future.[3] Clients often respond more openly, recognizing new possibilities and lowering their defenses. For example, instead of saying, "It will never happen," clients might share, "I feel more relaxed," or "My relationships are more harmonious" as evidence of their changed reality.[4]

In consultative sales, a similar approach can be transformative. Traditional future-looking questions often meet resistance due to perceived constraints. For instance, asking, "If you had a million dollars, how would you rearchitect your network?" might be met with, "I don't have a million dollars, so why would I answer that?" or "I don't have the authority to make those changes." These responses highlight the limitations clients feel, regardless of their validity.[5]

However, framing the conversation with The Miracle Question encourages clients to identify evidence of a new reality. They might say, "In this new and changed reality, our network is more efficient," or "We have fewer outages." This shift allows the salesperson and client to collaboratively explore what actions would have led to these changes. By identifying these actions, they can create a roadmap to achieve the desired outcomes. This backward exploration becomes a powerful tool for building a plan together, fostering a trusted-advisor relationship.[6]

The Miracle Question's simplicity belies its profound impact. By encouraging clients to look for evidence of change, it expands their thinking and breaks down limiting beliefs.[7] This approach not only helps in therapy but also transforms sales conversations, leading to deeper, more meaningful client relationships. I hope you incorporate this powerful solution-focused approach to build deeper, more meaningful client relationships. Remember to Ask Like a Therapist and then you will Sell Like a Pro!

ADDITIONAL BONUS TECHNIQUE: SILENCE

I can't end without sharing one final, **indispensable** therapeutic practice—one that, when applied to consultative sales, becomes a **game-changer: SILENCE**.

Although the concept of embracing silence during a consultative sales conversation has been mentioned throughout this book, its profound impact warrants further exploration and dedicated commentary.

After asking a **Therapy-Inspired** question, resist the urge to fill the space with more words. **Let silence do the work.** Give your customer the time they need—however long it takes—to absorb, reflect, and respond to what you've just asked. **Your silence is a gift.**[1] It grants the customer the mental space to engage deeply with your question rather than merely reacting to it.

If you break that silence too soon, two things often happen:

1. The customer **disregards** your question entirely, weakening rapport.

2. They attempt to process your question **while** you keep talking—causing them to miss everything else you say.

In both cases, you've **hindered** their ability to think rather than **guiding** them toward clarity. That's the opposite of everything this book teaches.

So take this to heart: **Ask. Pause. Wait. Embrace the silence.**[2] It is where the real breakthroughs happen.

STAY CONNECTED

I welcome the opportunity to hear how these approaches have transformed your sales career—and even your personal life. Join our community and share your success stories, insights, and experiences with us. Follow us on our social media channels and visit our website to stay updated on the latest strategies and discussions in consultative sales:

- **Facebook:** Ask Like a Therapist
- **Instagram:** @AskLikeaTherapist
- **Website:** www.asklikeatherapist.com

Wishing you continued success, growth, and inspiration in all your endeavors.

With respect, admiration, and appreciation,
Jared Kelner

ABOUT THE AUTHOR

Jared Kelner, M.Ed., is a seasoned sales professional with over 25 years of experience selling consulting services at Cisco Systems, Insight Enterprises, and Connection. His extensive career in sales is complemented by his expertise as a Mental Health Counselor, holding a Master's of Education degree in Counseling and Human Development. Jared's unique blend of skills allows him to integrate therapeutic modalities and questioning techniques into his sales approach, fostering deeper rapport and trust with clients.

In addition to his sales and counseling experience, Jared is a trained public speaker, a public speaking coach, the founder of The Mindful and Intentional Presentation Approach, and the creator of the P.R.E.S.E.N.T. APPROACH which empowers professionals who struggle with Imposter Syndrome and Public Speaking Anxiety to deliver impactful presentations with authenticity, confidence and clarity. Beyond sales, mental health counseling, and public speaking, Jared has worked in the acting industry for over 30 years. He is an award nominated playwright and a highly sought after acting coach who has been training actors around the world for over 30 years.

Jared is the author of "Line? The Creative Way for Actors to Quickly Memorize Monologues and Dialogues" and "The Chamberlain Negotiation Principles: A Tale of Five Must Know Negotiation Tenets and the Insight Behind the Principles to Help You Succeed." These works reflect his deep understanding of memory improvement and negotiation strategies, making him a valuable resource for sales professionals looking to enhance their careers through the integration of therapeutic techniques.

REFERENCES

FOREWARD

1. Beck, A. T. (1976). Cognitive therapy and the emotional disorders. International Universities Press.
2. Kahneman, D., & Tversky, A. (1979). Prospect theory: An analysis of decision under risk. Econometrica, 47(2), 263-292. https://doi.org/10.2307/1914185
3. Samuelson, W., & Zeckhauser, R. (1988). Status quo bias in decision making. Journal of Risk and Uncertainty, 1(1), 7-59. https://doi.org/10.1007/BF00055564
4. Cialdini, R. B. (2009). Influence: The psychology of persuasion. Harper Business.

OPEN–MINDEDNESS

1. Gottlieb, L. (2019). Maybe You Should Talk to Someone: A Therapist, Her Therapist, and Our Lives Revealed. Houghton Mifflin Harcourt.
2. van der Kolk, B. (2014). The Body Keeps the Score: Brain, Mind, and Body in the Healing of Trauma. Viking.
3. Harris, R. (2007). The Happiness Trap: How to Stop Struggling and Start Living: A Guide to ACT. Shambhala.
4. Koons, C. R. (2016). The Mindfulness Solution for Intense Emotions: Take Control of Borderline Personality Disorder with DBT. New Harbinger Publications.

WHY THIS APPROACH MATTERS

1. Cialdini, R. B. (2001). Influence: Science and practice (4th ed.). Allyn & Bacon.
2. Tversky, A., & Kahneman, D. (1974). Judgment under uncertainty: Heuristics and biases. Science, 185(4157), 1124-1131.
3. Rogers, C. R. (1951). Client-centered therapy: Its current practice, implications, and theory. Houghton Mifflin.
4. Brown, B. (2018). Dare to lead: Brave work. Tough conversations. Whole hearts. Random House.
5. Egan, G. (2019). The skilled helper: A problem-management and opportunity-development approach to helping (11th ed.). Cengage Learning.
6. Goleman, D. (1995). Emotional intelligence: Why it can matter more than IQ. Bantam Books.

FOSTERING TRUST WITH THERAPY-INSPIRED QUESTIONS

1. Covey, S. R. (2006). The speed of trust: The one thing that changes everything. Free Press.
2. Cuddy, A. J., Kohut, M., & Neffinger, J. (2013). Connect, then lead. Harvard Business Review, 91(7-8), 54-61.
3. Goleman, D. (2006). Social intelligence: The new science of human relationships. Bantam Books.
4. Brown, B. (2018). Dare to lead: Brave work. Tough conversations. Whole hearts. Random House.
5. Bandura, A. (1997). Self-efficacy: The exercise of control. W. H. Freeman.
6. Dweck, C. S. (2006). Mindset: The new psychology of success. Random House.
7. Tetlock, P. E. (2005). Expert political judgment: How good is it? How can we know? Princeton University Press.

8. Grant, A. (2021). Think again: The power of knowing what you don't know. Viking.
9. Lencioni, P. (2002). The five dysfunctions of a team: A leadership fable. Jossey-Bass.
10. Sedikides, C., Wildschut, T., & Arndt, J. (2008). "Nostalgia: Past, Present, and Future." Current Directions in Psychological Science, 17(5), 304-307.
11. Pennebaker, J. W., & Smyth, J. M. (2016). Opening Up by Writing It Down: How Expressive Writing Improves Health and Eases Emotional Pain. Guilford Publications.
12. Neff, K. D. (2011). "Self-Compassion, Self-Esteem, and Well-Being." Social and Personality Psychology Compass, 5(1), 1-12.
13. Schwartz, S. H. (1992). "Universals in the Content and Structure of Values: Theoretical Advances and Empirical Tests in 20 Countries." Advances in Experimental Social Psychology, 25, 1-65.
14. McAdams, D. P. (2001). "The Psychology of Life Stories." Review of General Psychology, 5(2), 100-122.
15. Bandura, A. (1997). Self-Efficacy: The Exercise of Control. W. H. Freeman.
16. Goleman, D. (1995). Emotional Intelligence: Why It Can Matter More Than IQ. Bantam Books.
17. Baumeister, R. F., & Leary, M. R. (1995). "The Need to Belong: Desire for Interpersonal Attachments as a Fundamental Human Motivation." Psychological Bulletin, 117(3), 497-529.
18. Deci, E. L., & Ryan, R. M. (2000). "The 'What' and 'Why' of Goal Pursuits: Human Needs and the Self-Determination of Behavior." Psychological Inquiry, 11(4), 227-268.
19. Rogers, C. R. (1961). On Becoming a Person: A Therapist's View of Psychotherapy. Houghton Mifflin.
20. Brown, B. (2012). Daring Greatly: How the Courage to Be Vulnerable Transforms the Way We Live, Love, Parent, and Lead. Gotham Books.
21. Tannen, D. (1990). You Just Don't Understand: Women and Men in Conversation. William Morrow.
22. Duckworth, A. L. (2016). Grit: The Power of Passion and Perseverance. Scribner.
23. Seligman, M. E. P. (2011). Flourish: A Visionary New Understanding of Happiness and Well-Being. Free Press.
24. Locke, E. A., & Latham, G. P. (2002). "Building a Practically Useful Theory of Goal Setting and Task Motivation: A 35-Year Odyssey." American Psychologist, 57(9), 705-717.
25. Ryan, R. M., & Deci, E. L. (2001). "On Happiness and Human Potentials: A Review of Research on Hedonic and Eudaimonic Well-Being." Annual Review of Psychology, 52(1), 141-166.
26. Neff, K. D. (2011). Self-compassion: Stop beating yourself up and leave insecurity behind. HarperCollins.
27. McAdams, D. P. (2006). The redemptive self: Stories Americans live by. Oxford University Press.
28. Gottman, J. M., & Silver, N. (1999). The seven principles for making marriage work. Harmony Books.
29. Durkheim, E. (1912). The elementary forms of the religious life. Free Press.
30. Seligman, M. E. P. (2002). Authentic happiness: Using the new positive psychology to realize your potential for lasting fulfillment. Free Press.
31. Pink, D. H. (2009). Drive: The surprising truth about what motivates us. Riverhead Books.
32. Tedeschi, R. G., & Calhoun, L. G. (2004). Posttraumatic growth: Conceptual foundations and empirical evidence. Psychological Inquiry, 15(1), 1-18.
33. Dweck, C. S. (2006). Mindset: The new psychology of success. Random House.
34. Csikszentmihalyi, M. (1990). Flow: The psychology of optimal experience. Harper & Row.
35. Kegan, R., & Lahey, L. L. (2009). Immunity to change: How to overcome it and unlock potential in yourself and your organization. Harvard Business Press.

36. Carucci, R. (2021). To be honest: Lead with the power of truth, justice, and purpose. Harvard Business Review Press.
37. Kabat-Zinn, J. (1990). Full catastrophe living: Using the wisdom of your body and mind to face stress, pain, and illness. Delta.
38. Peterson, C., & Seligman, M. E. P. (2004). Character strengths and virtues: A handbook and classification. Oxford University Press.
39. Duckworth, A. (2016). Grit: The power of passion and perseverance. Scribner.
40. Emmons, R. A. (2007). Thanks!: How practicing gratitude can make you happier. Houghton Mifflin.
41. Clear, J. (2018). Atomic habits: An easy & proven way to build good habits & break bad ones. Avery.
42. Brown, B. (2012). Daring greatly: How the courage to be vulnerable transforms the way we live, love, parent, and lead. Gotham.
43. Neff, K. D. (2011). Self-compassion: Stop beating yourself up and leave insecurity behind. HarperCollins.
44. Lyubomirsky, S. (2008). The how of happiness: A scientific approach to getting the life you want. Penguin.
45. McAdams, D. P. (2006). The redemptive self: Stories Americans live by. Oxford University Press.
46. Ericsson, K. A., & Pool, R. (2016). Peak: Secrets from the new science of expertise. Houghton Mifflin Harcourt.
47. Pink, D. H. (2009). Drive: The surprising truth about what motivates us. Riverhead Books.
48. Sen, A. (2009). The idea of justice. Harvard University Press.
49. Fredrickson, B. L. (2009). Positivity: Top-notch research reveals the 3-to-1 ratio that will change your life. Crown.
50. Bandura, A. (1997). Self-efficacy: The exercise of control. Freeman.
51. Dweck, C. S. (2006). Mindset: The new psychology of success. Random House.
52. Kouzes, J. M., & Posner, B. Z. (2017). The leadership challenge: How to make extraordinary things happen in organizations. Wiley.
53. Schein, E. H. (2017). Organizational culture and leadership (5th ed.). Wiley.
54. Tannen, D. (1995). Talking from 9 to 5: Women and men at work. HarperCollins.
55. Gottman, J. M., & Silver, N. (2015). The seven principles for making marriage work. Harmony.
56. Maxwell, J. C. (2018). Leadershift: The 11 essential changes every leader must embrace. HarperCollins.
57. Csikszentmihalyi, M. (1990). Flow: The psychology of optimal experience. Harper & Row.

BUILDING TRUST THROUGH MIRRORING

1. Cialdini, R. B. (2001). Influence: Science and practice (4th ed.). Allyn & Bacon.
2. Rogers, C. R. (1951). Client-centered therapy: Its current practice, implications, and theory. Houghton Mifflin.
3. Goleman, D. (2006). Social intelligence: The new science of human relationships. Bantam Books.
4. Chartrand, T. L., & Bargh, J. A. (1999). The chameleon effect: The perception-behavior link and social interaction. Journal of Personality and Social Psychology, 76(6), 893-910.
5. Bandler, R., & Grinder, J. (1975). The structure of magic: A book about language and therapy. Science and Behavior Books.
6. Brown, B. (2012). Daring greatly: How the courage to be vulnerable transforms the way we live, love, parent, and lead. Gotham Books.

7. Niedenthal, P. M., & Brauer, M. (2012). Social functionality of human emotion. Annual Review of Psychology, 63, 259-285.
8. Pink, D. H. (2012). To sell is human: The surprising truth about moving others. Riverhead Books.
9. Rogers, C. R. (1951). Client-centered therapy: Its current practice, implications, and theory. Houghton Mifflin.
10. Cialdini, R. B. (2006). Influence: The psychology of persuasion (Rev. ed.). Harper Business.
11. Brown, P., & Levinson, S. C. (1987). Politeness: Some universals in language usage. Cambridge University Press.
12. Bandler, R., & Grinder, J. (1975). The structure of magic I: A book about language and therapy. Science and Behavior Books.
13. O'Connor, J., & Seymour, J. (1995). Introducing NLP: Psychological skills for understanding and influencing people. HarperCollins.
14. Grinder, J., & Bostic St. Clair, C. (2001). Whispering in the wind. J & C Enterprises.
15. Knight, S. (2012). NLP at work: The difference that makes the difference in business. Nicholas Brealey Publishing.
16. Bandler, R., & Grinder, J. (1979). Frogs into princes: Neuro-linguistic programming. Real People Press.
17. O'Connor, J., & McDermott, I. (2001). The NLP workbook: The practical guidebook to achieving the results you want. HarperCollins.
18. Knight, S. (2012). NLP at work: The difference that makes the difference in business. Nicholas Brealey Publishing.
19. Grinder, J., & Bostic St. Clair, C. (2001). Whispering in the wind. J & C Enterprises.
20. Bandler, R., & Grinder, J. (1979). Frogs into princes: Neuro-linguistic programming. Real People Press.
21. O'Connor, J., & McDermott, I. (2001). The NLP workbook: The practical guidebook to achieving the results you want. HarperCollins.
22. Knight, S. (2012). NLP at work: The difference that makes the difference in business. Nicholas Brealey Publishing.
23. Grinder, J., & Bostic St. Clair, C. (2001). Whispering in the wind. J & C Enterprises.
24. Bandler, R., & Grinder, J. (1979). Frogs into princes: Neuro-linguistic programming. Real People Press.
25. Andreas, S. (2006). Transforming yourself: Becoming who you want to be. Real People Press.
26. Knight, S. (2012). NLP at work: The difference that makes the difference in business. Nicholas Brealey Publishing.
27. Grinder, J., & Bostic St. Clair, C. (2001). Whispering in the wind. J & C Enterprises.
28. Herz, R. S. (2007). The scent of desire: Discovering our enigmatic sense of smell. HarperCollins.
29. Gilbert, A. N. (2008). What the nose knows: The science of scent in everyday life. Crown.
30. Wilson, D. A., & Stevenson, R. J. (2006). Learning to smell: Olfactory perception from neurobiology to behavior. Johns Hopkins University Press.
31. Ackerman, D. (1990). A natural history of the senses. Vintage Books.
32. Shepherd, G. M. (2004). The synaptic organization of the brain (5th ed.). Oxford University Press.
33. Goleman, D. (2006). Social intelligence: The new science of human relationships. Bantam Books.
34. Shepherd, G. M. (2012). Neurogastronomy: How the brain creates flavor and why it matters. Columbia University Press.
35. Prescott, J. (2012). Chemosensory learning and flavor: Perception, preference, and intake. Physiology & Behavior, 107(4), 553–559.

36. Rolls, E. T. (2005). Taste, olfaction, and the central nervous system. Oxford University Press.
37. Stevenson, R. J. (2012). The psychology of flavour. Oxford University Press.
38. Kahneman, D. (2011). Thinking, fast and slow. Farrar, Straus and Giroux.
39. Simon, H. A. (1997). Models of bounded rationality: Empirically grounded economic reason (Vol. 3). MIT Press.
40. Gigerenzer, G., & Selten, R. (2002). Bounded rationality: The adaptive toolbox. MIT Press.
41. Kahneman, D., & Tversky, A. (1979). Prospect theory: An analysis of decision under risk. Econometrica, 47(2), 263–292.
42. Thaler, R. H. (2015). Misbehaving: The making of behavioral economics. W. W. Norton & Company.
43. Ariely, D. (2008). Predictably irrational: The hidden forces that shape our decisions. HarperCollins.
44. Zimbardo, P. G., & Boyd, J. N. (1999). Putting time in perspective: A valid, reliable individual-differences metric. Journal of Personality and Social Psychology, 77(6), 1271–1288.
45. Trope, Y., & Liberman, N. (2003). Temporal construal. Psychological Review, 110(3), 403–421.
46. Soman, D., & Ainslie, G. (2001). The psychology of intertemporal discounting: Why are distant events valued differently? Marketing Letters, 12(3), 217–228.
47. Eyal, T., Liberman, N., Trope, Y., & Walther, E. (2004). The pros and cons of temporally near and distant action. Journal of Personality and Social Psychology, 86(6), 781–795.
48. Charvet, S. R. (1997). Words that change minds: Mastering the language of influence. Kendall Hunt.
49. Hall, M., & Bodenhamer, B. G. (2005). The user's manual for the brain: The complete manual for neuro-linguistic programming practitioner certification. Crown House Publishing.
50. Andreas, S., & Faulkner, C. (1996). NLP: The new technology of achievement. HarperOne.
51. Chartrand, T. L., & Bargh, J. A. (1999). The chameleon effect: The perception–behavior link and social interaction. Journal of Personality and Social Psychology, 76(6), 893–910. https://doi.org/10.1037/0022-3514.76.6.893
52. Bernieri, F. J. (1988). Coordinated movement and rapport in teacher-student interactions. Journal of Nonverbal Behavior, 12(2), 120-138. https://doi.org/10.1007/BF00986930
53. Lakin, J. L., Jefferis, V. E., Cheng, C. M., & Chartrand, T. L. (2003). The chameleon effect as social glue: Evidence for the evolutionary significance of nonconscious mimicry. Journal of Nonverbal Behavior, 27(3), 145-162. https://doi.org/10.1023/A:1025389814290
54. Bailenson, J. N., & Yee, N. (2005). Digital chameleons: Automatic assimilation of nonverbal gestures in immersive virtual environments. Psychological Science, 16(10), 814-819. https://doi.org/10.1111/j.1467-9280.2005.01619.x
55. Neumann, R., & Strack, F. (2000). "Mood contagion": The automatic transfer of mood between persons. Journal of Personality and Social Psychology, 79(2), 211-223. https://doi.org/10.1037/0022-3514.79.2.211
56. Chartrand, T. L., & Bargh, J. A. (1999). The chameleon effect: The perception–behavior link and social interaction. Journal of Personality and Social Psychology, 76(6), 893-910. https://doi.org/10.1037/0022-3514.76.6.893
57. Lakin, J. L., & Chartrand, T. L. (2003). Using nonconscious behavioral mimicry to create affiliation and rapport. Psychological Science, 14(4), 334-339. https://doi.org/10.1111/1467-9280.14481
58. Bernieri, F. J. (1988). Coordinated movement and rapport in teacher-student interactions. Journal of Nonverbal Behavior, 12(2), 120-138. https://doi.org/10.1007/BF00986930
59. Bailenson, J. N., & Yee, N. (2005). Digital chameleons: Automatic assimilation of nonverbal gestures in immersive virtual environments. Psychological Science, 16(10), 814-819. https://doi.org/10.1111/j.1467-9280.2005.01619.x

60. Neumann, R., & Strack, F. (2000). "Mood contagion": The automatic transfer of mood between persons. Journal of Personality and Social Psychology, 79(2), 211-223. https://doi.org/10.1037/0022-3514.79.2.211
61. Hall, J. A., Murphy, N. A., & Mast, M. S. (2006). Nonverbal self-accuracy in interpersonal interaction. Personality and Social Psychology Bulletin, 32(12), 1675-1685. https://doi.org/10.1177/0146167206292089
62. Mehrabian, A. (1972). Nonverbal communication. Aldine-Atherton.
63. Pease, A., & Pease, B. (2004). The definitive book of body language. Bantam.
64. Ekman, P. (2003). Emotions revealed: Recognizing faces and feelings to improve communication and emotional life. Times Books.
65. Chartrand, T. L., & Bargh, J. A. (1999). The chameleon effect: The perception–behavior link and social interaction. Journal of Personality and Social Psychology, 76(6), 893-910.
66. Pease, A., & Pease, B. (2004). The definitive book of body language. Bantam.
67. Chartrand, T. L., & Bargh, J. A. (1999). The chameleon effect: The perception–behavior link and social interaction. Journal of Personality and Social Psychology, 76(6), 893-910.
68. Goman, C. K. (2008). The nonverbal advantage: Secrets and science of body language at work. Berrett-Koehler Publishers.
69. Kendon, A. (2004). Gesture: Visible action as utterance. Cambridge University Press.
70. Mehrabian, A. (1972). Nonverbal communication. Aldine-Atherton.
71. Scheflen, A. E. (1964). The significance of posture in communication systems. Psychiatry, 27(4), 316-331.
72. Bernieri, F. J. (1988). Coordinated movement and rapport in teacher-student interactions. Journal of Nonverbal Behavior, 12(2), 120-138.
73. LaFrance, M. (1985). Posture mirroring and rapport. Journal of Nonverbal Behavior, 9(1), 67-78.
74. Tickle-Degnen, L., & Rosenthal, R. (1990). The nature of rapport and its nonverbal correlates. Psychological Inquiry, 1(4), 285-293.
75. Lakin, J. L., Jefferis, V. E., Cheng, C. M., & Chartrand, T. L. (2003). The chameleon effect as social glue: Evidence for the evolutionary significance of nonconscious mimicry. Journal of Nonverbal Behavior, 27(3), 145-162.
76. Navarro, J., & Karlins, M. (2008). What Every BODY is Saying: An Ex-FBI Agent's Guide to Speed-Reading People. HarperCollins.
77. Pease, A., & Pease, B. (2004). The Definitive Book of Body Language. Bantam Books.
78. Morris, D. (2002). Peoplewatching: The Desmond Morris Guide to Body Language. Vintage.
79. Goman, C. K. (2011). The Silent Language of Leaders: How Body Language Can Help—or Hurt—How You Lead. Wiley.
80. Scheflen, A. E. (1972). Body Language and the Social Order: Communication as Behavioral Control. Prentice-Hall.
81. Mehrabian, A. (1971). Silent Messages: Implicit Communication of Emotions and Attitudes. Wadsworth.
82. Ekman, P. (2003). Emotions Revealed: Recognizing Faces and Feelings to Improve Communication and Emotional Life. Holt Paperbacks.
83. Hall, E. T. (1966). The Hidden Dimension. Doubleday.
84. Birdwhistell, R. L. (1970). Kinesics and Context: Essays on Body Motion Communication. University of Pennsylvania Press.
85. Chartrand, T. L., & Bargh, J. A. (1999). The chameleon effect: The perception–behavior link and social interaction. Journal of Personality and Social Psychology, 76(6), 893–910.
86. Hess, U., & Fischer, A. (2013). Emotional mimicry as social regulation. Personality and Social Psychology Review, 17(2), 142–157.

87. Ekman, P., & Friesen, W. V. (1975). Unmasking the face: A guide to recognizing emotions from facial clues. Prentice-Hall.
88. Niedenthal, P. M., Mermillod, M., Maringer, M., & Hess, U. (2010). The simulation of smiles (SIMS) model: Embodied simulation and the meaning of facial expression. Behavioral and Brain Sciences, 33(6), 417–433.
89. Lakin, J. L., Jefferis, V. E., Cheng, C. M., & Chartrand, T. L. (2003). The chameleon effect as social glue: Evidence for the evolutionary significance of nonconscious mimicry. Journal of Nonverbal Behavior, 27(3), 145–162.
90. Miles, L. K., Nind, L. K., & Macrae, C. N. (2009). The rhythm of rapport: Interpersonal synchrony and social perception. Journal of Experimental Social Psychology, 45(3), 585–589.
91. Stel, M., & van Knippenberg, A. (2008). The role of facial mimicry in the recognition of affect. Psychological Science, 19(10), 984–985.
92. Gregory, S. W., Jr., & Gallagher, T. J. (2002). Spectral analysis of candidates' nonverbal vocal communication: Predicting U.S. presidential election outcomes. Social Psychology Quarterly, 65(3), 298-308. https://doi.org/10.2307/3090123
93. Pentland, A. (2008). Honest signals: How they shape our world. MIT Press.
94. Nass, C., & Yen, C. (2010). The man who lied to his laptop: What machines teach us about human relationships. Current.
95. Cialdini, R. B. (2001). Influence: Science and practice (4th ed.). Allyn & Bacon.
96. Pentland, A. (2010). To signal is human. American Scientist, 98(3), 204-211.
97. Mehrabian, A. (1972). Nonverbal communication. Aldine Transaction.
98. Goman, C. K. (2011). The silent language of leaders: How body language can help—or hurt—how you lead. Jossey-Bass.
99. Berger, J. (2016). Contagious: How to build word of mouth in the digital age. Simon & Schuster.
100. Ekman, P. (2003). Emotions revealed: Recognizing faces and feelings to improve communication and emotional life. Times Books.
101. Kahneman, D. (2011). Thinking, fast and slow. Farrar, Straus and Giroux.
102. Pink, D. H. (2012). To sell is human: The surprising truth about moving others. Riverhead Books.
103. Goleman, D. (2006). Social intelligence: The new science of human relationships. Bantam Books.
104. Heath, C., & Heath, D. (2007). Made to stick: Why some ideas survive and others die. Random House.
105. Goman, C. K. (2011). The silent language of leaders: How body language can help—or hurt—how you lead. Jossey-Bass.
106. Cialdini, R. B. (2001). Influence: Science and practice (4th ed.). Allyn & Bacon.
107. Porges, S. W. (2011). The polyvagal theory: Neurophysiological foundations of emotions, attachment, communication, and self-regulation. W.W. Norton & Company.
108. Goleman, D. (2006). Social intelligence: The new science of human relationships. Bantam.
109. Cozolino, L. (2014). The neuroscience of human relationships: Attachment and the developing social brain. W.W. Norton & Company.
110. Siegel, D. J. (2010). The mindful therapist: A clinician's guide to mindsight and neural integration. W.W. Norton & Company.
111. Levine, A., & Heller, R. (2010). Attached: The new science of adult attachment and how it can help you find—and keep—love. TarcherPerigee.
112. Chartrand, T. L., & Bargh, J. A. (1999). The chameleon effect: The perception–behavior link and social interaction. Journal of Personality and Social Psychology, 76(6), 893–910.
113. Goleman, D. (2013). Focus: The hidden driver of excellence. HarperCollins.
114. Pentland, A. (2010). To signal is human. American Scientist, 98(3), 204-211.

115. Van Edwards, V. (2017). Captivate: The science of succeeding with people. Portfolio.
116. LeDoux, J. (1996). The emotional brain: The mysterious underpinnings of emotional life. Simon & Schuster.
117. Navarro, J. (2008). What every BODY is saying: An ex-FBI agent's guide to speed-reading people. HarperCollins.
118. Decety, J., & Lamm, C. (2006). Human empathy through the lens of social neuroscience. The Scientific World Journal, 6, 1146–1163.
119. Cialdini, R. B. (2006). Influence: The psychology of persuasion (Rev. ed.). Harper Business.
120. Goleman, D. (1995). Emotional intelligence: Why it can matter more than IQ. Bantam Books.
121. Goleman, D. (1995). Emotional intelligence: Why it can matter more than IQ. Bantam Books.
122. Cialdini, R. B. (2001). Influence: Science and practice (4th ed.). Allyn & Bacon.
123. Rogers, C. R. (1951). Client-centered therapy: Its current practice, implications, and theory. Houghton Mifflin.
124. Ekman, P. (2003). Emotions revealed: Recognizing faces and feelings to improve communication and emotional life. Henry Holt and Company.
125. Kahneman, D. (2011). Thinking, fast and slow. Farrar, Straus and Giroux.
126. Festinger, L. (1957). A theory of cognitive dissonance. Stanford University Press.
127. Thaler, R. H., & Sunstein, C. R. (2008). Nudge: Improving decisions about health, wealth, and happiness. Yale University Press.
128. Tversky, A., & Kahneman, D. (1974). Judgment under uncertainty: Heuristics and biases. Science, 185(4157), 1124-1131.
129. Covey, S. R. (1989). The 7 habits of highly effective people: Powerful lessons in personal change. Free Press.
130. Aronson, E. (2011). The social animal (11th ed.). Worth Publishers.
131. Rogers, C. R. (1957). The necessary and sufficient conditions of therapeutic personality change. Journal of Consulting Psychology, 21(2), 95-103.

APPLYING THERAPY TECHNIQUES TO SALES CONVERSATIONS

1. Beck, A. T. (1976). Cognitive therapy and the emotional disorders. International Universities Press.
2. Rogers, C. R. (1951). Client-centered therapy: Its current practice, implications, and theory. Houghton Mifflin.
3. Miller, W. R., & Rollnick, S. (2012). Motivational interviewing: Helping people change (3rd ed.). Guilford Press.
4. Ivey, A. E., Ivey, M. B., & Zalaquett, C. P. (2013). Intentional interviewing and counseling: Facilitating client development in a multicultural society. Cengage Learning.
5. Cialdini, R. B. (2009). Influence: Science and practice (5th ed.). Pearson.
6. Beck, A. T. (1976). Cognitive therapy and the emotional disorders. International Universities Press.
7. Ellis, A. (1962). Reason and emotion in psychotherapy. Lyle Stuart.
8. Linehan, M. M. (1993). Cognitive-behavioral treatment of borderline personality disorder. Guilford Press.
9. Segal, Z. V., Williams, J. M. G., & Teasdale, J. D. (2002). Mindfulness-based cognitive therapy for depression: A new approach to preventing relapse. Guilford Press.
10. Beck, A. T. (1976). Cognitive therapy and the emotional disorders. International Universities Press.
11. Shapiro, F. (1989). Eye movement desensitization and reprocessing (EMDR): Basic principles, protocols, and procedures. Guilford Press.
12. White, M., & Epston, D. (1990). Narrative means to therapeutic ends. Norton & Company.

13. Freud, S. (1910). The origin and development of psychoanalysis. American Journal of Psychology, 21(2), 181-218.
14. De Shazer, S., & Dolan, Y. (2012). More than miracles: The state of the art of solution-focused brief therapy. Routledge.
15. Glasser, W. (1965). Reality therapy: A new approach to psychiatry. Harper & Row.
16. Kelly, G. A. (1955). The psychology of personal constructs. Norton & Company.
17. Adler, A. (1956). The individual psychology of Alfred Adler. Basic Books.
18. Yalom, I. D. (1980). Existential psychotherapy. Basic Books.
19. Rogers, C. R. (1961). On becoming a person: A therapist's view of psychotherapy. Houghton Mifflin.
20. Frankl, V. E. (1959). Man's search for meaning. Beacon Press.
21. Seligman, M. E. P., Rashid, T., & Parks, A. C. (2006). Positive psychotherapy. American Psychologist, 61(8), 774-788.
22. Klerman, G. L., Weissman, M. M., Rounsaville, B. J., & Chevron, E. S. (1984). Interpersonal psychotherapy of depression. Basic Books.
23. Bowen, M. (1978). Family therapy in clinical practice. Jason Aronson.
24. Berne, E. (1964). Games people play: The psychology of human relationships. Grove Press.
25. Schwartz, R. C. (1995). Internal family systems therapy. Guilford Press.
26. Hayes, S. C., Strosahl, K. D., & Wilson, K. G. (1999). Acceptance and commitment therapy: An experiential approach to behavior change. Guilford Press.
27. Perls, F. S. (1969). Gestalt therapy verbatim. Real People Press.
28. Ogden, P., Minton, K., & Pain, C. (2006). Trauma and the body: A sensorimotor approach to psychotherapy. Norton & Company.
29. Segal, Z. V., Williams, J. M. G., & Teasdale, J. D. (2002). Mindfulness-based cognitive therapy for depression: A new approach to preventing relapse. Guilford Press.
30. Adler, A. (1956). The individual psychology of Alfred Adler. Basic Books.
31. Miller, W. R., & Rollnick, S. (2012). Motivational interviewing: Helping people change (3rd ed.). Guilford Press.
32. Seligman, M. E. P., & Csikszentmihalyi, M. (2000). Positive psychology: An introduction. American Psychologist, 55(1), 5-14.
33. Rogers, C. R. (1951). Client-centered therapy: Its current practice, implications, and theory. Houghton Mifflin.
34. Maslow, A. H. (1968). Toward a psychology of being (2nd ed.). Van Nostrand Reinhold.
35. Hayes, S. C., Strosahl, K. D., & Wilson, K. G. (2012). Acceptance and commitment therapy: The process and practice of mindful change (2nd ed.). Guilford Press.
36. Harris, R. (2009). ACT made simple: An easy-to-read primer on acceptance and commitment therapy. New Harbinger Publications.
37. Corey, G. (2016). Theory and practice of counseling and psychotherapy (10th ed.). Cengage Learning.
38. Hoffman, R., & McLeod, S. (2024). Adlerian therapy: Key concepts & techniques. Simply Psychology. Retrieved from https://www.simplypsychology.org/adlerian-therapy.html
39. Beck, J. S. (2020). Cognitive behavior therapy: Basics and beyond (3rd ed.). Guilford Press.
40. American Psychological Association. (2017). What is cognitive behavioral therapy? Retrieved from https://www.apa.org/ptsd-guideline/patients-and-families/cognitive-behavioral
41. Caddell, J. (2024). Constructivism in psychology and psychotherapy. Verywell Mind. Retrieved from https://www.verywellmind.com/constructivism-and-psychotherapy-2337730
42. GoodTherapy. (n.d.). Constructivism: Benefits, techniques & how it works. Retrieved from https://www.goodtherapy.org/learn-about-therapy/types/constructivism
43. Cleveland Clinic. (n.d.). Dialectical behavior therapy (DBT). Retrieved from https://my.clevelandclinic.org/health/treatments/22838-dialectical-behavior-therapy-dbt

44. Psychology Today. (n.d.). Dialectical behavior therapy. Retrieved from https://www.psychologytoday.com/us/therapy-types/dialectical-behavior-therapy
45. Corey, G. (2016). Theory and practice of counseling and psychotherapy (10th ed.). Cengage Learning.
46. Yalom, I. D. (1980). Existential psychotherapy. Basic Books.
47. Shapiro, F. (2018). Eye movement desensitization and reprocessing (EMDR) therapy: Basic principles, protocols, and procedures (3rd ed.). Guilford Press.
48. Miller, W. R., & Rollnick, S. (2013). Motivational interviewing: Helping people change (3rd ed.). Guilford Press.
49. Corey, G. (2016). Theory and practice of counseling and psychotherapy (10th ed.). Cengage Learning.
50. Yontef, G. M., & Jacobs, L. (2014). Gestalt therapy. In D. Wedding & R. J. Corsini (Eds.), Current psychotherapies (10th ed., pp. 299-336). Cengage Learning.
51. Corey, G. (2016). Theory and practice of counseling and psychotherapy (10th ed.). Cengage Learning.
52. Yontef, G. M., & Jacobs, L. (2014). Gestalt therapy. In D. Wedding & R. J. Corsini (Eds.), Current psychotherapies (10th ed., pp. 299-336). Cengage Learning.
53. Rogers, C. R. (1961). On becoming a person: A therapist's view of psychotherapy. Houghton Mifflin.
54. Maslow, A. H. (1970). Motivation and personality (2nd ed.). Harper & Row.
55. Schwartz, R. C. (1995). Internal family systems therapy. Guilford Press.
56. IFS Institute. (n.d.). What is internal family systems? Retrieved from https://ifs-institute.com/
57. Cleveland Clinic. (n.d.). Interpersonal psychotherapy (IPT). Retrieved from https://my.clevelandclinic.org/health/treatments/interpersonal-psychotherapy-ipt
58. Psychology Today. (n.d.). Interpersonal psychotherapy. Retrieved from https://www.psychologytoday.com/us/therapy-types/interpersonal-psychotherapy
59. Frankl, V. E. (1984). Man's search for meaning. Beacon Press.
60. Wong, P. T. P. (2012). The human quest for meaning: Theories, research, and applications (2nd ed.). Routledge.
61. Segal, Z. V., Williams, J. M. G., & Teasdale, J. D. (2013). Mindfulness-based cognitive therapy for depression (2nd ed.). Guilford Press.
62. Guy-Evans, O. (2024). What is mindfulness-based cognitive therapy (MBCT)? Simply Psychology. Retrieved from https://www.simplypsychology.org/mindfulness-based-cognitive-therapy.html
63. Miller, W. R., & Rollnick, S. (2013). Motivational interviewing: Helping people change (3rd ed.). Guilford Press.
64. Miller, W. R., & Rollnick, S. (2013). Motivational interviewing: Helping people change (3rd ed.). Guilford Press.
65. White, M., & Epston, D. (1990). Narrative means to therapeutic ends. Norton & Company.
66. Morgan, A. (2000). What is narrative therapy? An easy-to-read introduction. Dulwich Centre Publications.
67. Corey, G. (2016). Theory and practice of counseling and psychotherapy (10th ed.). Cengage Learning.
68. Rogers, C. R. (1961). On becoming a person: A therapist's view of psychotherapy. Houghton Mifflin.
69. Positive Psychology. (2024). What is positive psychotherapy? Retrieved from https://positivepsychology.com/positive-psychotherapy-research-effects-treatment/
70. GoodTherapy. (n.d.). Positive psychology: Benefits, techniques & how it works. Retrieved from https://www.goodtherapy.org/learn-about-therapy/types/positive-psychology

71. Corey, G. (2016). Theory and practice of counseling and psychotherapy (10th ed.). Cengage Learning.
72. Shedler, J. (2010). The efficacy of psychodynamic psychotherapy. American Psychologist, 65(2), 98-109.
73. Ellis, A. (2004). Rational emotive behavior therapy: It works for me—It can work for you. Prometheus Books.
74. Dryden, W. (2009). Rational emotive behaviour therapy: Distinctive features. Routledge.
75. De Shazer, S., & Dolan, Y. (2012). More than miracles: The state of the art of solution-focused brief therapy. Routledge.
76. Walter, I. R. (2020). Solution-focused brief therapy client types and their relevance to every session. Family Therapy Basics. https://familytherapybasics.com/blog/2016/9/27/solution-focused-brief-therapy-client-types-and-their-relevance-to-every-session
77. Salamon, M. (2023). What is somatic therapy? Harvard Health. Retrieved from https://www.health.harvard.edu/blog/what-is-somatic-therapy-202307072951
78. Psychology Today. (n.d.). Somatic therapy. Retrieved from https://www.psychologytoday.com/us/therapy-types/somatic-therapy
79. Corey, G. (2016). Theory and practice of counseling and psychotherapy (10th ed.). Cengage Learning.
80. Berne, E. (1964). Games people play: The psychology of human relationships. Grove Press.
81. Corey, G. (2016). Theory and practice of counseling and psychotherapy (10th ed.). Cengage Learning.

LEVERAGING MOTIVATIONAL INTERVIEWING

1. Miller, W. R., & Rollnick, S. (2013). Motivational interviewing: Helping people change (3rd ed.). Guilford Press.
2. Rosengren, D. B. (2018). Building motivational interviewing skills: A practitioner workbook (2nd ed.). Guilford Press.
3. Rollnick, S., Miller, W. R., & Butler, C. C. (2008). Motivational interviewing in health care: Helping patients change behavior. Guilford Press.
4. Moyers, T. B., & Martin, T. (2020). Therapist influence on client language during motivational interviewing sessions. Journal of Substance Abuse Treatment, 108, 29-38.
5. Rollnick, S., Miller, W. R., & Butler, C. C. (2008). Motivational interviewing in health care: Helping patients change behavior. Guilford Press.
6. Moyers, T. B., & Martin, T. (2020). Therapist influence on client language during motivational interviewing sessions. Journal of Substance Abuse Treatment, 108, 29-38.

UNDERSTANDING AND ADDRESSING BIASES

1. Kahneman, D. (2011). Thinking, fast and slow. Farrar, Straus and Giroux.
2. Tversky, A., & Kahneman, D. (1974). Judgment under uncertainty: Heuristics and biases. Science, 185(4157), 1124-1131.
3. Cialdini, R. B. (2009). Influence: Science and practice (5th ed.). Pearson.
4. Cialdini, R. B. (2009). Influence: Science and practice (5th ed.). Pearson.
5. Banaji, M. R., & Greenwald, A. G. (2013). Blindspot: Hidden biases of good people. Delacorte Press.
6. Staats, C. (2016). Understanding implicit bias: What educators should know. American Educator, 39(4), 29-33.
7. Ross, H. J. (2014). Everyday bias: Identifying and navigating unconscious judgments in our daily lives. Rowman & Littlefield.

8. Dovidio, J. F., & Gaertner, S. L. (2004). Aversive racism. Advances in Experimental Social Psychology, 36, 1-52.
9. Devine, P. G. (1989). Stereotypes and prejudice: Their automatic and controlled components. Journal of Personality and Social Psychology, 56(1), 5-18.
10. Fiske, S. T. (1998). Stereotyping, prejudice, and discrimination. In D. T. Gilbert, S. T. Fiske, & G. Lindzey (Eds.), The handbook of social psychology (4th ed., pp. 357-411). McGraw-Hill.
11. Paluck, E. L., & Green, D. P. (2009). Prejudice reduction: What works? A review and assessment of research and practice. Annual Review of Psychology, 60, 339-367.
12. Tversky, A., & Kahneman, D. (1974). Judgment under uncertainty: Heuristics and biases. Science, 185(4157), 1124-1131.
13. Furnham, A., & Boo, H. C. (2011). A literature review of the anchoring effect. The Journal of Socio-Economics, 40(1), 35-42.
14. Ross, L. (1977). The intuitive psychologist and his shortcomings: Distortions in the attribution process. In L. Berkowitz (Ed.), Advances in experimental social psychology (Vol. 10, pp. 173-220). Academic Press.
15. Heider, F. (1958). The psychology of interpersonal relations. Wiley.
16. Milgram, S. (1974). Obedience to authority: An experimental view. Harper & Row.
17. Cialdini, R. B. (2009). Influence: Science and practice (5th ed.). Pearson.
18. Tversky, A., & Kahneman, D. (1973). Availability: A heuristic for judging frequency and probability. Cognitive Psychology, 5(2), 207-232.
19. Schwarz, N., & Vaughn, L. A. (2002). The availability heuristic revisited: Ease of recall and content of recall as distinct sources of information. In T. Gilovich, D. Griffin, & D. Kahneman (Eds.), Heuristics and biases: The psychology of intuitive judgment (pp. 103-119). Cambridge University Press.
20. Kahneman, D. (2011). Thinking, fast and slow. Farrar, Straus and Giroux.
21. Tversky, A., & Kahneman, D. (1974). Judgment under uncertainty: Heuristics and biases. Science, 185(4157), 1124-1131.
22. Kahneman, D. (2011). Thinking, fast and slow. Farrar, Straus and Giroux.
23. Mather, M., Shafir, E., & Johnson, M. K. (2000). Misremembrance of options past: Source monitoring and choice. Psychological Science, 11(2), 132-138.
24. Kahneman, D. (2011). Thinking, fast and slow. Farrar, Straus and Giroux.
25. Plous, S. (1993). The psychology of judgment and decision making. McGraw-Hill.
26. Kahneman, D. (2011). Thinking, fast and slow. Farrar, Straus and Giroux.
27. Gilovich, T., Vallone, R., & Tversky, A. (1985). The hot hand in basketball: On the misperception of random sequences. Cognitive Psychology, 17(3), 295-314.
28. Kahneman, D. (2011). Thinking, fast and slow. Farrar, Straus and Giroux.
29. Nickerson, R. S. (1998). Confirmation bias: A ubiquitous phenomenon in many guises. Review of General Psychology, 2(2), 175-220.
30. Plous, S. (1993). The psychology of judgment and decision making. McGraw-Hill.
31. Camerer, C., Loewenstein, G., & Weber, M. (1989). The curse of knowledge in economic settings: An experimental analysis. Journal of Political Economy, 97(5), 1232-1254.
32. Hinds, P. J. (1999). The curse of expertise: The effects of expertise and debiasing methods on predictions of novice performance. Journal of Experimental Psychology: Applied, 5(2), 205-221.
33. Kahneman, D. (2011). Thinking, fast and slow. Farrar, Straus and Giroux.
34. Kruger, J., & Dunning, D. (1999). Unskilled and unaware of it: How difficulties in recognizing one's own incompetence lead to inflated self-assessments. Journal of Personality and Social Psychology, 77(6), 1121-1134.
35. Dunning, D. (2011). The Dunning–Kruger effect: On being ignorant of one's own ignorance. Advances in Experimental Social Psychology, 44, 247-296.

36. Kahneman, D. (2011). Thinking, fast and slow. Farrar, Straus and Giroux.
37. Kahneman, D., Knetsch, J. L., & Thaler, R. H. (1990). Experimental tests of the endowment effect and the Coase theorem. Journal of Political Economy, 98(6), 1325-1348.
38. Morewedge, C. K., Shu, L. L., Gilbert, D. T., & Wilson, T. D. (2009). Bad riddance or good rubbish? Ownership and not loss aversion causes the endowment effect. Journal of Experimental Social Psychology, 45(4), 947-951.
39. Kahneman, D. (2011). Thinking, fast and slow. Farrar, Straus and Giroux.
40. Ross, L., Greene, D., & House, P. (1977). The "false consensus effect": An egocentric bias in social perception and attribution processes. Journal of Experimental Social Psychology, 13(3), 279-301.
41. Marks, G., & Miller, N. (1987). Ten years of research on the false-consensus effect: An empirical and theoretical review. Psychological Bulletin, 102(1), 72-90.
42. Kahneman, D. (2011). Thinking, fast and slow. Farrar, Straus and Giroux.
43. Tversky, A., & Kahneman, D. (1981). The framing of decisions and the psychology of choice. Science, 211(4481), 453-458.
44. Levin, I. P., Schneider, S. L., & Gaeth, G. J. (1998). All frames are not created equal: A typology and critical analysis of framing effects. Organizational Behavior and Human Decision Processes, 76(2), 149-188.
45. Kahneman, D. (2011). Thinking, fast and slow. Farrar, Straus and Giroux.
46. Janis, I. L. (1982). Groupthink: Psychological studies of policy decisions and fiascoes (2nd ed.). Houghton Mifflin.
47. Esser, J. K. (1998). Alive and well after 25 years: A review of groupthink research. Organizational Behavior and Human Decision Processes, 73(2-3), 116-141.
48. Kahneman, D. (2011). Thinking, fast and slow. Farrar, Straus and Giroux.
49. Thorndike, E. L. (1920). A constant error in psychological ratings. Journal of Applied Psychology, 4(1), 25-29.
50. Nisbett, R. E., & Wilson, T. D. (1977). The halo effect: Evidence for unconscious alteration of judgments. Journal of Personality and Social Psychology, 35(4), 250-256.
51. Kahneman, D. (2011). Thinking, fast and slow. Farrar, Straus and Giroux.
52. Fischhoff, B. (1975). Hindsight ≠ foresight: The effect of outcome knowledge on judgment under uncertainty. Journal of Experimental Psychology: Human Perception and Performance, 1(3), 288-299.
53. Roese, N. J., & Vohs, K. D. (2012). Hindsight bias. Perspectives on Psychological Science, 7(5), 411-426.
54. Kahneman, D. (2011). Thinking, fast and slow. Farrar, Straus and Giroux.
55. Nisbett, R. E., & Wilson, T. D. (1977). The halo effect: Evidence for unconscious alteration of judgments. Journal of Personality and Social Psychology, 35(4), 250-256.
56. Kahneman, D. (2011). Thinking, fast and slow. Farrar, Straus and Giroux.
57. Thorndike, E. L. (1920). A constant error in psychological ratings. Journal of Applied Psychology, 4(1), 25-29.
58. Norton, M. I., Mochon, D., & Ariely, D. (2012). The IKEA effect: When labor leads to love. Journal of Consumer Psychology, 22(3), 453-460.
59. Kahneman, D. (2011). Thinking, fast and slow. Farrar, Straus and Giroux.
60. Norton, M. I., Mochon, D., & Ariely, D. (2012). The IKEA effect: When labor leads to love. Journal of Consumer Psychology, 22(3), 453-460.
61. Chapman, L. J. (1967). Illusory correlation in observational report. Journal of Verbal Learning and Verbal Behavior, 6(1), 151-155.
62. Fiedler, K. (2000). Illusory correlation. In A. E. Kazdin (Ed.), Encyclopedia of psychology (Vol. 4, pp. 1-3). American Psychological Association.

63. Dunning, D., Heath, C., & Suls, J. M. (2004). Flawed self-assessment: Implications for health, education, and the workplace. Psychological Science in the Public Interest, 5(3), 69-106.
64. Kruger, J., & Dunning, D. (1999). Unskilled and unaware of it: How difficulties in recognizing one's own incompetence lead to inflated self-assessments. Journal of Personality and Social Psychology, 77(6), 1121-1134.
65. Kahneman, D. (2011). Thinking, fast and slow. Farrar, Straus and Giroux.
66. Kahneman, D., & Tversky, A. (1979). Prospect theory: An analysis of decision under risk. Econometrica, 47(2), 263-292.
67. Thaler, R. H., & Sunstein, C. R. (2008). Nudge: Improving decisions about health, wealth, and happiness. Yale University Press.
68. Zajonc, R. B. (1968). Attitudinal effects of mere exposure. Journal of Personality and Social Psychology, 9(2), 1-27.
69. Bornstein, R. F. (1989). Exposure and affect: Overview and meta-analysis of research, 1968-1987. Psychological Bulletin, 106(2), 265-289.
70. Kahneman, D. (2011). Thinking, fast and slow. Farrar, Straus and Giroux.
71. Sharot, T. (2011). The optimism bias. Current Biology, 21(23), R941-R945.
72. Shepperd, J. A., Klein, W. M., Waters, E. A., & Weinstein, N. D. (2013). Taking stock of unrealistic optimism. Perspectives on Psychological Science, 8(4), 395-411.
73. Kahneman, D. (2011). Thinking, fast and slow. Farrar, Straus and Giroux.
74. Moore, D. A., & Healy, P. J. (2008). The trouble with overconfidence. Psychological Review, 115(2), 502-517.
75. Kahneman, D. (2011). Thinking, fast and slow. Farrar, Straus and Giroux.
76. Sharot, T. (2011). The optimism bias. Current Biology, 21(23), R941-R945.
77. Shepperd, J. A., Klein, W. M., Waters, E. A., & Weinstein, N. D. (2013). Taking stock of unrealistic optimism. Perspectives on Psychological Science, 8(4), 395-411.
78. Buehler, R., Griffin, D., & Ross, M. (1994). Exploring the "planning fallacy": Why people underestimate their task completion times. Journal of Personality and Social Psychology, 67(3), 366-381.
79. Kahneman, D., & Tversky, A. (1979). Prospect theory: An analysis of decision under risk. Econometrica, 47(2), 263-292.
80. Lovallo, D., & Kahneman, D. (2003). Delusions of success: How optimism undermines executives' decisions. Harvard Business Review, 81(7), 56-63.
81. Brehm, J. W. (1966). A theory of psychological reactance. Academic Press.
82. Miron, A. M., & Brehm, J. W. (2006). Reactance theory - 40 years later. Zeitschrift für Sozialpsychologie, 37(1), 9-18.
83. Steindl, C., Jonas, E., Sittenthaler, S., Traut-Mattausch, E., & Greenberg, J. (2015). Understanding psychological reactance: New developments and findings. Zeitschrift für Psychologie, 223(4), 205-214.
84. Tversky, A., & Kahneman, D. (1973). Availability: A heuristic for judging frequency and probability. Cognitive Psychology, 5(2), 207-232.
85. Schwarz, N., & Vaughn, L. A. (2002). The availability heuristic revisited: Ease of recall and content of recall as distinct sources of information. In T. Gilovich, D. Griffin, & D. Kahneman (Eds.), Heuristics and biases: The psychology of intuitive judgment (pp. 103-119). Cambridge University Press.
86. Cialdini, R. B. (2009). Influence: Science and practice (5th ed.). Pearson.
87. Regan, D. T. (1971). Effects of a favor and liking on compliance. Journal of Experimental Social Psychology, 7(6), 627-639.
88. Samuelson, W., & Zeckhauser, R. (1988). Status quo bias in decision making. Journal of Risk and Uncertainty, 1(1), 7-59.
89. Kahneman, D. (2011). Thinking, fast and slow. Farrar, Straus and Giroux.

90. Arkes, H. R., & Blumer, C. (1985). The psychology of sunk cost. Organizational Behavior and Human Decision Processes, 35(1), 124-140.
91. Thaler, R. H. (1999). Mental accounting matters. Journal of Behavioral Decision Making, 12(3), 183-206.
92. Kahneman, D. (2011). Thinking, fast and slow. Farrar, Straus and Giroux.
93. Taleb, N. N. (2007). The black swan: The impact of the highly improbable. Random House.
94. Brown, A. L., & Campione, J. C. (1994). Guided discovery in a community of learners. In K. McGilly (Ed.), Classroom lessons: Integrating cognitive theory and classroom practice (pp. 229-270). MIT Press.
95. Kahneman, D. (2011). Thinking, fast and slow. Farrar, Straus and Giroux.

PRESENTING YOUR SOLUTION

1. Hanan, M. (2011). Consultative Selling: The Hanan Formula for High-Margin Sales at High Levels. AMACOM.
2. Iannarino, A. (2022). Elite Sales Strategies: A Guide to Being One-Up, Creating Value, and Becoming Truly Consultative. Wiley.
3. Rapp, A., Agnihotri, R., & Forbes, L. P. (2008). The Sales Force Technology–Performance Chain: The Role of Adaptive Selling and Effort. Journal of Personal Selling & Sales Management, 28(4), 335-350.
4. Graziano, J. E., & Flanagan, P. J. (2004). Explore the Art of Consultative Selling. Journal of Accountancy. Retrieved from https://www.journalofaccountancy.com/issues/2005/jan/exploretheartofconsultativeselling.html
5. Brooks Group. (2024, May 9). 13 Best Consultative Sales Questions. Retrieved from https://brooksgroup.com/sales-training-blog/consultative-sales-questions/
6. Hanan, M. (2011). Consultative Selling: The Hanan Formula for High-Margin Sales at High Levels. AMACOM.
7. Rogers, C. R. (1951). Client-Centered Therapy: Its Current Practice, Implications, and Theory. Houghton Mifflin.
8. Iannarino, A. (2022). Elite Sales Strategies: A Guide to Being One-Up, Creating Value, and Becoming Truly Consultative. Wiley.
9. Graziano, J. E., & Flanagan, P. J. (2004). Explore the Art of Consultative Selling. Journal of Accountancy. Retrieved from https://www.journalofaccountancy.com/issues/2005/jan/exploretheartofconsultativeselling.html
10. de Shazer, S., & Dolan, Y. (2007). More Than Miracles: The State of the Art of Solution-Focused Brief Therapy. Routledge.
11. Beck, A. T. (1976). Cognitive Therapy and the Emotional Disorders. International Universities Press.
12. Adler, A. (1956). The Individual Psychology of Alfred Adler: A Systematic Presentation in Selections from His Writings. Basic Books.
13. Miller, W. R., & Rollnick, S. (2012). Motivational Interviewing: Helping People Change (3rd ed.). Guilford Press.
14. White, M., & Epston, D. (1990). Narrative Means to Therapeutic Ends. Norton & Company.
15. Frankl, V. E. (2006). Man's Search for Meaning. Beacon Press.
16. Brooks Group. (2024, May 9). 13 Best Consultative Sales Questions. Retrieved from https://brooksgroup.com/sales-training-blog/consultative-sales-questions/
17. Duffy, D. (2017). Consultative Selling: A Model for Sales Success: An Introductory Sales Development Program. CreateSpace Independent Publishing Platform.

18. Edinger, S. (2017). Sales Reps, Stop Asking Leading Questions. Harvard Business Review. Retrieved from https://hbr.org/2017/03/sales-reps-stop-asking-leading-questions
19. Graziano, J. E., & Flanagan, P. J. (2004). Explore the Art of Consultative Selling. Journal of Accountancy. Retrieved from https://www.journalofaccountancy.com/issues/2005/jan/exploretheartofconsultativeselling.html
20. Miller, W. R., & Rollnick, S. (2012). Motivational Interviewing: Helping People Change (3rd ed.). Guilford Press.
21. Rollnick, S., & Miller, W. R. (1995). What is Motivational Interviewing? Behavioural and Cognitive Psychotherapy, 23(4), 325-334.
22. Miller, W. R., & Rollnick, S. (2012). Motivational Interviewing: Helping People Change (3rd ed.). Guilford Press.
23. Beck, A. T. (1976). Cognitive Therapy and the Emotional Disorders. International Universities Press.
24. de Shazer, S., & Dolan, Y. (2007). More Than Miracles: The State of the Art of Solution-Focused Brief Therapy. Routledge.
25. Psych Central. (n.d.). What Is Solution-Focused Brief Therapy? Retrieved from https://psychcentral.com/health/solution-focused-brief-therapy
26. Perls, F. S. (1969). Gestalt Therapy Verbatim. Real People Press.
27. Palmer, W. (2007). Sales and Gestalt: Our Alienated Fragment. Gestalt Review, 11(1), 6-14.
28. Adler, A. (1956). The Individual Psychology of Alfred Adler: A Systematic Presentation in Selections from His Writings. Basic Books.
29. Hoffman, R. (2024). Adlerian Therapy: Key Concepts & Techniques. Simply Psychology. Retrieved from https://www.simplypsychology.org/adlerian-therapy.html
30. Sutton, J. (2024). 22 Most Effective Adlerian Therapy Techniques and Worksheets. Positive Psychology. Retrieved from https://positivepsychology.com/adlerian-therapy/
31. Beck, A. T. (1976). Cognitive Therapy and the Emotional Disorders. International Universities Press.
32. McPheat, S. (2024). Understanding Cognitive Biases in Sales. MTD Sales. Retrieved from https://www.mtdsalestraining.com/mtdblog/cognitive-biases-in-sales
33. Brines, C. (2024). The Impact of Cognitive Biases on Sales: Recognizing and Counteracting Biases in Buyer Behavior. Braintrust Growth. Retrieved from https://braintrustgrowth.com/the-impact-of-cognitive-biases-on-sales-recognizing-and-counteracting-biases-in-buyer-behavior/
34. Samuelson, W., & Zeckhauser, R. (1988). Status quo bias in decision making. Journal of Risk and Uncertainty, 1(1), 7-59.
35. Anderson, C. (2021). The Psychology of Doing Nothing: Forms of Decision Avoidance Result from Reason and Emotion. Psychological Bulletin, 129(1), 139-167.
36. Rius, A. (2021, October 26). What Is Status Quo Bias in Sales and Marketing? Corporate Visions. Retrieved from https://corporatevisions.com/blog/status-quo-bias/
37. Brontén, G. (2024). Here's why you need to understand confirmation bias in sales. Membrain. Retrieved from https://www.membrain.com/blog/confirmation-bias-in-sales
38. Brines, C. (2024). The Impact of Cognitive Biases on Sales: Recognizing and Counteracting Biases in Buyer Behavior. Braintrust Growth. Retrieved from https://braintrustgrowth.com/the-impact-of-cognitive-biases-on-sales-recognizing-and-counteracting-biases-in-buyer-behavior/
39. Brontén, G. (2024). Here's why you need to understand confirmation bias in sales. Membrain. Retrieved from https://www.membrain.com/blog/confirmation-bias-in-sales
40. Kahneman, D., & Tversky, A. (1979). Prospect theory: An analysis of decision under risk. Econometrica, 47(2), 263-292.

41. Costet, J. (2021, December 13). How to Use Loss Aversion in Sales: Tactics and Examples. Gong. Retrieved from https://www.gong.io/blog/loss-aversion/
42. Kahneman, D., & Tversky, A. (1979). Prospect theory: An analysis of decision under risk. Econometrica, 47(2), 263-292.
43. Hussain, A. (2025, February 27). What Is a Sunk Cost—and the Sunk Cost Fallacy? Investopedia. Retrieved from https://www.investopedia.com/terms/s/sunkcost.asp
44. Brines, C. (2024). The Impact of Cognitive Biases on Sales: Recognizing and Counteracting Biases in Buyer Behavior. Braintrust Growth. Retrieved from https://braintrustgrowth.com/the-impact-of-cognitive-biases-on-sales-recognizing-and-counteracting-biases-in-buyer-behavior/
45. Hussain, A. (2025, February 27). What Is a Sunk Cost—and the Sunk Cost Fallacy? Investopedia. Retrieved from https://www.investopedia.com/terms/s/sunkcost.asp
46. Dovetail Editorial Team. (2024, January 17). Understanding Authority Bias and How It Affects Decision-Making. Dovetail. Retrieved from https://dovetail.com/research/what-is-authority-bias/
47. Dovetail Editorial Team. (2024, January 17). Understanding Authority Bias and How It Affects Decision-Making. Dovetail. Retrieved from https://dovetail.com/research/what-is-authority-bias/
48. ProveSource. (2024). Authority Bias Explained: Psychology & Marketing. ProveSource. Retrieved from https://provesrc.com/glossary/authority-bias/
49. Brines, C. (2024). The Impact of Cognitive Biases on Sales: Recognizing and Counteracting Biases in Buyer Behavior. Braintrust Growth. Retrieved from https://braintrustgrowth.com/the-impact-of-cognitive-biases-on-sales-recognizing-and-counteracting-biases-in-buyer-behavior/

MOVING THROUGH OBJECTIONS

1. Kahneman, D. (2011). Thinking, Fast and Slow. Farrar, Straus and Giroux.
2. Beck, A. T. (1976). Cognitive Therapy and the Emotional Disorders. International Universities Press.
3. Kahneman, D., & Tversky, A. (1979). Prospect theory: An analysis of decision under risk. Econometrica, 47(2), 263-292.
4. Rogers, C. R. (1951). Client-Centered Therapy: Its Current Practice, Implications, and Theory. Houghton Mifflin.
5. Miller, W. R., & Rollnick, S. (2012). Motivational Interviewing: Helping People Change (3rd ed.). Guilford Press.
6. Iannarino, A. (2022). Elite Sales Strategies: A Guide to Being One-Up, Creating Value, and Becoming Truly Consultative. Wiley.
7. Rogers, C. R. (1951). Client-Centered Therapy: Its Current Practice, Implications, and Theory. Houghton Mifflin.
8. Miller, W. R., & Rollnick, S. (2012). Motivational Interviewing: Helping People Change (3rd ed.). Guilford Press.
9. Beck, A. T. (1976). Cognitive Therapy and the Emotional Disorders. International Universities Press.
10. Covey, S. R. (1989). The 7 Habits of Highly Effective People: Powerful Lessons in Personal Change. Free Press.
11. Miller, W. R., & Rollnick, S. (2012). Motivational Interviewing: Helping People Change (3rd ed.). Guilford Press.
12. Iannarino, A. (2022). Elite Sales Strategies: A Guide to Being One-Up, Creating Value, and Becoming Truly Consultative. Wiley.

13. Covey, S. R. (1989). The 7 Habits of Highly Effective People: Powerful Lessons in Personal Change. Free Press.
14. Beck, A. T. (1976). Cognitive Therapy and the Emotional Disorders. International Universities Press.
15. Kahneman, D. (2011). Thinking, Fast and Slow. Farrar, Straus and Giroux.
16. Rogers, C. R. (1951). Client-Centered Therapy: Its Current Practice, Implications, and Theory. Houghton Mifflin.
17. Pink, D. H. (2012). To Sell Is Human: The Surprising Truth About Moving Others. Riverhead Books.

CLOSING THE SALE

1. Rackham, N. (1988). SPIN Selling. McGraw-Hill.
2. Dixon, M., & Adamson, B. (2011). The Challenger Sale: Taking Control of the Customer Conversation. Portfolio/Penguin.
3. Covey, S. R. (1989). The 7 Habits of Highly Effective People: Powerful Lessons in Personal Change. Free Press.
4. Kahneman, D. (2011). Thinking, Fast and Slow. Farrar, Straus and Giroux.
5. Miller, W. R., & Rollnick, S. (2012). Motivational Interviewing: Helping People Change (3rd ed.). Guilford Press.
6. Bandler, R., & Grinder, J. (1979). Frogs into Princes: Neuro Linguistic Programming. Real People Press.
7. Bandler, R., & Grinder, J. (1979). Frogs into Princes: Neuro Linguistic Programming. Real People Press.
8. O'Connor, J., & Seymour, J. (1990). Introducing Neuro-Linguistic Programming: Psychological Skills for Understanding and Influencing People. Thorsons.
9. Andreas, S., & Faulkner, C. (1994). NLP: The New Technology of Achievement. William Morrow Paperbacks.
10. Dilts, R. (1999). Sleight of Mouth: The Magic of Conversational Belief Change. Meta Publications.
11. Dilts, R. (1999). Sleight of Mouth: The Magic of Conversational Belief Change. Meta Publications.
12. O'Connor, J., & Seymour, J. (1990). Introducing Neuro-Linguistic Programming: Psychological Skills for Understanding and Influencing People. Thorsons.
13. Andreas, S., & Faulkner, C. (1994). NLP: The New Technology of Achievement. William Morrow Paperbacks.
14. Beck, A. T. (1976). Cognitive Therapy and the Emotional Disorders. International Universities Press.
15. Miller, W. R., & Rollnick, S. (2012). Motivational Interviewing: Helping People Change (3rd ed.). Guilford Press.
16. Segal, Z. V., Williams, J. M. G., & Teasdale, J. D. (2002). Mindfulness-Based Cognitive Therapy for Depression: A New Approach to Preventing Relapse. Guilford Press.
17. Adler, A. (1956). The Individual Psychology of Alfred Adler: A Systematic Presentation in Selections from His Writings. Basic Books.
18. Perls, F. S. (1969). Gestalt Therapy Verbatim. Real People Press.
19. Berne, E. (1964). Games People Play: The Psychology of Human Relationships. Grove Press.
20. de Shazer, S., & Dolan, Y. (2007). More Than Miracles: The State of the Art of Solution-Focused Brief Therapy. Routledge.
21. Ellis, A. (1962). Reason and Emotion in Psychotherapy. Lyle Stuart.

22. Seligman, M. E. P. (2002). Authentic Happiness: Using the New Positive Psychology to Realize Your Potential for Lasting Fulfillment. Free Press.
23. Miller, W. R., & Rollnick, S. (2012). Motivational Interviewing: Helping People Change (3rd ed.). Guilford Press.
24. Yalom, I. D. (1980). Existential Psychotherapy. Basic Books.
25. Hayes, S. C., Strosahl, K. D., & Wilson, K. G. (1999). Acceptance and Commitment Therapy: An Experiential Approach to Behavior Change. Guilford Press.
26. Miller, W. R., & Rollnick, S. (2012). Motivational Interviewing: Helping People Change (3rd ed.). Guilford Press.
27. Yalom, I. D. (1980). Existential Psychotherapy. Basic Books.
28. de Shazer, S., & Dolan, Y. (2007). More Than Miracles: The State of the Art of Solution-Focused Brief Therapy. Routledge.
29. Beck, A. T. (1976). Cognitive Therapy and the Emotional Disorders. International Universities Press.
30. Hayes, S. C., Strosahl, K. D., & Wilson, K. G. (1999). Acceptance and Commitment Therapy: An Experiential Approach to Behavior Change. Guilford Press.
31. Seligman, M. E. P. (2002). Authentic Happiness: Using the New Positive Psychology to Realize Your Potential for Lasting Fulfillment. Free Press.
32. Ellis, A. (1962). Reason and Emotion in Psychotherapy. Lyle Stuart.
33. Perls, F. S. (1969). Gestalt Therapy Verbatim. Real People Press.
34. Mahoney, M. J. (2003). Constructive Psychotherapy: A Practical Guide. Guilford Press.
35. Hayes, S. C., Strosahl, K. D., & Wilson, K. G. (1999). Acceptance and Commitment Therapy: An Experiential Approach to Behavior Change. Guilford Press.
36. Beck, A. T. (1976). Cognitive Therapy and the Emotional Disorders. International Universities Press.
37. Frankl, V. E. (2006). Man's Search for Meaning. Beacon Press.
38. Miller, W. R., & Rollnick, S. (2012). Motivational Interviewing: Helping People Change (3rd ed.). Guilford Press.
39. Glasser, W. (2010). Reality Therapy: A New Approach to Psychiatry. Harper & Row.
40. de Shazer, S., & Dolan, Y. (2007). More Than Miracles: The State of the Art of Solution-Focused Brief Therapy. Routledge.
41. Miller, W. R., & Rollnick, S. (2012). Motivational Interviewing: Helping People Change (3rd ed.). Guilford Press.
42. Miller, W. R., & Rollnick, S. (2012). Motivational Interviewing: Helping People Change (3rd ed.). Guilford Press.
43. Beck, A. T. (1976). Cognitive Therapy and the Emotional Disorders. International Universities Press.
44. Rogers, C. R. (1951). Client-Centered Therapy: Its Current Practice, Implications, and Theory. Houghton Mifflin.
45. Covey, S. R. (1989). The 7 Habits of Highly Effective People: Powerful Lessons in Personal Change. Free Press.
46. Miller, W. R., & Rollnick, S. (2012). Motivational Interviewing: Helping People Change (3rd ed.). Guilford Press.
47. Covey, S. R. (1989). The 7 Habits of Highly Effective People: Powerful Lessons in Personal Change. Free Press.

Ask Like a Therapist, Sell Like a Pro: A Therapy-Inspired Sales Approach

MID-PROJECT CHECK-IN

1. Rogers, C. R. (1951). Client-Centered Therapy: Its Current Practice, Implications, and Theory. Houghton Mifflin.
2. Covey, S. R. (1989). The 7 Habits of Highly Effective People: Powerful Lessons in Personal Change. Free Press.
3. Nickerson, R. S. (1998). Confirmation Bias: A Ubiquitous Phenomenon in Many Guises. Review of General Psychology, 2(2), 175-220.
4. Kahneman, D., & Tversky, A. (1979). Prospect Theory: An Analysis of Decision under Risk. Econometrica, 47(2), 263-292.
5. Arkes, H. R., & Blumer, C. (1985). The Psychology of Sunk Cost. Organizational Behavior and Human Decision Processes, 35(1), 124-140.
6. Samuelson, W., & Zeckhauser, R. (1988). Status Quo Bias in Decision Making. Journal of Risk and Uncertainty, 1(1), 7-59.
7. Moore, D. A., & Healy, P. J. (2008). The Trouble with Overconfidence. Psychological Review, 115(2), 502-517.
8. Kahneman, D. (2011). Thinking, Fast and Slow. Farrar, Straus and Giroux.
9. Miller, W. R., & Rollnick, S. (2012). Motivational Interviewing: Helping People Change (3rd ed.). Guilford Press.
10. Beck, A. T. (1976). Cognitive Therapy and the Emotional Disorders. International Universities Press.
11. Rogers, C. R. (1951). Client-Centered Therapy: Its Current Practice, Implications, and Theory. Houghton Mifflin.
12. de Shazer, S., & Dolan, Y. (2007). More Than Miracles: The State of the Art of Solution-Focused Brief Therapy. Routledge.
13. Perls, F. S. (1969). Gestalt Therapy Verbatim. Real People Press.
14. O'Connor, J., & Seymour, J. (1990). Introducing Neuro-Linguistic Programming: Psychological Skills for Understanding and Influencing People. Thorsons.
15. Covey, S. R. (1989). The 7 Habits of Highly Effective People: Powerful Lessons in Personal Change. Free Press.
16. Bandler, R., & Grinder, J. (1979). Frogs into Princes: Neuro Linguistic Programming. Real People Press.
17. Rogers, C. R. (1951). Client-Centered Therapy: Its Current Practice, Implications, and Theory. Houghton Mifflin.
18. Covey, S. R. (1989). The 7 Habits of Highly Effective People: Powerful Lessons in Personal Change. Free Press.
19. Covey, S. R. (1989). The 7 Habits of Highly Effective People: Powerful Lessons in Personal Change. Free Press.
20. Kahneman, D. (2011). Thinking, Fast and Slow. Farrar, Straus and Giroux.
21. Nickerson, R. S. (1998). Confirmation Bias: A Ubiquitous Phenomenon in Many Guises. Review of General Psychology, 2(2), 175-220.
22. Beck, A. T. (1976). Cognitive Therapy and the Emotional Disorders. International Universities Press.
23. Miller, W. R., & Rollnick, S. (2012). Motivational Interviewing: Helping People Change (3rd ed.). Guilford Press.
24. Perls, F. S. (1969). Gestalt Therapy Verbatim. Real People Press.
25. de Shazer, S., & Dolan, Y. (2007). More Than Miracles: The State of the Art of Solution-Focused Brief Therapy. Routledge.
26. Rogers, C. R. (1951). Client-Centered Therapy: Its Current Practice, Implications, and Theory. Houghton Mifflin.

27. Covey, S. R. (1989). The 7 Habits of Highly Effective People: Powerful Lessons in Personal Change. Free Press.
28. Kahneman, D. (2011). Thinking, Fast and Slow. Farrar, Straus and Giroux.

POST-SOLUTION DEBRIEF

1. Rogers, C. R. (1951). Client-Centered Therapy: Its Current Practice, Implications, and Theory. Houghton Mifflin.
2. Bickley, L. S., & Szilagyi, P. G. (2017). Bates' Guide to Physical Examination and History Taking (12th ed.). Wolters Kluwer.
3. Rogers, C. R. (1951). Client-Centered Therapy: Its Current Practice, Implications, and Theory. Houghton Mifflin.
4. Kahneman, D. (2011). Thinking, Fast and Slow. Farrar, Straus and Giroux.
5. Covey, S. R. (1989). The 7 Habits of Highly Effective People: Powerful Lessons in Personal Change. Free Press.
6. Miller, W. R., & Rollnick, S. (2012). Motivational Interviewing: Helping People Change (3rd ed.). Guilford Press.
7. Beck, A. T. (1976). Cognitive Therapy and the Emotional Disorders. International Universities Press.

ROLE PLAY EXERCISES

1. Rogers, C. R. (1951). Client-Centered Therapy: Its Current Practice, Implications, and Theory. Houghton Mifflin.
2. Covey, S. R. (1989). The 7 Habits of Highly Effective People: Powerful Lessons in Personal Change. Free Press.
3. Kahneman, D. (2011). Thinking, Fast and Slow. Farrar, Straus and Giroux.
4. Miller, W. R., & Rollnick, S. (2012). Motivational Interviewing: Helping People Change (3rd ed.). Guilford Press.
5. Beck, A. T. (1976). Cognitive Therapy and the Emotional Disorders. International Universities Press.
6. Bickley, L. S., & Szilagyi, P. G. (2017). Bates' Guide to Physical Examination and History Taking (12th ed.). Wolters Kluwer.
7. Rogers, C. R. (1951). Client-Centered Therapy: Its Current Practice, Implications, and Theory. Houghton Mifflin.
8. Covey, S. R. (1989). The 7 Habits of Highly Effective People: Powerful Lessons in Personal Change. Free Press.
9. Kahneman, D. (2011). Thinking, Fast and Slow. Farrar, Straus and Giroux.
10. Rogers, C. R. (1951). Client-Centered Therapy: Its Current Practice, Implications, and Theory. Houghton Mifflin.
11. Covey, S. R. (1989). The 7 Habits of Highly Effective People: Powerful Lessons in Personal Change. Free Press.
12. Kahneman, D. (2011). Thinking, Fast and Slow. Farrar, Straus and Giroux.
13. Miller, W. R., & Rollnick, S. (2012). Motivational Interviewing: Helping People Change (3rd ed.). Guilford Press.
14. Beck, A. T. (1976). Cognitive Therapy and the Emotional Disorders. International Universities Press.
15. Covey, S. R. (1989). The 7 Habits of Highly Effective People: Powerful Lessons in Personal Change. Free Press.

16. Covey, S. R. (1989). The 7 Habits of Highly Effective People: Powerful Lessons in Personal Change. Free Press.
17. Rogers, C. R. (1951). Client-Centered Therapy: Its Current Practice, Implications, and Theory. Houghton Mifflin.
18. Miller, W. R., & Rollnick, S. (2012). Motivational Interviewing: Helping People Change (3rd ed.). Guilford Press.
19. Kahneman, D. (2011). Thinking, Fast and Slow. Farrar, Straus and Giroux.
20. Covey, S. R. (1989). The 7 Habits of Highly Effective People: Powerful Lessons in Personal Change. Free Press.
21. Rogers, C. R. (1951). Client-Centered Therapy: Its Current Practice, Implications, and Theory. Houghton Mifflin.

CLOSING THOUGHTS

1. Covey, S. R. (1989). The 7 Habits of Highly Effective People: Powerful Lessons in Personal Change. Free Press.
2. Dixon, M., & Adamson, B. (2011). The Challenger Sale: Taking Control of the Customer Conversation. Portfolio/Penguin.
3. Brooks Group. (2024, May 9). 13 Best Consultative Sales Questions. Retrieved from https://brooksgroup.com/sales-training-blog/consultative-sales-questions/

BONUS TECHNIQUE: THE MIRACLE QUESTION

1. de Shazer, S., & Berg, I. K. (1988). Clues: Investigating Solutions in Brief Therapy. Norton.
2. de Shazer, S., & Berg, I. K. (1988). Clues: Investigating Solutions in Brief Therapy. Norton.
3. Strong, T., & Pyle, N. R. (2009). Constructing a conversational "miracle": Examining the "miracle question" as it is used in therapeutic dialogue. Journal of Constructivist Psychology, 22(4), 328–353.
4. Metcalf, L. (2005). The Miracle Question: Answer It and Change Your Life. Crown House Publishing.
5. de Shazer, S., & Berg, I. K. (1988). Clues: Investigating Solutions in Brief Therapy. Norton.
6. Strong, T., & Pyle, N. R. (2009). Constructing a conversational "miracle": Examining the "miracle question" as it is used in therapeutic dialogue. Journal of Constructivist Psychology, 22(4), 328–353.
7. Metcalf, L. (2007). The Miracle Question: Answer It and Change Your Life. Crown House Publishing.

ADDITIONAL BONUS TECHNIQUE: SILENCE

1. Rogers, C. R. (1951). Client-centered therapy: Its current practice, implications and theory. Houghton Mifflin.
2. Voss, C., & Raz, T. (2016). Never split the difference: Negotiating as if your life depended on it. Harper Business.

Made in the USA
Las Vegas, NV
27 April 2025